CU00894596

Thy Will be Done
by
Peter Conway
ISBN: 978-1-9997646-9-2

Front cover photograph is of the author in 1999.

Published by

i2i Publishing. Manchester. UK.
www.i2ipublishing.co.uk

To my father, Peter Conway
to my mother, Jane,
and
to all the people who helped me stay alive
and
in memory of
Rob Reynolds

ACKNOWLEDGEMENTS

I could not have written *Thy Will be Done* without the support, encouragement and persistence of my uncle, **Colin Armstrong**. You, the reader, like me, owe him a huge debt of gratitude for giving you the opportunity of reading about my amazing time in South Africa and elsewhere in the world over a period spanning some forty years.

Following my return from South Africa at the age of forty-six, adjusting to life in England has not been easy. In that regard, I owe my partner, **Jane Bennison**, an incalculable vote of thanks. She has stood by me and, when as has happened from time to time, I have felt low, she has cheered me up and given purpose to my new life in such a different environment.

Thy Will be Done, as originally written, comprised nearly 440,000 words, far too long for publication. I record my thanks to my publisher, **Lionel Ross** of **i2i Publishers** for his patience while *Thy Will be Done* was painstakingly prepared for publication; to **Patrick Sims**, the editor Lionel Ross asked to prune *Thy Will be Done* to a manageable length; and to **Peter Morrell**, who, from his perspective as both novelist and lawyer, has further edited and fine-tuned *Thy Will be Done*.

I am enormously grateful to **Graeme Lamb**, for his generous *Foreword*. He has been a tower of strength when I have needed it.

Last and by no means least, I express my thanks to my parents, **Peter and Jane Conway**, for their love, coupled with long-suffering patience, which my antics tested almost beyond endurance.

Peter Conway
January 2018

FOREWORD

Sir Winston Churchill took just fifteen words in the opening to *The Gathering Storm*, the first of his six volumes titled *The Second World War*, to frame World War Two. The theme is typically Churchillian; a simple short and seemingly unremarkable statement but one which draws the reader to ponder on his simple use of words, so innocently arranged as follows:

'How the English-speaking peoples through their wisdom, carelessness and good-nature allowed the wicked to rearm.'

This assertion unashamedly puts the guilt of World War Two with Adolf Hitler, the Nazi Party and Germany, but unmistakably, and with exquisite clarity places the blame for a war that ruined Europe and took over 60 million lives on us. We, the English-speaking people, allowed the wicked to re-arm and fought a global state-on-state war for over 5 years.

Thy Will Be Done is about a very different war. Not a war of armies set against armies, but war nevertheless. A war set in train and carried out by a state and its institutions in political transition against its own people and its neighbours. So return to Winston's grand theme, his *opus magnum*, and review it against this account of Peter Conway's wars, for while the guilt for his violent behaviour lay with Peter, the blame for his and for the courses of action of others, lies squarely on those responsible; the State of South Africa and its faltering institutions. This is the lesson and insight that makes this book essential reading for so many interested minds, be they students, academics, professionals, and across so many walks of life, rather than it just being bought by the 'Filthy Few' and the others who feature in its pages.

Thy Will Be Done is an account of violence, of murder, of revenge and retribution, of power abused and misused. It provides a fascinating insight of how a nation, in order to function, can stray from legitimately enforcing its national agenda on its own people and its neighbours to where it drifts, unchecked and unconstrained, into a situation where all ends justify all means. This uniquely shines a light onto so many of the world's faltering states, infected by organized crime, corruption and cronyism, increasingly operating by a design unrestricted, and without an accountable jurisdiction. *Thy Will be Done* provides an insight to what happens and is happening if 'Thomas Hobbes' takes root and allows the state to lose its moral compass and incite brutal violence on its behalf, as just another tool in maintaining temporary control, as it spirals out of it.

I met Peter John Conway in South Africa in a social setting over a long weekend. Peter is highly intelligent, commensurately articulate and unsurprisingly interesting company. He is, I would suggest to those very few to whom he claims to be close, a 'foul weather' friend, totally dependable but do not mistake him for something he is not. For Peter Conway is a dangerous man, the result of events, and one whom Alfred, the Lord Tennyson's poem, *Ulysses*, captures perfectly in the simple line: 'I am a part of all that I have met'.

Peter Conway's life from his formative years has been shaped by others, be they individual, family, institution or state. Peter is simply the sum of his experiences; the part he has met, guilty without doubt; but I sense not to blame – you should be the judge.

Graeme Lamb
Lieutenant General (Retired) Sir Graeme Lamb, KBE,
CMG, DSO
January 2018

Glossary of Abbreviations

AK 47	Mikhail Kalashnikov 47 (Assault Rifle)
ANC	African National Congress (South Africa)
BOSS	Bureau of State Security (South Africa)
DJ	Disc Jockey
DRC	Democratic Republic of Congo
FAA	Forces Armada Angolan (Angolan Army)
FAPLA	Armed Forces for the Liberation of Angola
FBI	Federal Bureau of Investigation (US)
FN-FAL	Belgian Battle Rifle
H&K	Heckler & Koch (Rifle)
HAMC	Hells Angels Motorcycle Club
ID	Identification
IFP	Inkatha Freedom Party (South Africa)
IV	Intravenous
JEM	Justice and Equality Movement (Sudan)
MK	uMkhonto we Sizwe (ANC armed wing)
MPLA	Popular Movement for the Liberation of Angola
NASCOM	National Commissioner of the Police Services (South Africa)
NIA	National Intelligence Agency (was BOSS)
R (As in R100)	Rand (Currency of South Africa)
SADF	South African Defence Force (before May 1994)
SANDF	South African National Defence Force (after May 1994)
SANAB	South African Narcotics and Alcohol Bureau
SAPU	South African Policing Union
SLM	Sudan Liberation Movement
SPLA	Sudan People's Liberation Army
SWAPO	South West African People's Organisation
UDF	United Democratic Front (South Africa)
UNITA	National Union for the Total Independence of Angola
US$ (as in US$100)	United States Dollar

Africa

Southern Africa
with major population centres

Chapter 1

This book is dedicated to my parents who had to move back to England from South Africa to escape the burden I became to them.

My father grew up in Richmond, North Yorkshire, and was one of seven brothers and two sisters. His group of brothers were known as The Fighting Conways and my father became a well-known tough guy in the area. Although I'm not saying this is a mitigating factor of what I did with my life, it could explain why I felt the necessity of not embarrassing my dad by being bullied. As I'm writing, I think that, if making him proud meant being violent, then he must be very proud.

I was born in England into a family of Mom, Dad, sister and me. My parents worked hard which supplied my privileged background and we emigrated to South Africa when I was three.

How do I explain my life? There was nothing strange about my upbringing. My parents were decent, respectable and upstanding members of society. I went to school and got into trouble; not the bad kind of trouble. That would come later. I don't remember too much about my early childhood, but I'm going to narrow it down to a few decisive but limiting choices.

I started school at the age of five and attended an excellent, and expensive, Catholic convent. Nothing very interesting happened in those times. I applied and was accepted into an all-boys feeder school. For the next three years, this would become my school-home and my initial experience of violence.

In 1978, at the age of twelve, I was in the final year of my primary school. I was doing fine academically, but socially I was not happy. By that time, in an upmarket Catholic school, I had no political beliefs and no awareness that my surroundings were contrived into a Utopia that made everything look great on the surface. In fact, the Bush War, in which South Africa was embroiled, would change me forever. It never occurred to me at the time that the way white South Africans lived was wrong or different. Europeans and Africans were inhabiting parallel universes.

One day, while waiting for our Zulu teacher to enter the room, I decided to take a sandwich out of my case. He entered the room whilst I was taking the sandwich from my lunchbox and when I looked up he was storming down the aisle towards me. He grabbed my sandwich from me and, as much as I reflect upon it, I do not know exactly why I reacted as I did. I remember hitting him unconscious and the expressions of horror on the faces of the other kids. Mostly I remember feeling justified. I don't think any of the boys took sides on what I'd done. It just happened.

As a result I was sent to a school with high fences and locked gates attended mostly by boys who had transgressed their Catholic school system. This led to my induction into a group of mostly violent boys and a continual church regime. I have nothing against Catholicism, but when it's used as a punishment, you run from it whenever you can.

My time in that school started with a fight with a boy nick-named "T-shirt". He was made the guy in charge by the older boys and took to it like a duck to water. By the time I arrived he was totally in charge of the new boys.

Then came the inevitable clash, but at that point I had no experience in violence. I was dropped to the ground and beaten senseless. I remember that afternoon as a turning point. I'm a quick learner and this was lesson one. The boys in this institution discovered quickly how to survive. I learnt to use everything at my disposal to keep the predators at bay. The predator analogy states, "Divide the weak, herd them away and make good choice of the prey." I was later part of a unit whose motto was "Fear is for prey". I was now improving fight by fight, a learning curve on how to knock people out. It would never be a necessary talent for a budding accountant, but it is a necessity for a future soldier and well-known bouncer.

My next school was a state-run, over-populated classroom environment. English-speaking Edenvale High School was separated from Afrikaans-speaking Edenvale Hoer School by an establishment named Norman House Reform School. This was a setup I would later come to know as "The Model". It was designed to create conflict and conflict there was. As life went on at my new school I formed new relationships. Socialising in that environment was easy and I was happy again. I had an entire cross-section of friends.

Then came a shock.

My Uncle Norman was killed in an accident at the Modderfontein dynamite factory. This was significant as I began to spend more time with my cousin Paul and his younger brother Gary. After school hours and at weekends, we always seemed to be together. I remember the funeral as the first time I would see someone I had an emotional attachment to lying in a coffin. It was the first of many to come.

Aunt Jean decided to move the family back to England, which included Paul and Gary. It was a sad day for me as I lost half the small family I had become used to in South Africa. After this I started to seek out new boys to be with on weekends and holidays. This would lead to more influential decisions in my life and the narrowing of my choices.

I found myself a new group of guys who had a formed a gang called "The Panthers". They were a small group, all younger than me, but we would become more famous than we ever imagined. The induction was a process of being beaten by two members. This had never been done before as nobody new had tried to join. More likely nobody had wanted to. I passed induction by changing the rules so that no one older than the oldest member could be inducted this way.

The Panthers had their first official meeting. I was put in charge of operations and it took all four other members to over-rule me. I came up with things to do within these new boundaries. We started off by doing petty theft in corner shops. Then we started stealing motorbikes and breaking into houses. We would only fight if we had to.

It was at this time that I had my first sexual experience. I had money and was so full of myself that I attracted an older girl into my world. She was my first sexual partner. I found myself confiding in her and she helped me get through that awkward first time.

As a result of my exploits with The Panthers, I was wearing an expensive watch, had enough alcohol to stun a horse and the cash from multiple houses in my pocket. This was enough bounty to get anyone to admire you at fourteen.

The boys in The Panthers were my best friends. However, a boy called Brian was my favourite member. He is now married and father of a little girl, but one specific incident involving Brian is crucial to this story. One day we were messing around in a park, drinking in the afternoon during the summer holidays. The residents had started a community group that was designed to keep the park clear of vagrants. One of them, the local tough guy, came out of his house to confront us. He had been waiting for this all day. The incident happened quickly. Our group all hit him at the same time. He became another adult who misjudged his own place in a fight. Now, every housewife on the street felt it necessary to come to his aid and all I can remember is a lot of threats being passed between us and them.

There are many ways to look at that afternoon, but we were in a public place drinking, which was not a serious offence. We were threatened in that public area, won the fight and yet we were going to pay for the egos that were trashed that day. By the time Brian and I had returned to his parents' house, the police had not only been informed, but had been to tell Brian's mother they were looking for us. She was absolutely freaking out. The first thing she did was to phone the eldest of Brian's brothers, Gary. The major outcome of this incident was my introduction to Gary. Gary was a well-known street fighter at the time and was extremely unhappy at being blamed as a bad influence. He was pissed off and looking for us. I paid for that day, not only by upgrading my status with the local police, but with an introduction to the older boys and an acceleration into a world where I was heading anyway.

Gary eventually rounded us up. Fortunately, this took a few hours and he was much calmer than he would have been, had he found us sooner. Luckily, he was very fond of Brian and had worked out a strategy for us. I wonder why his mother had believed it was best to contact Gary. We were just small-time thugs, but now we had a planner who was going to take us a lot further. He told us to remain calm and not go home. We were to remain at the dam, where we had a fort, and at no stage show up. Gary then went to see the representatives of the neighbourhood watch and convinced them we were making a stand. I think they were more afraid of being beaten up again and losing all the credibility they had gained. Gary managed to fix that afternoon and was quite proud of Brian, deep down.

This episode caused so much tension in this upper middle class suburb that it made us famous for a short while. More importantly, it created a link between the younger guys, Gary and the older guys. We became a force of different ages and some would stay in my circle of friends for the rest of my time in South Africa.

Chapter 2

Our little gang was ready to branch out. There were nine of us aged between fourteen and eighteen. It was with one boy called Colin that I became especially friendly. He was heavy-set with a huge neck and short cropped hair. At the age of fifteen, he even had a tattoo. Colin was an enigma to me and a constant rebel.

Our gang was ready to be elevated from minor mischief and common assaults to the world of real crime. We were pretty much ready to do anything and everything. By this time, most of us were carrying guns. The thing about the South African gun laws was that anybody over the age of twelve could carry a licensed firearm with written permission from the owner. As long as you had a letter from the owner of the weapon you were carrying, it was legal to possess that weapon. At this time, I was in possession of a Taurus .38, courtesy of my dad.

We were violent youngsters and in some weird way violence seemed to be encouraged. We weren't being pro-actively encouraged. It was just that we seemed to get away with it, so we became worse. Right up to the first murders, we were given enough rope to hang ourselves. This was literally true. South Africa was adept at hanging people and, as we would later find out, a token white person would be walked to the gallows every now and again.

The South African Police Force was so stretched with violent uprisings in the black townships, that it appeared to be numb to our level of violence. The local courts were filled with political cases, so we carried on. We mistook this lack of justice for apathy. I would later find out we were being watched with great interest by the security branch, whose existence was unknown to us at the time.

Our first big event was a robbery. I was fifteen when it was planned one Friday afternoon. There were two roadhouses in our town where you could order food and have it delivered by a waiter to your car window. The concept of a roadhouse might be more familiar to some more than others. Least to say, we ate at them as often as we could afford it. Today, ordering via a drive-thru is commonplace, but in 1981 this was a Friday night's special event and we were broke.

We chose The Airport Star, because it was a big roadhouse situated at the juncture of three major highways. The plan involved Robin's dark brown Alfa Romeo Juliette, and a motorbike, loaned to us by a boy called Michael, courtesy of his mother. We thought it was a great plan. Robin would drive the Alfa into the service area. We would order a whole lot of food and, as it was being served to our window, Michael would race past on his motorbike and steal it. Robin would then stall at the exit, preventing Michael being chased. Robin would act dumb-founded and not have to pay. It was the most over-planned robbery possible of a cheap food outlet.

Everything went to plan, until the owner began shooting at Michael on the bike, but, unable to hit a barn door under pressure, he redirected fire at the stalled car at the exit. I guess he saw through the plan. I started returning fire with my dad's Taurus .38 and we managed to get away. Although we fucked it up, we managed to enjoy the food. We seemed to get away with it just as school boys but, and there's always a "but", later that night one of our band of brothers, Bernard, decided for some unknown reason to confess to his parents. They took him to the local police station where he made a statement. However, the police couldn't care less about another shooting in Johannesburg, where nobody got hit. The operation was a mixture of bad planning and, even worse, bad personnel. I received eight lashes of State corporal punishment with a heavy cane. The scars remind me every day of how foolish we were to not to use better people in our endeavours.

Nine months before my sixteenth birthday in June 1982, I took my friend's driver's licence and forged a motorbike licence in my name. It was a poor forgery. My dad had told me he would buy me a bike when I got a licence and with this forged licence in his hands he kept his promise. With a motorbike between my legs, I was now going places, literally and figuratively. I had gained a freedom I'd only dreamed of before.

This only lasted a couple of weeks, because there were only two policemen who could have signed the licence and they patrolled the streets of the township where I lived. It didn't take them long to realise there was a new motorbike on their streets and they knew I hadn't been given a licence. When I was stopped one afternoon, I stupidly produced my forged licence. The policeman looked at it and blew a gasket. It was his signature. He escorted me back to my house and informed my dad of the forgery. My motorbike was taken away from me until I passed the real test and I was relegated to the back of Colin's bike.

Then, in November 1981, my life was turned upside-down. That night, Colin and I were so drunk it was about to backfire. I was on the back of Colin's bike as he overtook a vehicle on the outside. The driver made a right turn and we collided. I remember flying through the air and crashing through a pain barrier I had never experienced before. I landed on the road and the pain intensified. My left femur was broken and I mean broken. I remember seeing it sticking through my jeans. The real cluster fuck that night was the paramedics. They put us into the ambulance and, in all their glory, they switched our names. I needed an operation which involved having a blood transfusion. However, I was admitted under Colin's name and his parents were Jehovah's Witnesses. They didn't believe in blood transfusions and said "No" to the operation.

Need I say more?

South African bureaucracy nearly killed me that night. Thank God my parents arrived and cleared up the confusion. I was operated on in the early hours of the morning, but later that day, the marrow from the fractured femur leaked into my blood and I was put in intensive care. It was the first time I would receive an electric shock into my heart to restart it. I had three pins put into my femur and would lay up in hospital for the next four months in traction, undergoing more surgery as I got infections and skin transplants. I was restricted and very unhappy, but, most of all, I was in constant pain. I had plenty of time to think. My main thought was, 'Would I ever be able to walk properly again?' To people who have never had that thought process, let me tell you, it's mind altering. I wondered whether I would have the same quality of life. Was I going to get shit out of my life and not just get into shit for the hell of it? I became very determined.

My great uncle, Jimmy Clark, advised my parents to pursue an insurance claim. He introduced them to a firm of lawyers I would use again. They were very thorough. I spent every afternoon off school at one consultancy or another but it paid. With the money I bought a better motorbike, but most of all I learnt the value of good representation.

I was on crutches for three months after I was released. Once I started walking again, I immediately started at the gym, strengthening my entire body. Although I missed my final exams, I passed by my previous results.

Chapter 3

The remainder of our crew from that night at the roadhouse were still going strong and, by now, we had all bonded in the aftermath of our failure. We had learnt a healthy lesson about personnel choice and were ready to branch out again. It was around this time we started going out to nightclubs. As we had friends old enough to have cars, this was the next logical step in our search for entertainment.

During the early eighties, the liquor laws were so tight in South Africa, that nightclubs didn't have a liquor licence. Instead, they would sell you the mix and add alcohol for free. It was an ingenious way of getting around the conservative laws at the time. With the police having free entry and free alcohol, it was in the interest of their busy schedule and low wages to turn a blind eye.

Star Gazer was the first club we started to visit. Even though it was located in a small suburb east of Johannesburg, it was successful. They hired the toughest of guys to keep it safe. It was at this nightclub that I would be exposed to another type of fighting and to the bouncer mentality. My introduction to this new level of violence started with a bar fight where I ended up in casualty. There were about thirty of us going for each other. I had a broken beer bottle in my hand and was using it to stab a guy in the chest and arms. When the lights came on and everybody was told to sit down, I didn't realise it was an order I had to obey. I was deemed to be threatening the bouncer and, as I moved towards him, he broke my jaw. Suffice to say, I was hit over a few tables and woke up in Casualty in Johannesburg General Hospital.

Mandy's was another club we went to and I would be linked to it for the next twenty-three years. The name and the music kept changing, but the address stayed the same. I started working there when I turned seventeen. I was old enough to bounce, but too young to drink. Saturday nights were a warzone, with so much blood on the floor that it smelt like a butcher's shop. As a doorman I was expected to get involved in any fights that broke out. Our crew eventually became known as the wolf-pack of that nightclub, attracting the attention of the police and of the hospitals we were sending our victims to. The thing about Johannesburg in those days was that, due to conscription, everybody had been desensitised to violence by white South Africans. So, we got worse and worse. The funny thing was that Mandy's was becoming hugely popular despite the amount of fights. To this day I have only worked in one other nightclub that had so much blood flowing every Saturday night.

We were no longer a blip on the police intelligence radar. We were now an operation. The newly formed South African Narcotics and Alcohol Bureau (SANAB) had been alerted to an assault on a policeman we had previously beaten. Mandy's was their first operation. Their plan was simple. Some unit members would come into the club and interact and then the rest of the team would rush the door at a designated time. The real problem was that they had no real way of communicating. At the time of the raid, there were only two of them who managed to gain entrance to the club. What happened next was a nightmare for them. As they started the operation, they were isolated inside and were attacked by customers on their announcing their intent. The commanding officer, who had been held up outside, proceeded to rush the door with the other undercover guys. He was beaten senseless. When the blue lights arrived, the entire unit was bleeding on the floor, inside and outside the club. We were all arrested and handcuffed outside in the street. That night we made enemies who would become more powerful and would not forget us.

Their first operation was handled so badly that they resorted to tried and tested methods they knew well. The commanding officer was treated for his wounds and once he had his senses back, proceeded to beat us, while handcuffed in the street. Some of the uniformed policemen got involved and stopped the SANAB unit from assaulting us. Some were embarrassed by their behaviour, but I think most were conscious that the patrons of the club and newspapers were getting a full view of police tactics and becoming hostile. The newspapers came to our aid as they exposed the whole débacle. We were charged with assault, defeating the ends of justice and selling liquor without a licence. We pleaded not guilty. The magistrate gave us bail and adjourned our case for two weeks. We had all the charges dropped on the next appearance, but we didn't escape the attention of the powers that be.

With all the newspaper coverage, I was now famous. Every left-wing reporter was interested in this new unit. This would only make things worse as, instead of being invisible, I was now part of a police fuck-up. The machine was starting to take notice.

Mandy's reopened. We all went back to work, but it didn't take long before the next incident. Brothers had been terrorising another nightclub, The RES, and we were asked by the owner to keep them out. After consulting with our new friends we decided to take it on and divide up the money. We went to the The RES in force the next time the brothers arrived. In hindsight, it was asking for trouble and trouble we found. We arrived and the staff was already nervous. Strangely, they had a female bouncer at the door. Cutting a long story short, she started shooting. We started shooting and she was hit critically and died. All I remember was that it was a .38 special with a two-inch barrel that killed her. A lucky shot in that lighting and at that distance.

This brought a new kind of policeman into our lives, Brixton Murder and Robbery. Up until that point I didn't even know they existed. They were mostly National Intelligence Service operators, who had a ninety-eight per cent success rate, solving murders within twenty-four hours. Needless to say, we were in shit this time. I arrived at school that Monday morning and it happened during my first class. The classroom door opened and four large members grabbed me, beat me with a nightstick and handcuffed me. That was one of eighteen arrests that Monday morning, all co-ordinated and carried out in much the same way. Their station was a medieval looking building with cells and a charge office situated next to the Brixton

Tower. They had the first *Ware Kamer* (Truth Room) I was to encounter. Looking back, I had no idea what was in store for me.

I was thrown into the cell nearest the charge room. There were no charges at this point. Over the next few hours they filled up that cell. They didn't bother separating us. Interrogation started in the colonel's office. We were taken in by threes, stripped naked and made to wait. There's something intimidating about being naked and not being offered any other clothing. Naked, we stood in a row. Eventually the warrant officer entered and we were told that someone was going to the *Ware Kamer*. In later years, he would tell me we were the first and only white gang they ever did this to. To tell the truth I didn't want to be the first one, but it turns out we were all in for a visit to the Truth Room.

These days, people complain about water-boarding, but in the early eighties in South Africa, the security police had become adept at half-drowning you, with electronic shocks included at the same time. One by one, we were taken to the Truth Room. We had electrodes attached to our testicles and a threaded sack put over our heads. Then they put your head into a bucket of water. At first you hoped they wouldn't get the timing wrong and kill you, but after a while you stopped caring. I tried drinking as much as I could and hoping for the best, but they were just giving me "another night in paradise", as they put it. I realised why their success rate was so good. You would have confessed to anything just to get it over. When I wasn't asleep or being "paradised", I would sit at the barred door of the cell and watch the charge office. They knew we had no idea who had fired the shot that killed the female bouncer that night. It could have been any one of us. They were going to wait for the forensics to link the murder to the weapon. Mostly they were like us, but on the other side of the coin; insensitive to what they were doing, due to repeating it over and over again. We were gradually released on police bail. The guy who was charged with the murder, crossed the border into Botswana and obtained political asylum in England.

Soon after my release, I applied to study Commerce at two prominent universities, namely the University of Cape Town and the University of Witwatersrand. I was accepted by both and left the final decision up to the Senates of the Education Board. I didn't want to relocate to Cape Town, but I was seriously reconsidering my path after that short stay at the hands of the National Intelligence Service.

Just before my final exams, I was called into a meeting with the headmaster. He led me into his office where three men I didn't recognise were sitting. I would soon find out that these men were from the National Intelligence Service. When the headmaster excused himself, I knew something was wrong. I wasn't asked to sit, so I just stood there, waiting for the hammer to fall. The first question was something I will never forget.

"Do you understand the Conscription Act?"

Blunt and to the point. I thought it best to keep quiet. I was seventeen and not that confident around authority anymore. I knew enough to know that every white South African male had a choice. Either receive call-up papers and obey them, or be a conscientious objector and receive five years in a military prison. I hadn't received any registered post so I didn't know where this conversation was going. I was going to university which was the only way of stalling conscription. I was all ears. I was told that they owned two years of my life at some point, either when I finished university or dropped out. At some time in the future, I was going to become "State Property". I was everything they were looking for. Seventeen years old, doing exceptionally well at school, but, even more appealing, with a violent streak. I was told I could put away all thoughts of making beds, polishing boots, marching in unison, basically the entire robotic machine that is the making of a soldier and I was offered another deal, another route I could make a difference in. I had had enough of this kind of manipulation and without any real understanding of what I was being offered, I just said,

"Yes."

Chapter 4

Life went on. I tried to forget about what I had signed up for that morning, but it played on my mind almost every day. I knew it depended on my gaining entrance into Witwatersrand University, so I went all out for my final exams. I wrote my exams in October and November of 1984. I knew I had done well, hoping my good results would keep those men in the headmaster's office at bay, but it was quite the opposite.

On the morning of my last exam, I was visited at my parents' home by a man in army uniform. He had a parcel for me and demanded I sign his receipt. I was given a train ticket to Upington for the next evening. I remember arriving at the station and being met by a man in civilian clothing. He looked uncomfortable, which made me feel uncomfortable. After a short greeting, he led me to a white Mercedes. He didn't say much on the drive to a little fishing village north of Cape Town.

My first impression was not good. The whole camp was fenced off with only one gate. It looked like a low-level prison and I felt dismayed. This would be my home for the next five months. During my time here, my parents believed I was on holiday in Durban. They didn't even question it. I had been so good on the run-up to finals that they were relieved, I suppose. The driver read my apprehension and I remember his words.

"Just keep quiet, remain calm and don't answer back."

These words would see me through the upcoming ordeal. When I arrived I was introduced to the other conscripts. We were a small group, aged between eighteen and twenty-five. I was the youngest and the only English speaker. Everything from that moment on was taught in Afrikaans.

This type of training should never be confused with what is taught to soldiers in the first three months of basic training. Here, physical tests were rare, but academic tests were continuous. Sure, we were punished with running if anyone did anything stupid, but mostly we were put under pressure to regurgitate information we had been lectured upon. Sometimes we were fucked around by disinformation, but most of my training was, in hindsight, brain-washing. I was being trained to observe situations and write reports about them. The reports had to be relevant to the situation at hand. Although it may seem basic, it surprises me how few people can do it. I left that fishing village a military intelligence officer, equipped with an identity card and the rank of second lieutenant. That is all I'm going to say about those five months of my training, except that, during it, I received my acceptance to the University of Witwatersrand, but missed the initiation period.

So, onto Wits University. The University of the Witwatersrand was the only tertiary education establishment not receiving state funding. It was financed by big business. This allowed business to filter its recruitment and selection process. As a result, the campus was a hotbed of political dissent, with lecturers from all over Africa to give the rich, mostly white, students an alternative opinion and perspective on South Africa as it then was.

The students were mostly upper middle class and, although they regarded themselves as radical, the few token black students were pretty much just a tax write-off for big business. The black students were mainly from middle class backgrounds and were being groomed for the new South Africa.

My first mission was to find out where the relevant lecture halls were and what my roster was. As a first-year student, my subjects were set. They were economics, business economics, law, mathematics, statistics and accountancy. I soon settled and played a role in the University Event Rag Week which consisted of floats parading through the streets of Johannesburg. I also found myself a central role in the logistics of distributing the student magazine.

My mission at this university was to give reports on events to my handler whom I met in restaurants. I made progress on the reports by listening to Wits Radio Station at Tuesday and Thursday lunchtimes. There was one DJ, whom we shall call Bruce to save him from the embarrassment of his liberal thought process in 1985. Bruce made careful political rants in-between songs. I applied to the Wits Radio Station, volunteering for administration work at Tuesday and Thursday lunchtimes. My relationship with Bruce blossomed. He was a liberal's liberal. He had radical ideas on Bantu education and was surrounding himself with black students from across the campus. He was also a member of the United Democratic Front (UDF), the only organisation that hadn't been banned by the South African government at this time. I joined it with Bruce's sponsorship, in order to make my new masters happy. There was little I was exposed to at first. I wrote very low-level reports to my National Intelligence Service handler, but he hardly ever came back to me, so I presumed all was well.

At this time in my life, everybody I knew was either a conscripted soldier or a university student. I was both, but this was something I kept quiet. Colin had been conscripted to a maintenance regiment in Kimberly and we managed to stay in touch as much as possible. Brian on the other hand was still a year behind me and with my new found military influence I managed to get him conscripted into the air force. The South African Air Force was a place for privileged kids. They had the lowest work rate during basic training, the best food and, most importantly, the most time off from camp.

I was given a pager and chose a code. As new communications were taking off in South Africa, I needed to be aware. I was sent to the Limpopo Province and given a course in how to map telephones. It scared me. Although only land-lines were available at that time, I was taught how they were open to configuration, if you were on the radar. It was only basic stuff, but it showed me that walls truly did have ears. Now I could be paged at any time and I had to respond immediately. The reins were pulled in. This led to my next interaction with the military. Brian, although enjoying basic training, was having problems with two guys, who had their families pay their way into the Air Force Academy at Valhalla, Pretoria. His air force training headquarters were located on the same road as a military intelligence farm, in turn situated next to a farm owned by Police Intelligence. These two farms would later become notorious during the Truth and Reconciliation process of the Mandela Government.

As it happens, I was being briefed by the general in charge of that farm the evening Brian paged me. I phoned him back and he told me he was about to fuck a couple of big guys in the bungalow next to him. I told him to wait for me as I was close and in the mood. I left the farm filled with brandy and armed with an assault rifle. This was always going to be a recipe for disaster. A toothache looking for a tooth. By the time I arrived at the air force base I was late. I used my military ID access to the base and headed towards Brian's bungalow.

I woke Brian and we drank some wine I had taken from the Police Intelligence farm. Eventually, Brian told me about the two guys in the bungalow next to him. They were giving him a hard time because of Gary's reputation. As we got drunk, we got stupid and it ended with me entering their bungalow and beating them with a knuckleduster while they were asleep on the floor. Nobody came to their assistance. I went home. The next morning I was woken by the buzzer on the gate. It was the South African Air Force Police. I was arrested for sedition and taken in for questioning. They processed me into their cells, but I didn't give them a statement. Brian was brought in later that morning. He looked worried as they paraded him past my cell.

I was eventually taken before a judge. He had been given my status by my handler, but it was up to him inevitably how to rule on the case. By lunchtime I was offered a deal. I would plead guilty to two counts of grievous bodily harm and all sedition charges would be dropped. I pleaded guilty, was given a fine and released. Brian was also released. He returned to his Air Force regiment and upon graduating basic training was drafted into the South African Air Force Police. He would spend the next eighteen months of his conscription as an enforcer. We were all relieved and happy.

When you are constantly pulled out of shit, it will only make you worse. Absolution from guilt gives you a curious sort of confidence. I went back to university having no sense of responsibility for anyone or anything.

Chapter 5

Currently my life consisted of going to lectures, working weekends at a nightclub and attending UDF meetings. All those meetings simply rehashed the same story about resisting the corrupt and evil minority government. I continued to make weekly reports on them.

I had just finished my mid-year exams, when I was contacted on my pager. The number was new, but the voice was the same. I was told to report in person at an address he gave me by 13h00 the next day. The address turned out to be the new police headquarters in Johannesburg. That was the first time I walked into a police station out of choice and, just as I had been taught only a few months earlier, if you act as though you're supposed to be there, it usually runs smoothly. I met my handler. I liked him. He was wearing a well-worn, military police uniform, which would become familiar to the citizens of South Africa very soon. The police would never return to the old Cordeaux uniforms.

I remember that day like it was yesterday. I signed the Official Secrets Act for the second time and sat down. I was told the South African State President was about to declare a partial state of emergency in the Eastern Cape and areas of the old Transvaal, now renamed Gauteng. Life was about to change for all South Africans, but all I could think was, 'Fuck, just my luck.' The new powers to be given to the police and army would be, arrest, 24/7 house arrest, search and seizure, and the ability to prevent people working and participating in political activity. I remember leaving that building with the first headache I had ever had, thinking, 'What the fuck!' This was no longer a game. It had become very real and serious.

I had instructions to step-up contact with the UDF. To gain the organisation's confidence, I would inform my handler of my next UDF meeting and be arrested with all of them. Like all intelligence plans it was simple, yet bizarre. No more written reports were to be submitted and all briefings and debriefings would be done at different locations and off the record. I attended a small UDF meeting, paged the address to my master and we were all arrested. There was no safety-net put out for me. The cells were overcrowded and we were all beaten. Not badly, more like bullies flexing new-found authority. The cells filled up with more people. I was later informed that eight thousand UDF members were arrested that week, mostly in the Western Cape. Do you know how many people could be put into an eight-man cell? A lot.

Most of the detainees had wives and young children and the uncertainty of being separated from them escalated their paranoia and disillusionment. The new powers of detention, of imposing curfews and control of the media were slowly being drip-fed into increasingly overflowing cells. By this, the police were going to test the backbone of the UDF members. We all started to chat with each other and I was surprised by how unprepared they were. There were dentists, lawyers, printers, architects and they told me how consumer boycotts of white-owned business were going to be the way forward. It would be all non-violent protest. I remember thinking how conflict escalation was not something that anybody I met in those cells had any idea about. This was going to be a long haul for them and I felt sorry for them with their innocent outlook.

For me, the arrest was successful. I had gained the confidence of the leaders of the UDF operating around Johannesburg. It was amazing how quickly they confided in me. The real pity was that most of them would not attend a political meeting ever again. They had been criminalised and had felt the weight of the State's stick. I promptly debriefed all I knew to my handler. Things started to accelerate. Consumer boycotts took off in the second half of 1985, mostly against white-owned businesses. Although these boycotts were supposed to be peaceful, there was always going to be violence to enforce them. The UDF was in disarray. Many of their leaders were in prison and paranoia had set in. The way they communicated changed after those arrests and they began to show signs of militancy. I wanted a break from it. I saw my five years in Military Intelligence being nothing but bad and I was only seven months in. I was given time off to study for my final exams. I wrote my finals and knew I had passed all five subjects at first-year level.

I had kept in touch with Gary, who was still working at Mandy's night club, and went to see him one night. That caused another incident that would change my life. Gary had started to tax people he was fighting at Mandy's and his method was unique. Once he had beaten someone up, he would take their jewellery. That night he took a gold chain from the neck of the guy who started on him, but, as it turned out, the gold chain had been left to the guy by his deceased grandmother. As we were leaving we were surrounded in the car park by his team. I pulled out my .357 Magnum revolver and they all went quiet. They left but not before recording my car number plate. The problem was that the boy's father was a magistrate and his uncle an up-and-coming prosecutor in the Johannesburg High Court. This was not going to go away.

I was approached by a Brixton policeman, who told me he would make it go away if I returned the gold chain. I thought it best to report to the army, which I duly did. I wasn't able to get hold of my handler however and was passed off to a junior officer. He told me not to hand it back. It would be an admission of guilt. So, I was arrested and, as usual, made no statement, so no bail. I was sent to the police cells at Hillbrow and waited to be prosecuted by the boy's uncle. It was two days before I was brought in front of my handler and a man wearing the rank of major general. Although I had been familiarised with the ranking system during training, I had only ever seen this rank on a dedicated information board. I was in awe.

They were livid at the junior officer's advice and told me the courts were resisting new laws and, until new legislation was broadened, I would have to wait it out. He assured me bail was inevitable but to intervene was impossible. So, I was put back into the police cells in Hillbrow and given access to a high-powered lawyer. Spending those weeks in the cells I saw that the arrests were still ongoing and people outside the system had no idea how determined the state had become. I was given bail and went back to lectures, waiting for the upcoming court case.

Chapter 6

The trial was eventually set for 1 June 1986. My father attended with me, as did some of my friends. I was facing two counts of assault with intent to inflict grievous bodily harm, pointing a firearm in a built-up area, theft and perverting the course of justice. This was all because of a fight I hadn't even started with someone over his stupid gold chain. The first three days consisted of prosecution witnesses, who all painted a bleak picture of my actions. The last witness was the son of the magistrate. He gleefully told the courtroom how I had taken his chain from him, after I had assaulted him for no reason. My lawyer absolutely ripped into his testimony, but he remained steadfast and stuck to his story. I was cross-examined by the uncle, who had no interest in the trial and knew I would be found guilty no matter how he performed. I was convicted on all four counts with each having up to a five-year sentence. I was to be sentenced the next day.

That's when the major general came to see me again. He said this stupid court case wasn't going to fuck-up his domestic operations. He intervened and, invoking powers that could be considered Martial Law, he took my sentencing out of the hands of the magistrate and gave it to a group of three judges and two assessors. It struck me that this was quite some power-play. They were waiting for me the next day. My sentence comprised three years for assaults, six months for being unfit to possess a firearm and fines for petty theft and perverting the course of justice. However, the sentences were suspended for five years. Checkmate. Justice had been seen to be done.

Soon after this trial, I turned twenty and felt everything was in the realm of accomplishment. I started to breathe again, but a few weeks later another hammer hit me. I was being debriefed at Johannesburg central command during my mid-year holiday when I was told there was a different plan for me. The court case had made me subject to unnecessary exposure. I had been in the newspapers during the trial and the victory of the sentencing was only going to make me more vulnerable.

Therefore, the plan was to leave university and undergo further military training. I signed up, as it couldn't be any worse than a lengthy jail term. Upon the completion of training, I would be promoted and start operations in a different Province.

On Friday of that week, I was introduced to a lieutenant colonel. He told me he was going to take over my training. I was to sign a form that had already been completed and was on his desk. It was a G5 Physiological Discharge form that would complete my leaving university and being called-up. It was pre-stamped by the Medical Battalion in Pretoria and all it needed was my signature. He told me he would accept my application and I would no longer be under any constraint for my conscription, but he reminded me I still was under contract with the military for another three years. 'Things just get better and better,' I thought sarcastically, as I signed it.

I took a DC10 military transport plane to the Military Base of Uitenhage, situated south of Port Elizabeth. The Eastern Cape was a hotbed of political activity and, more importantly, the international point of operations by all factions.

I was given a private sleeping area and left to sleep in. I had food with me and thought it best to keep off the radar. At 10h00, the lieutenant colonel came in and politely asked if I was happy before instructing me to go and requisition my new uniform from the store. At the store, I was given a new set of uniforms and lapels with one pip on the shoulders, denoting second lieutenant. I was now an active lieutenant. It was the first time I had worn any rank in the South African Defence Force (SADF). What a difference it was going to make.

I attended my first lecture the following Monday morning. To my dismay I would be trained on a one-on-one basis by the lieutenant colonel. He smiled when I walked into the office and informed me I could address him as "Peter" or "Colonel" in the classroom, but only as "Colonel" anywhere else.

He told me that, on successful completion of this experiment, he would be promoted to full colonel and I would be awarded the rank of first lieutenant. Together, we were going to go through one module a week. I would write an exam every Friday afternoon, remembering that "the little green men" who set these exams made sure one hundred percent was not possible, but I was expected to get close. Failure was not an option for either of us. I decided to excel for him. He handed out my first reading material and told me that anything I felt I should read would be accessed for me, within reason. I was told to be careful what I asked for, as the walls had ears. He then said,

"There are two ways to wade through the crap. Reading the books in their entirety or an idiot list. Which one do you want?"

As I had no idea what an idiot list was, I asked if I could have both. He smiled for the first time since I had met him and we seemed to get closer. It isn't important what the subject matter was in the next eighteen weeks, but it is important that, by the beginning of week three, the colonel started to lunch with me. I learnt more in those hours than I could have done from all the different books I had to read. During our third lunch, I asked the colonel if the walls in the mess had ears. He replied,

"Why?"

I asked him to get me a book by Tom Sharpe titled *Riotous Assembly*. It was the first time he laughed with me. The book arrived that Friday morning and I looked forward to reading some banned material that weekend. After my exam that Friday afternoon, he asked me if I would like to spend the weekend off-base with his family at his house in Port Elizabeth. I could think of nothing more appealing. His wife was absolutely lovely and his daughter and son were revelations. We all went out to a restaurant that evening and, after being told that shop talk was out until Monday, I enjoyed one of the best evenings of my life. My mind absorbed the family small talk and my taste buds absorbed flavours prepared by a very good chef. After three weeks living with officer types, I was happy to be amidst the normality of family life. I was very grateful. I spent every weekend after that at his house. At the end of the eighteen week course, I hadn't been home for months and didn't care much any more.

I wrote my final exam two days before Christmas 1986, and we had a party at the officer's mess. I was awarded the rank of first lieutenant and Peter was wearing the rank of full colonel. We had become firm friends and had both completed our tasks successfully. I was saluted with vigour that afternoon and had a strongly warm feeling of being part of the biggest gang I knew. But with every high, there comes a low. I was about to receive my orders.

Chapter 7

I flew to Windhoek and was directed to a convoy of vehicles heading for a military base outside a town called Rundu on the border with Angola. I jumped into the front of a SAMIL 20. The next morning, I took my physical and was given a G1 K1, "Fit for Duty". I was then told I was being moved to a base in Kapako and that my travel had been arranged. It was all very whirlwind, but seemed to have purpose.

The next day I was collected by a very friendly corporal driving an armoured vehicle. He told me we would be in Kapako in about two hours. We arrived just before lunch and I was dropped off outside a small lodge about a kilometre outside the town. There I was greeted by a woman with a German accent. She booked me into a room and offered me lunch. Her husband was soon to make my acquaintance. He was very pleasant towards me and offered to have my kit cleaned.

The following morning, I was approached in the breakfast-room by the German owner with an envelope. I would be picked up outside the front of the lodge just after lunch and instructed to be wearing full military uniform with my ID on hand. After lunch, I waited in the reception, making small talk with the maid, who had cleaned my uniform and given me a haircut the previous afternoon. She brought me a magazine to read while I waited. A driver came into the reception, as I was finishing an article. He drove me to the biggest building in Kapako. At the reception, I was greeted by a young first lieutenant and taken up to the first floor. I was shown into a small classroom, where another officer with lapels denoting a Panzer Battalion (Mechanised Regiment) was already seated at one of the desks. The classroom eventually filled up with about thirty boys, all eager to find out what was in store.

A very fat, middle-aged colonel came in, accompanied by a corporal carrying a large hot water dispenser. He was followed by a soldier carrying jars of coffee and sugar and a third soldier carrying milk cartons in buckets of ice. Whilst writing on the board at the front of the room, the colonel told us to help ourselves to coffee and not to ask permission for anything that would disrupt the briefing. I realised this briefing was going to take a while. Files were handed out. He started by giving a brief outline about his motivation. There would be no written exam and we were to ask no questions until he finished. He told us this briefing would bear neither on his record nor on his conscience, so he couldn't care less if we all fell asleep, so long as we didn't snore. I was the only English-speaking officer in the room, but the lecture was going to be in English anyway. Nobody complained, as he wouldn't have cared less. I liked him.

We were briefed on the history of colonization in Africa. We spent about an hour on the topic, looking through our files as he spoke. It was much like school history and pretty easy to absorb, as there was nothing new to know. We were first taught about the country that we were in. South West Africa, now Namibia, had been a German colony from 1884, but after the First World War the League of Nations had mandated South Africa to administer the territory. After the Second World War, the League of Nations was dissolved and its successor, the United Nations, instituted a trusteeship to bring all former German colonies in Africa under United Nations control. South Africa objected, arguing that the majority of the people living in South West Africa were content with South African rule. For the next twenty years, there was legal argument. In October 1966, the United Nations General Assembly decided to end the South African Mandate. It declared that South Africa had no right to administer the territory and it would take responsibility for South West Africa.

In 1966, the South West African People's Organisation (SWAPO), the military wing of the People's Liberation Army of Namibia, began guerrilla attacks on the South African forces in South West Africa. These attacks were mostly launched from bases in Zambia, but after Angola became independent in 1975, SWAPO established bases in Southern Angola and the threat became more severe.

In 1977, Canada, West Germany, France, the United Kingdom and the United States launched a joint diplomatic effort to bring about an internationally acceptable transition to independence in South West Africa. Unilaterally held elections were held in 1978, but were boycotted by the SWAPO. They declared elections illegal, unless they were part of them. After those elections, South Africa continued to administer South West Africa through coalitions and their appointed Administrator General. We were told that, as long as there was a threat to South Africa or its territories, we would be ordered to fight.

We broke for supper and I think we all felt a little apprehensive about that afternoon's final lecture. After supper, we went back to the classroom. There was very little said between us. It was the least social atmosphere I had ever encountered in the SADF. The colonel came back in and told us to pay specific attention to the history of Angola, as we needed to understand the threat this country could exert on South Africa. Angola had been a colony of Portugal. He explained that the Carnation Revolution in Portugal had resulted in a new government there, which legislated immediately to abandon all overseas Portuguese territories, including Angola. On 11 November 1975, a transitional government was established in Angola, which caused infighting between the three parties contesting the approaching election. The result of that election had been that the Popular Movement for the Liberation of Angola (MPLA) would rule the Northern Provinces and the National Union for the Total Independence of Angola (UNITA), the South-Eastern Provinces. Between 10 September and 7 October 1987, the Armed Forces for the Liberation of Angola (FAPLA), the armed wing of the MPLA, advanced into South-Eastern Angola to attack UNITA at its Mavinga headquarters.

The SADF's primary objective was to protect UNITA in Southern Angola and to prevent SWAPO from using this region to launch attacks into South West Africa. The SADF would intervene on UNITA's behalf. The Soviet and Cuban influences in Angola were encouraging South Africa to delay any change to the status quo by dominating large tracts of land in Southern Angola and providing surrogate forces for UNITA.

There were very few questions asked at the end of that briefing, mostly because everybody was tired, but the lecture had been self-explanatory. We were about to intervene in the Angolan Civil War. This would lead to the largest battle on African soil since the Second World War. I couldn't wait.

We were all handed orders on the way out of the building. I was to report to the armourer the next morning and would be collected after breakfast by a maintenance corporal. I was impressed by the efficiency of the military. For the first time, I could see how it worked. If you missed one order and did not attend, you would not be there to receive the next one. What Peter had taught me in Uitenhage, I was now witnessing at work.

The next morning, I was taken to the armoury of a large military camp. I signed for a Vector R1 7.62 calibre assault rifle, with five spare magazines and a Colt 1911 .45 calibre pistol, with three spare magazines. I was given a webbing belt with a holster and asked to pick out a *dooiby* (plastic helmet) and a *staaldak* (metal helmet) to fit over it. I collected a new pair of boots, a pair of sunglasses and a bush hat.

The captain in charge of the stores asked me if I wanted to go to the range to fire in my new weapons. I jumped at the chance. I hadn't worked an R1 since my basic training at Upington. We walked over to a massive firing range and waited for the troops to finish. I stripped the two weapons down, re-assembled them and filled the magazines while we waited. I remember feeling a little apprehensive about shooting in a one-on-one situation, but the captain seemed very cool about everything and I relaxed. I shot off all the rounds I had been given for both weapons that morning. While I was shooting there was another officer shooting from behind and to the left of us. I was just firing rounds through the barrel but he seemed to be making more considered shots down the range. I went back to the stores and signed for the same amount of ammunition I had just used.

A car was waiting to take me back to the lodge. I was heavily armed and apprehensive about the future. That night, I was given orders that, the next morning I would be transported to a camp at Mupini. A very happy English-speaking corporal collected me the next morning and drove me to the camp. It struck me immediately how new it was. The entire camp was a demarcated tented area with a nine-metre wire fence around it. There were a couple of troops doing guard duty at the gate, who both saluted me and let me in without any checks. I remember thinking how happy and relaxed everyone I met seemed to be.

The camp was situated on a small tributary on the south side of the Okavango River, which separated South West Africa from Angola. Whoever had decided the location of the camp was more interested in the efficiency of access rather than the defence of the camp. Clearly, its purpose was not to absorb an attack.

I was greeted by a staff sergeant, who saluted me with gusto and seemed happy to see me. His enthusiasm soon turned cold when he addressed me in Afrikaans and I responded in English. He took me to a tent in silence and told me the colonel expected all new officers to meet him in his office before the lunch of the day. He pointed out the colonel's office which was just another tent close by. I went to see the colonel and his opening line was,

"I don't trust people who don't drink or smoke, Lieutenant."

He proceeded to pour me a drink and offer me a cigarette. I took both. This was a very different type of officer, less polished but very sure of both his position and authority. He told me he had requested an intelligence officer to gather information on the enemy from a mission nearby. He had expected someone with more experience, but I would have to do. I gave him a brief outline of my years in schools run by priests and nuns. He seemed satisfied and, pouring himself another stiff whisky for the walk, told me to follow him to lunch.

The colonel and I arrived at lunch with two officers sitting at a table wearing nothing but shorts and sandals. They were introduced to me as a major and a captain. I was told there were two other lieutenants in the camp but the major and the captain were in charge of the comings and goings in the camp. The captain told me to report for roll call that evening, when he would introduce me to the troops. I was not to wear my rank from that time on and there would be no more saluting.

I was told to visit a Christian mission nearby the next day, so I went to the stores to get some kit. The sergeant in charge of the storeroom had been working on a motorbike outside, at the back. He proudly showed me his prized possessions, ten Honda CR200 off-road motorcycles. They had been painted army earth brown and were lovingly parked in a row. After acquiring what I wanted, I went to see the colonel and told him I needed one of the bikes to enable me to engineer a chance meeting at the mission. He signed a requisition form between finishing off his whisky and pouring another one. That afternoon, I went back to the store room and commandeered one of the bikes. The sergeant was unhappy that his little routine had been disrupted, but he put up minimal resistance

Chapter 8

I found the path to the mission and followed it to a small group of buildings and a very run-down church. I knocked on the door of a small building which had some signs of life in the form of smoke coming out of a very dangerous looking chimney. A Scandinavian priest welcomed me in for a cup of tea. I could have done with an alcoholic drink but accepted the invitation. I was wearing fatigues, boots and a vest. He was very friendly and took me to be a prospective convert, looking for somewhere to talk. He told me there were two priests, one Catholic and himself, an Anglican. He was from Finland and the Catholic priest was Portuguese. The Catholic priest presided over funerals in the area and travelled a lot of the time, but he would be there to see me the next day. I went back to the camp and made a report which was submitted that night at supper. The colonel seemed impressed at my progress. Luck appeared to be on my side, but anyone who had gone there would have been welcomed. I was just the first to try.

The next day I went back to the mission by another path. I just wanted to ride the bike. The Portuguese priest was very pleasant and poured out information about funerals he was called upon to take. He didn't realise I was making conversation for a very different reason than he was and proceeded to tell me more than I could ever have imagined; information that directly involved what was going on in South Eastern Angola. SWAPO were coercing the locals for food and shelter. They would execute people in the villages from time to time to make a point of their strength.

That night I submitted another report at supper and my obvious ability at getting a priest to talk was the topic of the evening. I was accepted into the fold of officers and remember thinking how easy it all was. My years in a Catholic school were paying off in a way I had never imagined. I was well versed in bible studies and to the Catholic priest, I appeared very religious. He couldn't tell me enough. Each day I would use a different bike and the sergeant, realising I was going to bring the bike back to him in one piece, became more and more friendly. It's amazing how lonely it would have been if I had been excluded just because I was English. That was something about South Africans I never got used to.

After a couple of weeks of submitting information and knowing when there was a funeral in the area and what the cause of death was, I was approached by the colonel in the Mess. He told me I was to go back to the lodge in Kapako. There I would be debriefed by an intelligence officer. I had made an impact that probably should have been drawn-out more. I liked being the gatherer of information and I had more to talk about than the rest of the officers combined. I felt wanted, but this sudden success in the area had made me realise I was on somebody's radar. I believe the colonel had thought I would survey the mission from afar. Nobody thought of just knocking on the door. Success has its own rewards.

That Thursday morning, I was sent back to Kapako. The lodge was as I had left it. At supper I got drunk with an officer from Johannesburg. He was seriously overweight with greasy hair and acted like a pig. Although we had very little in common, other than that we had grown up in the same city, I drank with him for the night. He had very different experiences and memories of Johannesburg, but we got on really well. The next day I slept the hangover off and read in my room, trying to get ready for my oral debriefing.

On Saturday morning, there was a knock on my door. It was the same officer I had got drunk with on the Thursday night. He was now wearing full military uniform and sporting the rank of a major. I realised he was the person I was expecting. He had profiled me that Thursday night and I should have seen it coming. In Uitenhage, Peter had taught me that if you have a good-looking girl and a bottle of brandy to throw at the problem, everybody will eventually talk. That night I had talked. Although I had not said anything about the operations, I still had given him an insight into my mind. I was a bit embarrassed that I had been duped so easily by him. Most of all I was now wary of his methods. I mistrusted him. I answered his questions about the mission as best as I could, but in brief sentences so far as possible. He was less impressed with my progress than the colonel at the camp had been. He made notes all the time.

When he appeared satisfied with the intelligence I was confirming, he told me to put on my uniform. We would lunch together at a restaurant in the town. Over lunch, we made small talk. I wanted to return to my room at the lodge as there was nothing more I felt I could help him with, or so I thought. After lunch, he ordered a bottle of whisky to be sent to our table, but I wasn't going to fall for that again. I ordered water. After he downed a large whisky, the hammer fell. He told me the nuns at the mission were harbouring SWAPO operators, giving them food and sometimes even basic medical help. He wanted to interrogate the nun who was in charge of the infirmary and told me I would be given a car outside the lodge the following morning. Taped to the underside of the steering column, I would find a packet of capsules. Once I had made friends with the nun in charge, I would break one of the capsules into her food and she would become violently ill. I would then rush her to the military hospital in Rundu, about a fifteen-minute drive at night, where he would be waiting each evening from the following day onwards. The next day I went back to the camp in my issued car, a white Toyota Corolla. It was very under-powered but I presumed that was all part of the plan.

On Monday, I drove to the mission and was met by the Scandinavian priest. He told me his colleague was across the border taking a funeral service. It was amazing how trusting they were. If only they had known what my intentions were that day, I might have seen another side to their religious principles. I had brought them food from the camp, which I had done before, and offered to cook supper for everyone. That afternoon I made a roast chicken dinner and while I was cooking in the kitchen, the nuns came in one after the other, giving me advice and approval. There were fewer than ten, so far as I could tell. Only two were white, but it was apparent who was in charge. I laced her food and served it to her. It shocked me how quickly the crushed pill I had put in her food worked. She began to throw up almost immediately and then defecated in her clothes. It was obvious she had been poisoned, yet nobody pointed a finger. Everyone was concerned by the symptoms, not by the possible cause. I offered to take her to hospital. The Scandinavian priest insisted on accompanying me. On the way to Rundu, I thought the nun was going to die. She threw up and retched throughout the journey. The poison was crude but effective. On arrival at the hospital, we were questioned at the reception, until the major arrived in a white coat and acted as though he was admitting her. Everyone at the casualty seemed to know him and he wheeled her away with the priest in tow. I found out later that, later that night, she had been moved to military hospital in Pretoria and was never seen again.

When I went back to the mission a few days later, the Portuguese priest told me the nun had been sick on and off for a while. He was glad she was in good hands. He was absolutely thankful I had been there to help her. I couldn't believe it had all worked so simply. The fact that she was the only person to get sick from the food aroused no suspicion of foul play. I suppose she was acting out of Christian conviction, but in reality she was just a cog in the machine that was the South West African border during those years. She had been servicing both sides and must have known the dangers involved.

I continued going to the mission every day. Now I was really part of the family. The other nuns, believing I had been the saving grace that afternoon, started to talk to me. They told me there was a huge SWAPO presence in the area just north of the river. They were moving around and forcing villages to assist them at night. I filed reports consisting of relevant information from conversations with the priests and the nuns. The colonel of my camp was very happy with me and, after a couple of weeks, I was informed I would be flying to Pretoria with him. At that time, I couldn't have cared less. It was August and the days were hot and the nights deceptively cold. I was happy to get away for a few days. Upon arrival at the Air Force base in Valhalla, Pretoria, the two of us were driven to Military Headquarters at Pelindaba. There, we were taken immediately to the administration block and greeted by a very old colonel. He looked tired and unwell, but friendly. We followed him to his office and I was given a cup of coffee while they both had a stiff whisky. I was relieved that the two colonels not only seemed to know each other, but were friends. I was told I had done a good job and was being allowed to go home for a couple of days. As I was dismissed, I was told,

"Lieutenant, it's war. If you have any regrets you should remember that the game needs to be shot, not the players."

I just wanted to go home and sleep. During the next three days back at home, I never even went out of the house apart from going to buy a cake at a bakery in town. To this day I believe it sells the best cream cakes I have ever tasted. I was happy at my parents' house. I had both silence and privacy and rested with my thoughts.

Three days later I flew back to South West Africa. Upon arrival at the camp, there were a few changes. There were new personnel but, more noticeably, supplies were continually being brought through the gates. Anybody observing this sudden activity would know something was on. After a week or so, SAMIL 20 trucks started to arrive. Infantry soldiers began arriving and the noise was deafening. They were assigned beds and equipment. It had been a while since I had heard parade ground orders being issued. They came fast and furious, with as much swearing as possible. I was just happy to get on my bike and go riding.

The following week, more senior non-commissioned officers arrived, along with junior infantry officers, doing their best to look as though they were in charge. Then came the Puma helicopters, with more senior officers on board. The choppers landed on the parade ground and the officers they brought that day gave it all away. They were focussed, fresh and determined. I met one of them at supper that night. He seemed to be in his element with what was happening. He told me he had been training for a year for this. It's difficult to understand how much things are changed in an isolated environment by an influx of about 800 males. The whole camp suddenly became alive, noisy and distracting.

At supper, the camp colonel asked me to join him at his table, where I was accompanied by the battalion colonel and a lieutenant colonel. I was told I would have to wear full combat uniform from the next morning onwards. There were to be no exceptions to wearing rank at all times. I was not to interfere with training in any way and would be expected to be available at the shooting range in Kapako every Thursday afternoon. More importantly, I would continue to visit the mission, reporting information concerning SWAPO movements to the colonel and fending off any of the priests' concerns about the huge number of men at the camp. Furthermore, I could requisition to have lunch with the colonel's table, if I had anything important to talk about, but otherwise not to waste a seat.

That evening, when I returned to my tent, all seven beds apart from my own which, since my arrival, I had previously had to myself, were occupied. Their occupants were familiar with each other and didn't interact with me much, so I just listened and read. I was the ranking officer in the tent, so I felt it better for them to approach me on a personal level at a later stage. The next morning I attended roll call at 06h00 on the parade ground. Assembled that day were six companies, 120 men in each one. Each company had four corporals, a sergeant, a second lieutenant and a first lieutenant. There were three captains assigned to two companies, to whom the lieutenants reported, and one major, to whom the captains reported. Heading the parade were the colonel and his executive officer. A further section from the signal regiment consisted of twelve signalmen, two corporals, one sergeant, one senior staff sergeant, two lieutenants and a captain. The camp was full.

Later the same morning, I went to the mission in full combat uniform. The priests didn't mention the number of troops in the immediate area, so I brought it up. I told them I was being made to wear army regulation uniform at all times and couldn't wait for these war games to be over. I wanted to go back to less formal times. The Catholic priest was suspicious of my rank. He tried hard to cover the fact, but I knew it was going to be the end of my infiltration. I wrote a report to the colonel explaining that I felt I was compromised and would not be able to sustain my initial progress. My contact with the mission ended.

I attended roll call on the parade ground every morning and evening and ate the mandatory three meals a day in the Officers' Mess. The conversation at my table was repetitious beyond belief and I mostly kept myself to myself. On the next Thursday, when I joined the shoot at the range in the camp at Kapako, the only thing that stood out was that the same officer as before was shooting with deliberation from further back. It seemed strange, but I didn't care too much and let it go. Shooting is always fun and I had been taught to shoot from an early age.

The officer, who had been shooting from behind me, a captain, came to speak to me afterwards. He had read about me in the newspapers but did not seem at all put off. He was from Johannesburg, short, heavy-set with a black beard and short-cropped hair. I liked him. He told me to requisition a four-day pass to Kapako. He would make sure it got authorised as the battalion colonel at my camp was his uncle. I filled out the forms later that evening and on Friday afternoon I was issued four days liberty in Kapako. As the sun was setting and surrounded by military vehicles, I set off in my Toyota for Kapako.

I was put into the same room at the lodge. I went to supper that evening and was shown to the table of the captain, who had arranged my pass. We ate, made small talk and then I drank with him through the night, marking the beginnings of a friendship that would last all my time in South Africa. When we were alone, he told me to call him Sean. I asked him why he had been shooting from a distance on the range and he told me that, if I wanted, he'd show me the next day. The following morning, a Saturday, he woke me very early and told me we had the shooting range all to ourselves. I couldn't think of anything I would have rather done than go shooting with him. Once there, he requisitioned a FN-FAL assault rifle for me which fired the same 7.62x51 mm NATO round as the R1 assault rifle I had been trained with. It had a telescopic sight welded to the dust cover and was beautiful to look at. He opened the boot of the vehicle and removed a bag with the exact same weapon inside. I shot one thousand rounds that morning, with my sights being adjusted after every thirty rounds. I loved it. It was better shooting that rifle than being in bed with any girl I had ever been with up to then. I still think it surpasses any experience since. I got better and better as the morning went on, shooting from further and further distances. Sean was delighted at my progress with the rifle and gave me as much encouragement as he could. We had lunch together in the town and he asked me if I was willing to operate with him, if something came up. I could think of nothing more appealing and replied,

"Of course."

He told me to keep the rifle. I might need it soon. I went back to Mupini on the Tuesday evening and was given orders upon entering the camp. I had been moved to a two-man tent next to the camp colonel. My belongings had already been moved. I spent most of the last week of August 1987 by myself in that tent and it wasn't until the following week that Sean moved in. It was a Saturday morning and when I returned to the tent after breakfast, Sean's kit was there. All his rifles, a Vector R1, a FN-FAL and a Heckler and Koch G3 were neatly stacked up against the bed. I was reading when he came into the tent. He was in a great mood and had a bottle of whisky, which we drank that morning. He told me I was going to have to spend some time in the signals tent to familiarise myself with the personnel and the codes being used. We got on so well that I was very happy to have someone to talk to beyond the day-to-day military chatter. He was not only well educated, but also very funny when he wanted to be. The way he portrayed his thoughts was a breath of fresh air and I was truly grateful to be back in the loop with somebody in that camp.

The next morning, we each took a motorbike. I was impressed by his ability to ride and we went to the mission. We didn't go in, or stop to speak to anyone. He knew about my previous operation here, but we went on and crossed the river into Angola. It was my first time and I was apprehensive, but I followed him across. Once we had cleared the vegetation on the north bank of the river, we found a trail and followed it to a small village. We were greeted by delighted villagers. I understood how rural they were by the way they revered two bikes being brought into their world by two strange white people. We handed out chocolate and became the life and soul of the village. It struck me it wasn't Sean's first time that side of the river, as he took it all in his stride.

We stopped for lunch at an ancient, disused copper mine about twenty kilometres into Angola. Sean brought out a couple of ration packs, called "rat packs". I hadn't opened and eaten one since my basic infantry training at Upington and had no fond memories of them. They consisted of dehydrated food and were more of a lucky dip. When we had finished, he passed me a water bottle and said flippantly,

"You better get used to this type of food Peter. It's gonna be all we have soon."

That afternoon, when we returned to the camp, he told me to park the bike at the entrance of our tent, as we were no longer answering to the maintenance unit for our comings and goings. The next day after breakfast, we rode to Kapako. That afternoon was spent on the shooting range. There were squads of infantry men coming all day, but we took up position behind them and spent the whole day taking specific shots at targets set up for us. We repeated it every day that week. I became so familiar with the new rifle that it became second nature to load the magazine, count the rounds and fire a consistent shot at different ranges.

The next week we did it again. This time we kept contact by touching feet, with no talking. We interacted with hand signals and attracted each other's attention with our feet. All five rifles, Sean's three and my two, shot the same ammunition, so we used each other's rounds without thinking. It's amazing how simple uniformity is, and how necessary. Each day of the second week we would only speak to one another at lunch.

The third week we went to the range, armed only with our service pistols. Once there, we were given AK-47s. We occupied the mornings doing drills with our handguns and the afternoons with the AKs. At that time, nothing seemed strange about what we were doing but, looking back, I realise how specialised it was.

Those three weeks were about as pleasant as they could be in northern South West Africa. We were left alone unless we asked for anything and, when we did, it arrived as soon as it could. No reports were submitted and I felt more freedom than I had in a while. My friendship with Sean became stronger and stronger and when he asked me if I had any questions, I generally remained silent.

One Thursday afternoon after lunch, Sean appeared seemingly animated, but I had become used to his highs and thought little of it. The next day we drove to the Kapako camp in the Toyota with only our handguns, my FN-FAL, and Sean's H&K G3. We were met at the gate by a stern looking major and followed him on foot to his office. The camp was very quiet and strangely empty. On entering the office, I immediately noticed the equipment on the floor. Sean started going through it and, at first, he said very little. Then, once he had sorted it, he turned to me and said,

"We are now operational."

There was a glint in his eye that made me queasy, but I said nothing. We packed up the equipment he had chosen and walked with it to the shooting range. It was as though I was not being told everything, but I had become used to how the army worked.

We spent the next three days on the range, all by ourselves. We spent every day lying under a tarpaulin and moving to another part of the range at early evening. We practised moving without conversation and using a marker fixed to a pad that could be wiped clean after every interaction. We ate only rat packs and hardly slept. By the time we had finished those seventy-two hours, we were absolutely in sync with each other. We communicated perfectly and were able to eat, drink and move around in absolute silence.

On Monday morning, I was asked by the major to come and see him privately in his office. I wanted to get back to my base to wash, shave and eat a good meal. The major told me I was to draw anything of interest I observed in the coming days. At this point my fears were starting to make sense. I had spent the best part of a month doing highly specialised training and now I knew why. I was going behind enemy lines to gather information. This was a long way from the deal I had struck in my headmaster's office nearly three years earlier, yet I felt strangely excited.

The next day, we were choppered out of the camp to a point about thirty kilometres north-east of the river. We had full packs and although we walked approximately ten kilometres in total silence for each of the following three nights, we rested during the day. It was all very exciting. Sean seemed to know exactly where we were going and I kept making notes on the terrain to keep the major happy. Just before dawn on the third night, we stopped on high ground to the north of a town. Although there was very little activity when we passed the town at night, by dawn we watched the town come to life. The day in early September was very hot. When the sun rises in rural southern Africa, it clears the chill very quickly. We were under a tarpaulin with our feet touching, just as we had practised. I was hot and uncomfortable, but I started taking notes.

The town was a hive of activity. Women were collecting water. Small boys were taking goats out to pasture. There were military vehicles parked in the forest on the other side of a stream. They were transport vehicles for an MPLA unit, with Cuban and Russian advisors. The personnel appeared relaxed and confident. I remember thinking about how, during all the years of my training, I had been taught about the Red Peril. Today, as the sun rose, I was only some 500 metres from it. The Russians and Cubans were fighting with and advising very poorly trained and poorly motivated MPLA African soldiers. The Cold War was being played out in Africa.

Later that afternoon, it started to rain. At that time of year, it's almost guaranteed to rain in the afternoon. Although it was a relief from the heat, it was Sean's signal to go to work. Sean used his foot against mine to alert me. He pointed to the area where the forest was closest to the stream. I took my binoculars and focussed on where Sean had pointed. There was a middle-aged European man washing his face. He had short cropped hair, military fatigues that I recognised as Russian, and a well worn-in set of boots. Sean shot him in the chest as he stood up. Watching a man die instantly through a pair of binoculars is cold reality. Although seeing someone being shot dead wasn't new to me, it was the last thing I had expected. I suppose it was naïve of me, but it's the truth. I wasn't moved by the sight of the entry wound so much as I was by the role we were playing that day. We were there to kill a specific advisor.

There was a flurry of activity in the forest and I watched with interest to see the response time. At first there was confusion. Three more Russian officers and six Cubans appeared. Sean shot the next one almost immediately. Most people would think this might have disclosed our position, but on humans it has quite the opposite effect. The unexpected froze their minds and it was only when Sean shot the third one, that they began to take cover.

Everything went eerily quiet in the forest below us. By moving his pointed finger up to the sky in a circular motion, Sean motioned me to start packing. I couldn't have agreed more. We packed up as quickly and quietly as possible, but, with that much adrenalin running through your body, it's difficult to stay calm and think. We retreated about 500 metres and waited for the sun to set. Sitting there as the light faded, I shrugged my shoulders with my palms upward, asking him, "What was that?" He copied my signal exactly and had a huge grin on his face. I knew then that I had been had. Although I was getting used to being told only what I needed to know, this was not at all funny. There is something about someone trusting you enough to watch him kill someone however, and we would stay friends.

We took a week to walk back to South West Africa, moving only at night. On the first night, we headed northwards. It seemed the best plan, as they would have expected us to go south. Just after midnight, we altered direction to the east. By now it was not a shave and a shower that I wanted, but to get back. We ditched our equipment on the third night, keeping only our weapons and light kit. It rained every afternoon, but the ground usually dried by evening. I was sure we were being chased, but Sean was calm, judging that they weren't organised enough. He told me there had been intelligence about that convoy's movements and they had to be stopped at that town. The best way to create confusion was to kill the officers. I agreed.

Now I wanted a proper meal. I remember thinking that if I were killed, I wouldn't need to worry about my next meal, but if we were captured, I would have to eat prison food for a very long time. Once we crossed the river into South West Africa, we ran into a SADF convoy heading for Rundu. We had walked about 100 kilometres over the past ten days and I was pleased to see the inside of a vehicle. As we were wearing no rank on our shoulders, we were ordered to get into the back of the second vehicle. Upon arriving in Rundu, we were turned over to the Military Police as deserters and put in a cell. My worst fears had come true. My first meal back was prison food. That evening a duty officer came into the cells and Sean gave him contact details of a brigadier general in Pretoria. Within the hour, we were visited by the colonel in charge of the detention barracks. Later that evening, back in the comfort of the lodge outside Kapako, we spoke properly for the first time. Sean laughed it off and told me that now I was a real soldier, no longer bullying the guys back home, but earning my pay. I hadn't looked at what I was doing as a job until then, more of a route through conscription. We were given a fourteen-day pass and I went home.

When I arrived home, I had my first really heated argument with my mother. It was one of many to come. Until then, I could do no wrong in her eyes, but things and emotions had changed. I spent the rest of my pass sitting in the sun, reading. I met up with Colin who was working as a bouncer for a nightclub called The Thunderdome. I went to take a look. The thing about Johannesburg at that time was that violence was never far from where alcohol was sold. The country was at war, the natives were restless and free flowing alcohol made my first night back on the town a bloodbath. After that night, I actually wanted to go back to Angola. It seemed to have more of a point to it than the carnage that was Johannesburg night life. My hands hurt and I had pulled a muscle in my left thigh. I had suffered more injuries that night, than I had during my first ten days at war.

Chapter 9

When I arrived back at the camp, an entire company of paratroopers, called parrabats, had moved in. The camp was full. The ablution blocks were full. The mess was full and there was a huge amount of friction between the infantry troops and the parrabats. Sean explained to me that a certain amount of respect should be given to troops who had volunteered for parrabat training and looked down on regular troops with a superiority complex.

That weekend I was briefed on all decisions being made around me. We were about to go into a different type of contact. All we seemed to know was that the MPLA, backed by Russian and Cuban advisors, were gathering at a town called Cuito Cuanavale. They were planning a push against the UNITA forces in Mavinga so they could unify the country under an MPLA Government. We were going to support UNITA with ground forces, but would consider everything to be hostile. This was nothing new to me, but it seemed the timing was a smokescreen. Sean and I would be a small team seconded to a section of parrabats. When we ran into anything hostile, we would move to high ground and engage their officers. I would find them and Sean would kill them. We were just glorified assassins.

By October 1987 I was officially deployed to Southern Angola. Sean and I shared a room at a rundown hotel in the town. It wasn't ideal but it was better than being in makeshift camps. During the first week there, we spent most mornings sleeping off the alcohol we had consumed the night before. Afternoons were taken up by American and English advisors giving us updates on the advancing MPLA army. They seemed to be coming quickly as well. We eventually got the nod from Jonas Savimbi, the leader of UNITA. He had resigned himself to the fact that he was not only under attack, but had little chance of holding on, unless he became more proactive. We were given intelligence on an advanced group of FAPLA troops with an estimate of their strength, their predicted coordinates, and the direction we would take to engage them.

On 21 October 1987, Sean and I deployed with the parrabats, a SADF signalman and about 150 UNITA troops. We walked north through the bush for the first day. October in southern Angola is the beginning of summer and it was so hot, that we kept stopping for water. The UNITA troops were loud and badly disciplined and I felt exposed. That night, Sean and I left the column and made a small camp on high ground above the ground-water where the rest were encamped.

The next morning the firing started. A small group of FAPLA troops had wandered into the UNITA guards, deployed around their very obvious position. There were only a few of them but, by the amount of rounds let off, I thought they were surrounded. The perception of victory that came after that initial contact stopped all UNITA units in their position. By mid-morning the UNITA troops hadn't come close to moving and the SADF parrabats had moved to their flank about one kilometre east of them. It was mid-afternoon when the UNITA forces, still celebrating their small victory, encountered the main force. These FAPLA troops were much better prepared and, although they were smaller in numerical terms, they seemed much more determined. There was a running battle going on below us and it's hard to explain how disorganised a battle scene is in that type of terrain. The sporadic noises of distinctive calibres being fired was our only measuring stick.

Just before sunset, our participation in this complete mess of firing and screaming changed. FAPLA set up a command structure about one kilometre from our position. Sean and I then went to work. Before the sun had set, we claimed three Cuban advisors and twelve leaders killed. Sean and I had a position that was only attacked once that afternoon. They must have been looking for the high ground but never made it. We worked like poetry and, with the failure of their command structure, the battle was won. I would learn later that this was SADF's first real accomplishment in stopping the advancing FAPLA troops. The FAPLA commander, who was left in charge that night, made a strategic decision to retreat. The UNITA troops mopped up the surrounding area with much excitement. The commander of the UNITA forces explained to the second lieutenant of the parrabats, that he wanted to go back and report this victory to his leader and regroup. He had lost twelve men and had nearly thirty wounded. Sean stepped in and took command of the SADF troops, telling the UNITA commander in no uncertain terms that we would split from them and make our own way back to Mavinga. It wasn't as though he were asking permission. It was how it was going to be.

The parrabats had not had much contact on the flank, but the little they did, left one of them, a corporal, dead and three wounded. Two had been hit in the shoulder and the other in the leg and a tourniquet put around his upper thigh. The wounded were given painkillers and were being attended by the medic. They were put onto makeshift stretchers, as was the dead corporal. These parrabats were no longer first-timers. They were battle-hardened. We set off eastwards first, working well together. We carried the stretchers as a tag team. Once away from the UNITA troops, Sean called in immediate casualty evacuation. We arrived back at Mavinga in the early hours of the morning. The stress of the whole endeavour had taken its effect on everybody. We were all very tired. We took our wounded to a SADF medical tent where they were stabilised and given an immediate casualty evacuation to Rundu. The following afternoon, Sean and I caught a chopper back to Rundu.

I was amazed at the amount of armoured vehicles, auxiliary vehicles and artillery G5 cannons crossing the river northwards. Once back at Mupini I had a shower, but I didn't shave. I had endured the itchy part of growing a beard and decided to keep it. Sean and I resumed training and on Friday night, we went to Kapako for supper. We were met by two colonels and were given an update on the battles going on north of Mavinga. The SADF, primarily the Sixth Mechanized Regiment, had stopped the armed wing of the MPLA from advancing any further south. In turn they had advanced to a town north of Cuito Cuanavale, where we had been the previous week. Most importantly the SADF had captured a member of the African National Congress (ANC) and of its armed wing, uMkhonto we Sizwe (MK), co-founded by Nelson Mandela in the wake of the Sharpeville Massacre in March 1960.

Sometime after eating, we were told SWAPO had assumed the demise of UNITA and had moved some reconnaissance units into Angola. We were given a set of coordinates that was to be their rendezvous point with the MK operator, who had talked. I was impressed at how quickly it was all done. Both of us went back and familiarised ourselves with the area on the map and set off that night. As dawn approached, we took cover. By the light of day, we could hear the SWAPO operators talking amongst themselves, waiting patiently for the MK operator. There were six of them with nobody on guard. They were a ragtag group, who had slept on mats under the trees that night. They had left their AK-47s behind and seemed to be having a meeting. At lunchtime, they all were huddled around a smokeless fire. One, a large man, had a watch on his wrist. By using hand signals we decided to begin with him.

I spotted the range distance and Sean started shooting them. The first two died where they were sitting. The third was hit while taking cover behind an ant hill. The fourth was hit running for the trees. The fifth was hit in the thigh, diving blindly towards his AK-47. It had taken us less than seventy-five seconds to kill four of them. We waited patiently for a sixth to break cover. I worked out that if he was going anywhere, it would be towards the trees just south-east of us. To my surprise he returned to the shooting area. There was something there more important than the rifles. We allowed him to go for what he wanted. Sean's discipline came out there and then. He had a perfect sight of the guy, yet we both knew it was important to see why he had come back. It was a brave but stupid thing for him to do.

He picked up a leather bag and then, when he stopped to bend down and speak to the one with the wounded leg, Sean shot him. We waited and watched for the rest of the afternoon. Nothing moved. Now came the difficult bit. We both knew we had to get that bag and finish the wounded operator off. As the sun set, we walked slowly down towards the bodies. It's difficult to explain how differently you feel as a prospective target. We were now the prey rather than the hunter. We were on the low ground and, if we were being observed, we wouldn't have lasted any longer than the guys who were lying dead on this killing field. The wounded SWAPO operator was still alive when we got down to the area. He was in shock and bleeding heavily. He had propped himself against a tree with his rifle in his hands. It was my first experience of a human-being knowingly resigning himself to death. I shot him in the chest and, as I turned him over, he looked into my eyes. He didn't seem at all perturbed as he took his last breath, gurgling on his blood. The most important thing I remember about that experience was the lack of hatred he seemed to have for me in his eyes.

The leather bag was filled with maps of Southern Angola and Northern South West Africa. They had names and codes written crudely on them in Portuguese. I didn't understand the language enough to make either head or tail of it and, if Sean did, he wasn't letting on. We both took an AK-47 with us as a trophy. I still don't understand why we did this, but years later I would clean it and try to rationalise that action. An AK-47 is not light by any means and is unwieldly at the best of times. We reloaded each weapon's magazine before we left. I suppose it was just the done thing. When we crossed the river we flagged down a SADF convoy heading east on the road to Rundu. This time neither of us was in any mood for another arrest. I had thick, black blood from the SWAPO operator's head all over my left boot and hand. I had smelt the iron in the blood on me for too long to explain the presence of the AKs, or what we were doing there. We were taken to the Administration Block and Sean was immediately ordered to take the leather bag to Pretoria. He was to leave on the next flight out from Grootfontein and I was left to calm down by myself in the lodge at Kapako. I bought a bottle of whisky and retreated to my room to get drunk by myself.

At some stage before the next weekend, Sean returned and had something to tell me. He had been redeployed to another unit. I was to be given a new guy as my spotter and I would assume the position of shooter. My new team would be going north to Cuito Carnavale very soon. He must have seen the look on my face and said,

"Don't worry, bud, because I'll choose the new guy myself and you'll be in charge of the team up there."

The next day he left and it would be a while before I saw him again. On parade the next morning, I was awarded the rank of captain by the camp colonel. I remember thinking it would have been nice if the parade ground had been a little fuller.

I went back to my tent, making conversation with Rob Reynolds, my new partner. He was a second lieutenant and was big. More importantly, he came across as highly intelligent.

After the parade, I was to have a meeting with the colonel. When I met him, he behaved differently towards me. When I saluted him, he responded,

"No formalities any more, Captain. We're all men now. Have a drink and let's go to lunch."

The two of us sat down together at his table and he immediately came to the point.

"What do you need, Captain?"

I wanted a two-man room for Rob and me at the lodge in Kapako, range time for the next three weeks and freedom to requisition any equipment I needed. He told me to come past his tent later that afternoon and it would all be arranged. I asked if I could take two of the motorbikes to use and he laughed, writing the orders out before I left. As promised I was given a letter, signed by a lieutenant general, giving me carte blanche at the range and stores. I was told the two-man room at the lodge had been arranged for an indefinite time from that afternoon onwards and I would be given a new car for transportation.

Chapter 10

Rob and I spent the next three weeks going through the same routine I had done with Sean. However, it was not exactly the same, as I was now the shooter and Rob the spotter. On the range, we took up position behind the troops being brought in and didn't interact with anybody else unless we had to. We ate our meals together and trained every day. This helped us become good friends and, although he was by far the better shot, he was happy to be on the team with me as shooter. I learnt his dad had died during Rob's last year at school. He hadn't processed the information and, some days, he spoke of his dad in the present tense. He had two sisters whom he adored and a mother on the brink of a breakdown after his dad's death. I realised how lucky I was that all my immediate family were still alive. Before then, I had never thought about it.

In early December 1987, the two of us were deployed about twenty kilometres north of the border, where there was to be another meeting between the ANC's MK and the SWAPO. I knew we weren't the only small team operating in that area and was a little surprised at how much information was obviously flowing to Military Intelligence. It would be our first time out and I decided to approach it differently from when I had been with Sean. Instead of Rob thinking he was going out to gather information on the ground, I told him exactly what to expect. I was going to shoot the guys whom we found and, if I were wounded or incapacitated, he was to take over and finish them off. We would remain on target until the job was done. Any information obtained at the scene would be brought back and handed in for analysis. Rob was not in the least perturbed. Quite the contrary. He was champing at the bit.

There was no difference in operational procedure from the previous time. We walked for two nights, found the coordinates and took the high ground. I killed the four SWAPO terrorists I found. It took me five shots to kill the four of them and I would be subjected to ridicule by Rob for missing that one shot until the day when sadly he died. We waited for movement until the evening, before going down to collect information to be passed on. This time I decided not to carry home a trophy AK-47, but Rob did. The first time doing what we did together was an odd experience and I watched Rob's response. He took it all in his stride.

Taking a very roundabout route, we made it back to South West Africa. When Rob and I shared our rations, I realised how determined he was. He would eat anything and was not at all emotional. I remember thinking how lucky I was to have him. I thought he had no idea it was my first time in that role. Years later, when we talked about those days, he smiled and said he had known it had been my first time as the shooter. It was the beginning of a friendship that would lead us into taking over the nightclub scene in all the major cities in South Africa.

I knew deep down that it wasn't possible to carry on stopping the flow of information between the ANC and SWAPO in the way we were doing it. It would only be a matter of time before they realised that intelligence was being leaked. At first it could be written off as bad luck, but no organisation could continue losing operators and information at that rate without investigating the reason why.

For about ten days, Rob and I lived at the lodge, training every day on the range. Then, one night, the hammer fell. I picked up an order at the front desk. I was to be at SADF Headquarters in Rundu the next morning. That morning, whilst riding one of the bikes into town, the weather was perfect. The sun was shining and, as it had been raining most afternoons, both banks of the river were as green as I had ever seen them.

When I arrived, I was shown to a briefing room, where there were two captains. I recognised them from the lodge, but had never spoken to them. We said nothing to one another and I sat down and waited. A man wearing the rank of brigadier general came in. The general was about as intimidating as any man I have ever met. He told us to address him as Keith. He spoke in English, but with a strong South African accent. He was the general in charge of operations in South Eastern Angola. His manner wasn't rude, but I had the feeling that, although any questions would be answered, we should shut up. It was not a question and answer session. It was all restricted information and nothing was to be discussed between the three of us after the briefing was over. He told us the information we were working on had been compromised. Military Intelligence believed we were being baited by the ANC informant.

Apparently, the ANC had flown one of their operatives in from Russia to the Angolan capital, Luanda. In Russia, this guy had trained in counter-intelligence for nearly five years. Ours was no longer an intelligence-led operation. We were being set up. This was the last time we would be using information from the source, but if we didn't turn up, the ANC would know which of their members was passing on the information. So, we were going, but it would be different. The plan was to counter their intelligence operation.

Each of us would have a team and all three teams would deploy to the locations given to them. Each team would be given a different place to be but, to begin with, one team would do the shooting. The other two teams would back up the shooting team, once the trap was set. As soon as the firing began, we could expect backup from SADF Special Forces. Under no circumstances were we to be taken prisoner. There was to be no marching of us through Luanda in front of cameras. It would be out of the question for us to be interrogated by this Russian trained intelligence officer. He ended by saying,

"Gentlemen, go out there and kick some heads in."

We were all somewhat apprehensive. I could sense anxiety in the room. Our job was dangerous enough without walking into a trap with open eyes. We were each given an envelope containing our orders and, as instructed, we didn't talk to each other afterwards. I could sense that we all hoped this general knew what he was doing. When we were back at the lodge, I opened the envelope with Rob. The coordinates were barely six kilometres north of the river. We both discussed how sloppy SWAPO was, being that close to us. The coordinates were the location of the disused mine Sean and I had driven to during my first time in Angola. It seemed ironic that my first meal in that country might be where I had eaten my last. Even more so that it would be the same rat pack.

We decided to take with us no equipment except weapons, replacing the weight saved with extra ammunition. We took enough food and water for forty-eight hours and enough ammunition to kill off a whole company. We set off on foot on the afternoon of 14 December 1987. I wondered where the other two teams were and hoped they were planning well, as we weren't the team that was going to start the game.

We took up position before midnight and waited out the next day and night. Then the SWAPO troops came in and set up camp. They were confident in their own way. It was obvious to us they had no idea they were the bait to attract the bait. This time we watched the ANC operators actually meet their SWAPO friends, but there was nothing friendly about it. The two sides were not at all happy to see each other and seemed nervous.

The shooting started to our left. The ANC operators were picked off first and the SWAPO operators moved very quickly. Rob and I held our fire, watching through our 'scopes. The entire area suddenly came alive. The position that had opened the shooting drew fire from the low ground almost immediately after the first volley. We watched as the mine became active. The building covering the disused shaft was holding twelve men and the trees to our right were filled with troops. How we had all made it there without stumbling upon them was probably more by luck and good timing than stealth. I tapped Rob's foot with mine and we started shooting the SWAPO operatives as they emerged from the mine. By the time we had finished and were looking for new targets in the bush around us, it had become alive. Screams from the wounded seemed to come from everywhere.

Three teams of shooters had made a huge impact on this disorganised attack. The SWAPO had expected to overrun one team, but by being hit from both their flanks they were caught in cross-fire, called "blue fire" in South Africa. It made it almost impossible for the group below to find a safe place to hide and their response was chaotic. The strange thing about that shooting was how quickly the returning fire stopped. Everybody below us seemed stunned and shocked. Their ambush had been the defining issue in their minds, and they had no plan B, if it went wrong. We kept picking them off for the rest of the day. Years later, Rob told me he had at least seventeen kills that day. I don't remember how many I had, but it was a turkey shoot. The cross fire was devastating for them and the fact that the hunters became the victims as soon as they exposed themselves, made them easy targets.

The Pumas arrived just before sunset. Twenty-four members of the reconnaissance regiment abseiled down ropes from the helicopters and took control of the area. I turned my radio on and waited. The sporadic firing that followed as the teams swept the area was the dismal end of a SWAPO ambush party that, for SWAPO, had gone horribly wrong.

I was hailed on my radio. At first, I didn't respond. When I did, we were all told to break cover and come down towards the chopper. Rob wrote on his pad, "Fucking cowboys, they will probably take a shot at one of us." We stayed where we were, as did the other two teams. Eventually we were hailed by groups and we all responded at almost the same time. We walked casually down to the choppers. Everybody was full of adrenaline. We waited in the nearest Puma. One of the captains from the briefing in Rundu, with his team member, climbed into the helicopter soon after us, wearing huge grin on his face. Maybe it was more a smile of relief that the day had worked out so well, rather than bravado. The SADF had turned a SWAPO plan to kill and capture the snipers who were breaking up the flow of information in South Eastern Angola into a massive victory. The fallout to this plan was going to be bad for SWAPO and the ANC. It would be a major concern for everyone who had planned it.

That weekend Rob was promoted to the rank of first lieutenant at the camp in Mupini and we proceeded to get as drunk as we could to celebrate the end of the operation. We were both still alive with nothing to show for the operation but our memories.

The following Monday morning, I was summoned to the camp colonel's tent. He told me I was being given the command of another operation. I was allocated thirty-six troops, divided into three squads of twelve. I was to use them to gather as much intelligence as possible and, more importantly, to engage the MPLA troops being held back for the Christmas festivities. My troops set out marching the next day and, on the evening of 24 December 1987, Rob and I flew by helicopter to rendezvous with them. Rob jumped first when we arrived at the point. I followed immediately afterwards. On the ground, while sliding down an embankment on my arse with my rifle held above me, I heard a loud crack and passed out. I had slid into probably the only fixed piping in South Eastern Angola. Both my left and right tibiæ were broken by the impact. The piping was about eight inches high where I hit it and my shins still have the scars to remind me.

My first time leading men into battle had ended in less than a minute. To this day I wonder what those troops must have thought of their leader, passed out on the ground with two broken legs. The whole plan had been utterly compromised. I remember waking up for a brief period on the chopper. I had an IV drip in my forearm and was in no pain. Rob, I would find out later, had pumped me full of the nearest medic's morphine. Back at Rundu, I was stabilised and my legs set in plaster of paris up to my groin. On Boxing Day, I was transferred to a military hospital in Pretoria and felt as embarrassed as could be. The wounded around me all had war stories to tell. I just had a tale of bad luck. Most of the boys around me had very severe injuries and there were a lot of limb amputees. The boy in the bed next to me had had both legs amputated below the knee.

This was the first time I had any idea about the damage to my legs. They had X-rayed my old motorbike injuries as well. I was told the initial impact had been to my right leg, where the fracture was more compound than in my left leg. All I wanted to do was to get out of bed and out of that hospital. After five days, the doctor relented and gave me heels on the casts, crutches and physiotherapy. Once I had convinced him I could move about, I would be given discharge forms.

I was eventually discharged from hospital and given orders to present myself at Johannesburg Command by the end of February. I was on a medical pass until then. I stayed with Gary in his flat until mid-February, when the casts were taken off. By the end of February, I was officially discharged from military sick leave. One Monday morning, I reported to Johannesburg Command. After sitting around all morning, I was seen by the colonel in charge. He told me I was to report to Pretoria the next day for further orders.

Chapter 11

I spent the following six months infiltrating the Congress of South African Trade Unions, after which, in September 1988, I was paged to meet a lieutenant colonel at Johannesburg Command. He was a pig of a man and didn't care who knew it. I could not have disliked him any more that day than I would at any time afterwards. As the face of Military Intelligence in the SADF, he had been given operational oversight of Special Operations in Europe and the United States of America. He told me I was being sent to Seattle to co-ordinate with Boeing. I would be a messenger boy and send as much information as was given to me back to South Africa.

I was to fly to Los Angeles first. There I met a very young major who identified himself as from South African Military Intelligence. He took me to a motel in Orange County and gave me a credit card. I was to wait there for further orders. Nine days later, I was summoned to a very opulent house in the hills just north of Sunset Boulevard. There, I was given instructions to go to Seattle, book into a hotel and wait for an employee from Boeing to contact me. I was back on the clock.

When most people think about the company Boeing, if at all, it's usually when one of their commercial aircraft crashes or has a major operating fault. That's how I had viewed Boeing right up to the day I met Kurt. He was an engineering lecturer at the University of Washington by day and an operational link between the United States and South Africa by night. I met him at night. Kurt was highly intelligent and the moment we met, we became firm friends. I started gathering the information that he had been cleared to give me by the Government of the United States of America. The information was basic knowledge of Russian military equipment, mostly about the MiG aircraft being used over Angola and Mozambique. He also informed me about Boeing's new development, the Stealth Bomber. I would send the information to the address of the house in Los Angeles and presumed it went from there to the relevant departments in South Africa. It opened my eyes to

73

what the United States were prepared to offer in the pursuit of winning the Cold War. Ronald Reagan was President and the cowboy mentality was prevalent.

At the end of November 1988, Kurt told me he was giving me a file on the impending launch of the Northrop B-2 Spirit, the Stealth Bomber. It featured low observable stealth technology designed to enable it to penetrate anti-aircraft defences. The bomber could deploy both conventional and thermonuclear weapons and would be introduced before the following summer, 1989. The planned deployment of this aircraft was to be the four aces that would move the stalemate in Africa towards a political solution. I was told to deliver this file, personally and by hand, to the house in Los Angeles. It took three days for me to drive there. When I arrived, I reported to the house in the hills. The package was opened and I was thanked.

Then I was given the address of a makeshift forge where I went, signed for some gold bars and left. After taking the newly minted bars to the house in the hills, I was invited to stay the night, as there was a party going on. I could think of nothing worse. I was dirty and tired, but I took a shower and was given clean clothing. I decided to grin and bear it. That night I met the South African Ambassador to Canada. We got on well and he was impressed when I fixed a problem his drunken date had caused by throwing the trouble-maker out.

That night would change my life again. I probably should have gone home, as I was very tired and didn't want to be there anyway, but fate has a way of rearing its ugly head, when least expected. I was asked to be part of the security detail for the South African Diplomatic Services during the period they were in town. I accepted and, after signing some forms in the office, I was handed a new driving licence, identification and a Beretta 9mm pistol. That night I drove the ambassador and the gold bars to his residence in Malibu. I was armed and under cover of diplomatic immunity. Diplomatic immunity is a great feeling but certainly a responsibility. I spent the next seventy-two hours either riding shotgun in the ambassador's car or playing nanny to his kids. I enjoyed both tasks equally. The gold was eventually passed on and he and his family's posting in Los Angeles ended. I realised South Africa was paying gold for bullshit from the United States.

The ambassador asked me if I were interested in working for him in London, where he was taking a lower profile position in a couple of weeks' time. I was a little surprised as he hardly knew me. I told him I would go with him to England, but he didn't reply. Two weeks later, I learned I was being sent to London. I had seventy-two hours to finalise my affairs in the States so I sold my car and bought a ticket to London via JFK, New York. I arrived in London the next day and caught a taxi to South Africa House for a meeting. I had to walk through a picket of anti-apartheid protestors to get to the front door. The building and location of the South African Embassy impressed me.

My meeting was brief. I was told I would be responsible for gathering information on the protestors outside the embassy and the organisations funding them. I was given a house in Hammersmith and a job working for Sky. Sky was saturating London with satellite dishes and hiring Australians and South Africans to sell them. I was given a vehicle with a Sky logo and a team of South Africans with it. It was easy to do and we were paid per signature. We targeted the poorer areas in South London. Our quota was twenty signatures a day and most days we hit the mark by lunchtime. The team would go home and I would go to South Africa House and join the protests. It was strange for me that there were so many people protesting. More importantly, few of them were South African.

I easily made friends with the protest organisers. I had the perfect in, as I had actually been fighting for the government they were protesting against. I was immediately accepted and gained the confidence of the Swedish organiser. She was young, blond and sure she was doing the right thing. All I wanted to know was who was funding her. I eventually embarked upon a relationship with the Swedish girl. Although she was older than me, she was not paranoid about being infiltrated.

I managed to do the job and produced full documentation on where the money for the protests was coming from. I was elevated to being the ambassador's blue-eyed boy and asked to join a covert operation being run from a house in Knightsbridge. The thing about the protests wasn't so much their aggressive nature, but the fact that hardly any of the people protesting were South African. This was a cause of concern in the house in Knightsbridge. International public opinion was becoming increasingly more important to the incumbent South African Government.

I decided to form a splinter group with the main protestors and, instead of just bleating out slogans, we started throwing eggs at cars entering South Africa House. Then we upped our game by throwing paint at both the cars and the employees entering the building. I was eventually arrested with two Scandinavians for breach of the peace. My credentials were now perfect. The South African Diplomatic Security Corporation would not release the video of our actions to the police and eventually all charges were dropped.

The series of events that followed that arrest can at best be described as opaque. I was approached by a large retail company based in Denmark, which supported the protests. It contacted me via its legal team in London and offered me a budget. I accepted and was given full legal representation, along with a four-storey house in Earls Court from which to run my operation. I liaised with them twice a week and told them there were ex-military personnel living in South Africa that were as despondent as I was about the situation in South Africa. I was given funds to bring some guys out of South Africa and relocate them. I was basically recruiting my friends. It all ran very smoothly.

I was given more and more funds for air fares and the relocation of my new friends and, by Christmas 1989, I had my own gang in London, paid for in full from Denmark. We made more and more trouble outside South Africa House and were given a bigger and bigger budget. With a heavy-handed legal team behind us, protesting became less important. I flew a locksmith in from Johannesburg and one of my guys got employment at a removals company. We started to breach the squatting laws. Under English law, once seventy-five percent of the furniture was moved from a house, we could move in and change the locks, effectively taking temporary ownership of the property. Most owners settled out of court and paid us, but a few took us to court and we became more visible. Looking back, it wasn't that clever, yet it turned a massive profit. I was living a very lucrative lifestyle and keeping the SADF happy at the same time, feeding it banking details of the protesters' funders and not asking for any legal help. Everybody was happy.

Then came the incident that changed everything in London. There were three of us on the tube one Saturday night. We were drunk but minding our own business when the youngest of the South African guys lit a cigarette. Those days, the no-smoking rules on the London Underground were rarely enforced after midnight, but there's always one concerned citizen. There were only the four of us in the carriage and he must to this day regret playing transport policeman. I was caught on camera at the White City Underground station, beating him with a fire extinguisher taken off the wall. This time there was no safety net to save me. The three of us were arrested on the main road out of Shepherds Bush and we were all charged with assault inflicting grievous bodily harm. I woke the following morning with a headache and a custodial sentence looming over me. We were shipped from Hammersmith police station to a very hostile court, denied bail and remanded in custody to Her Majesty's Prison, Wormwood Scrubs. This time I had gone too far.

Chapter 12

HMP Wormwood Scrubs was a lot less scary than I thought it would be. In South Africa, I was used to the heavy-handed approach of being transferred from one cell to another. In England, the attitude towards incarceration is more civilised, but not knowing what's coming is sometimes a more daunting prospect than you're used to. We were the last prisoners to arrive at Wormwood Scrubs that night and the whole prison was in lock down. English prisons are about as boring as anything I have ever experienced. They work like a Swiss clock. You wake at the same time, lights out at the same time and even the food, although better than anything I was used to in custody, is boring. Although I was used to being locked up, the first thing that struck me upon entering the cell, was that there was no toilet. Even though the conditions in an African prison in some ways are much more brutal, you're not expected to use a bucket for ablutions.

After two weeks, we went before the judge. He granted bail for the two South Africans but refused my bail application on the ground of further police investigations. My cellmate's lawyer paid their bail immediately and they were released before I even went back down to the cells. That night I was alone.

I had been in Wormwood Scrubs for exactly two months, when my cell door was opened by new guards. It was time for food and I hardly noticed there were three guards as opposed to the usual one. Instead of being served food, I was taken to a room where my supper was already on a plate on the table in the middle. I started eating. The fat colonel from my old unit came in and sat down. He had two cups of coffee and when he placed one in front of me, I swapped it for his. I didn't trust him one bit and remember thinking he had put on more weight, if that were possible. For a man in his late thirties he was enormous.

It was December 1989 and my five years in the SADF were over. I hadn't expected to hear from it and I think I had been truly relieved I wasn't answering to it any longer. He produced an identification card, showing he had been promoted to the rank of full colonel. I addressed him as Craig. I felt nothing but animosity towards him and no longer cared about his rank. He told me he could get the Crown to blink on the assault charges if I co-operated with him. So, the game remained the same. I was costing Her Majesty's Prison Service to keep me and the Crown to prosecute me and yet they were willing to give me bail if I would go back to South Africa and pick up my commission for another year. That night I was in no mood for negotiations but listened to what he wanted me to do. He showed me photos of the Scandinavian girl I had befriended. She looked great in her cheap student type clothing and as determined as I remembered her. I would spend Christmas and New Year in South Africa then come back to the United Kingdom, under different passport details, and carry on with my infiltration of the protesters. He explained that the Crown was confident it could make a case for the offence at the tube station. In the prison library during my first two weeks, I had read the sentencing precedents on previous grievous bodily harm cases and knew that the likely minimum was eighteen months. Either way I was going to give up a year of my life. I accepted but requested to make a phone call to my father in Johannesburg. After finishing my supper, I was taken to a room and allowed to call him. I now knew the colonel had been granted some leeway in the prison.

As promised I was granted bail, given back my clothes and left on a one-way ticket to Johannesburg. To me, the co-operation between the British Authorities and South Africa House at that time didn't seem to be anything out of the ordinary. I was off the hook for the time being and happy to be heading towards the sun. That Christmas I spent living at my parents' house. They were happy to see me yet, working the hours they did, we were distant.

On 3 January 1990, I was to attend a briefing at the Brixton Murder and Robbery Station. They had stopped the façade that they were a police unit or that the building they were using was a police station. They were now openly working as a National Intelligence Services unit. The war in Angola was over, but the domestic situation in South Africa was turning into something new and the SADF was at full stretch. I was going to England however. At Brixton I was photographed for a new passport. My name on it was Peter Colony, which was appropriate as I was still working for one.

I flew to London the next day and was collected by the same major I had met at Los Angeles airport. I was given back my house in Hammersmith and a new credit card. I was to buy some winter clothes and start work the following Monday. On the Monday evening, I attended a meeting with a diplomat at the house in Knightsbridge. I was under the impression at the time that this would be a one-on-one meeting but we were joined by a middle-aged man, whom I had seen in the reception earlier. He was in full police uniform. I was offered a drink but declined.

"Have a drink Peter. You're going to need it," the diplomat said, so I asked for a double scotch and soda.

It's pretty easy to remember the sequence of events that night, as they were pivotal to my future and I was very aware of it. Again, I decided to say as little as possible. The format was like a military briefing. I was informed that the South African government was about to release Nelson Mandela from Victor Verster prison in Paarl. There would be a victory parade in South Africa, but, in due course, Nelson Mandela would visit England and would be a security concern for the British Government. I sat there and listened. South Africa House was the main point of concern, as Nelson Mandela would ultimately make an appearance there and nobody wanted anything to go wrong when he did.

I was shown surveillance photos of new groups of South Africans protesting outside the building. I was then told I would be given access to video footage of recent events that had taken place. I gulped down my whisky at that point and was handed another. I knew then that both sides were looking for an angle. More importantly, it meant they didn't have a clue where to start. It seemed my Scandinavian friends were being out-performed by South African personnel and it made them somewhat nervous.

At the end of the briefing, I was asked if I had any questions. I had many, but kept it brief. I only needed to know the boundaries of what I was supposed to do. I was told in no uncertain terms that this project was going to be worked from the inside out. Anything I needed would be given to me. Really? Anything? They must have been desperate. I was left in that office with my third whisky and a strange feeling of excitement. This was going to be a challenge. The office door opened and my first instructor, Peter, entered. He looked a little older with grey hairs at his temples and had put on some weight. I pointed that out to him after shaking hands. He sat on the couch next to me and said,

"Peter, this is important. We can both go anywhere we want, if we get it right."

He would be my contact and I must say I was relieved that fat Colonel Craig was out of the picture. In three months, the nationalities of the protestors outside the South African Embassy had become a huge priority at many levels for many different reasons. The South Africans had arrived and nobody trusted their motives. Peter told me the British had tried in vain to infiltrate the South African Bureau of State Security (BOSS), but with very little success. It all started making sense. The incumbent Government of South Africa was by day, appearing to be more receptive of the inevitability of a transition. By night it had a different agenda.

Peter rose, opened the office door and introduced me to the four South African ex-pats who would make up my team. They did not have Afrikaans accents, but definitely sounded South African. They were all young first lieutenants, who couldn't see how blurred the lines of our State were becoming back home. They were the cream of what I could expect. They were very polite and disciplined and, after the first hour, we started to understand each other's sense of humour.

This would be the second time I was expected to lead soldiers into a battle. This time it was on foreign ground and I intended to keep my legs in one piece. Although it was a much smaller deployment, I was going to get the job done. At the house in Hammersmith they split up, two to a bedroom, and we went to sleep. The next day, everybody was happy with the arrangements they had sorted out with one another. The washing-up was done and the dirty linen was on the washing-line. Off we went to South Africa House.

In three months, the mood had changed. The initial thing that jumped out at me was the police presence, closely observing the protests. Soon we witnessed the new and much more aggressive South African presence. The only way forward was to align ourselves with the South Africans there and work it, one step at a time. Peter agreed and by the beginning of February 1990, the five of us actively joined the protests. We split up and went in. On the first weekend, we had to overcome the paranoia of the South Africans which was, to say the least, a massive jump from the previous Scandinavian organisers. Paranoia is very infectious when you're doing something you want to keep secret, but we answered all questions posed to us. We were all ex-pats, just interested in getting the message across.

On 11 February 1990, Nelson Mandela was released. We watched the whole fanfare on the BBC in silence, huddled around the television in the front room. The five of us knew our project was going to be accelerated, yet I don't recall any of us mentioning it. I remember a knot in my stomach and I would have dearly loved to have known what was going through other people's minds that afternoon. I knew I was going to have to come up with a plan quickly, as attending the protests was not going to be enough for much longer.

The weather was poor the following weekend, but that was the last concern of many hitherto half-hearted protesters. It was as though they had secured Mandela's release single handedly. There was a sense of accomplishment, but not of completion.

Every two weeks I received new footage from the security cameras on the outside of South Africa House. We focussed on the protestors who turned up most frequently. This involved hours of watching the tapes, making notes and cross-referencing results. It was laborious and we began to get on each other's nerves. I managed to recover still photos of the South Africans, who seemed to be the most ardent supporters. We put them up in each of our bedrooms in the hope that by becoming familiar with their faces, we would notice someone new. I suppose it was at the end of March when the biggest development occurred. Peter told me that Nelson Mandela and his wife, Winnie, had been given diplomatic status. Many of the world's capitals had invited him but he had declined for the time being. We knew we were on a much longer timeline. I could see the relief on Peter's face and I'm sure he saw it on mine.

There was an immediate reaction to the news. The South African faces in the crowd seemed to be fewer. By July 1990, we were the veterans in the crowd. One of us attended the vigil every weekday and all five of us attended at weekends. The truth was we were getting nowhere and it felt like a dead-end project. We were just going through the motions. By the end of the summer, Peter was getting impatient. The operation had been going on for nearly seven months and everything seemed to be flat. I came up with a plan. An impending visit to London by the Mandela family should be leaked to a newspaper in the hope we would see a reaction.

The next morning *The Washington Post* ran an article on the front page that Nelson Mandela would be leaving South Africa for an official visit to London. It went viral and over the next twenty-four hours, the intensity outside the embassy became chaotic. Although it was a long shot, it worked. The faces on our walls appeared out of nowhere. Peter cross-matched them with flight records into Heathrow on South African Airlines flights and now we had a mark. It wouldn't be long before somebody would refute the claims so we needed to work fast. Peter came to the house the next morning. He said he needed not only names, but proof. When I asked him what my boundaries were, he said,

"Just get me something that sticks. You have carte blanche on this one."

I was given passport photos of four guys, their names and ages. I didn't have a plan, but sometimes winging it is a plan itself. It all happened very quickly that day. The four of them were together and we introduced them to other regulars. That night I invited them back to the house. We fed them sleeping pills in their drinks and within an hour they were all asleep. They were tied up and put in each of the bedrooms. The leader went in the bathroom. We systematically beat them all night until they were ready to tell us anything. That's the problem with that kind of interrogation. If you hurt someone enough they will tell you they come from Mars to persuade you to stop.

The following morning, I took them one by one to their banks and made them transfer money into an account that had been opened in Hong Kong in my name. First Pacific had a fortune transferred into my account during the course of that morning. The thinking was that the accounts they were using could be traced back to their funders. We let them go the following evening and I told the rest of the team to stay with their families until the following week. We had established that the guys we had interrogated were gathering information for BOSS. They didn't know what the agenda was and had lost their funds. I thought it was a job well done and went to sleep.

Sometime during the early hours of that morning, I was woken by armed police and taken to Hammersmith Police Station. I didn't care as I thought it would be sorted out eventually. I wondered how much fallout we had caused back home. Anyway, one problem at a time was what I thought as I sat in a police cell that night.

Chapter 13

When the shift changed that morning I was taken out of the cell and fingerprinted. It didn't bother me too much and I expected the cavalry at any time. It never came. By mid-morning, I was charged with entering England bearing a false passport and re-charged, under my real surname, with the assault that had taken place nearly a year ago at the tube station.

It was all a little strange. I had exposed the fact that there were people working for BOSS, who were trying to destabilize the transition process back home. Although my methods were crude, the previous day I had been put under enormous pressure to get a quick result and had proof of a trail for the Defence Ministry to follow. The bank accounts that had transferred the money to mine were a start for an investigation and I believed it wouldn't be too difficult to take it from there.

By the end of the first weekend, my concern turned to anger. I was interviewed by two different sets of detectives about my identity and the previous assault case. I was absolutely impossible and said nothing. I had never been that uncooperative before but I didn't care. During the first week, I was angered by the fact that I hadn't been visited by anyone from the house in Knightsbridge. It is a very harsh reality to be let down. As the days went on I got worse. I refused to clean out my cell and was given an internal hearing for being aggressive and using profanity towards the guards. I was being fed alone, exercising alone and was left on my own.

The night before my first bail hearing, Peter finally came to see me. He was in full dress uniform and I stood at attention as he walked in. That was because I respected him and not the uniform. I had spent nearly fourteen days in isolation for a mission to keep a politician I didn't care about alive and to help the London Metropolitan Police save face from a potentially embarrassing incident. More importantly I was going to be free from the SADF agreement in a couple of months' time and wanted nothing further to do with it after that. Peter told me I would be given bail the next morning. It would be paid out of a budget and I would be flying home. I told him I was sick of the game we were playing and had decided to let the whole affair go to trial. Even as I said it, I knew it was stubborn, but it seemed the way to go. I was twenty-four and didn't have a clue that I didn't have clue. That morning I was denied bail as the court decided I had no real fixed address.

The next week, I got a visit from my sister, along with her newly born son, Matthew. My sister has a very determined personality and she wasn't at all perturbed by the surroundings of the prison. My nephew was great. I can still remember holding him on my lap and thinking how lucky she was. Then came the bombshell. She had been contacted by the prison authorities to come and speak some sense to me. She told me I would be released on bail at the next hearing if I calmed down. I knew what that meant. By now I only had about six weeks left of my extended contract with South African Military Intelligence and it was unhappy about having my noose removed and for me to go public in front of an English judge.

My sister told me she thought it would be best for me to get bail, think and make a decision on my future. I agreed and was bailed to her house in Bournemouth. Peter arrived at the house about three days before my next court appearance. He had taken my new address from the courts and had booked into a local hotel. He asked me to have a drink with him at his hotel later that evening. When I met with him I was surprisingly pleased to see him. He took very little time before asking me what my plans were. I asked him what my options were and he told me to come back and see him the next night. We arranged a time at the same hotel and I left.

The following evening, I was open to suggestions. Peter told me that, if I were accepted into a university in South Africa, then the Crown Prosecutors would drop all charges and I would be allowed to leave England under my own name as proof there were no outstanding charges. The South African Military would expect me to take up my commission again, until the first democratic elections were held. I didn't mind the choice of going back to university but was not prepared to go back into any uniform whatsoever. I told Peter I would think about it and he could contact me in a month, after I had applied to a couple of universities. I sent application forms to the University of Witwatersrand and the University of Cape Town. I then wrote to the London School of Economics asking for an application to be sent to me.

Although I was doing the odd night at a local bar in Bournemouth as a bouncer, I spent most days looking at television by myself. I watched as Margaret Thatcher lost her position as Prime Minister and leader of the Tory party and returned to the back benches of the House of Commons. Her successor, John Major, would have his hands full filling her shoes. I listened to BBC Radio 4 every day and the winds of change were everywhere. I watched as Germany seemed to be suspended by its unification and reflected that transition is never easy. I also went to a local tattoo artist and acquired a huge dragon tattoo on my back.

Peter had left a London contact number. I called it and arranged with him a time and place for us to meet in Bournemouth the following afternoon. I would have to decide my future in the next twenty-four hours. When I met Peter, he seemed very positive and we spoke for hours. He was being promoted to the rank of brigadier general in the SADF and his ideas for a new unit had been approved. I made some comment about him now being a politician, but I was actually happy for him.

What came next was something I should have seen coming. He wanted me to enrol back into the University of the Witwatersrand and work for his new unit. As fate would have it, I had received acceptance letters from both South African Universities I had applied to, as well as offered an interview at the London School of Economics. Although I trusted him, I knew the pressures of a new position meant he would be cutting corners to please whoever had promoted him. I didn't relish being part of any arse-kissing operation. He offered me promotion to the rank of major, if I passed all my first-year exams. I could think of nothing less appealing than being given more leeway to implement the will of the South African Ministry of Defence. I decided to hear him out and listen to his plan. I knew he would have one. He guaranteed that all charges against me, both old and new, would be dropped. Everything that had taken place outside South Africa House during the past year would be lost. I didn't feel that confident, but he continued,

"Come on Peter, think. You did it all under a different name. It works."

It's amazing how you can remember the exact words used when you are being talked into making a big mistake. We ended that night with my promising to write a letter of acceptance to the University of Witwatersrand to read economics and, if I gave him the letter to send home, he would arrange for a new passport to be issued. We were on again.

I listened to as much as I could on BBC Radio 4 about South Africa. It seemed the country had become a war zone since the release of Nelson Mandela. I didn't take too much notice, as I had seen how reporters sensationalise news. I suppose news is like any product you want to sell. It needs to be marketed correctly. I felt very far from home and the consequences of my not getting a new passport approved was a sword of Damocles hanging over me. By the beginning of December 1990, I received a letter to collect my passport from Weymouth. I had another tattoo done on my calf that day and met Peter with the letter.

I flew to Johannesburg. My parents were prepared to let me live with them while I studied. They had sold my car, as they thought I would be away for a while, but were prepared to buy me another. I opted for a high-powered motorbike. We used the money I had accumulated from my army pay and my dad filled the gap. We bought a Kawasaki GPZ 1100 and I loved it. Years later I would give it to a member of the Hells Angels for him to meet the required minimum membership requirement.

I spent most evenings watching the local news with my dad. He was working from Johannesburg and building roads in the biggest township in Southern Africa. The news told us that pretty much all was well, but as my dad worked every day in a bullet-proof vest, I wasn't convinced. He used to grunt at the reports and told me it was urban warfare in the townships.

In the first week of January 1991, I attended a briefing at Johannesburg Command. Peter looked good, wearing the swords and one pip of a brigadier general. I was the only one not in uniform and hadn't cut my hair in more than a year, so I was given strange looks by the team I was going to work with. After a short welcome, we were introduced to the concept of a "third force". The idea was that, although the government was talking transition, elements of it were working behind the scenes to derail it. We were told we would each receive assignments from individual team leaders. It was the same shit I'd walked into a year before.

My assignment came from a very young lieutenant colonel. I was to attend university and befriend any black students from upper middle class families. I knew there wouldn't be too many of them. They called them, Black Diamonds. If you believed the propaganda, then they were the future of South Africa. I was dismissed and told to report to Peter before I left the building. When I knocked on his door, he was fiddling around in his filing cabinet. He told me to sit down and handed me the file on the London operation. It was a series of my reports. The tracking of the bank accounts had led nowhere. Basically, I had spent a year of my life doing something nobody wanted to follow up. I asked him what he wanted me to do. The situation was complex and they had only suspicions of what was going on, but the army had been deployed with the police in the townships. We owed it to both to find out anything helpful. I saw his point but wondered what I wasn't being told. He then opened up.

"Peter, we're only getting half the story. We need to know how to make it safer in this mess for our troops."

He told me that I was now working part time for the Customs Department and gave me a new identification card. Peter also gave me the key to a house in the southern suburbs of Johannesburg and a Toyota Hilux pickup. Last, but not least, he gave me a credit card and bank details. I left thinking it was all a waste of time. The next day I went to the administration block of the university, enrolled and applied for a student loan. I then went to the house and started the Toyota. It was brand new and, for the first time, I felt confident about this new unit. I kept that vehicle until the day I left South Africa.

The weekend before my first lectures, I was invited to a house party in an affluent suburb north of Johannesburg. When I arrived there were so many familiar faces that I decided to stay. It seemed the best way to keep out of trouble. The alternative was to visit the nightclub scene in downtown Johannesburg. I branched off with a group of guys smoking grass from a broken bottle neck, which made the intake of the drug much more intense. I hadn't smoked that way in many years and was immediately very high. The problem with getting high that quickly is that you get paranoid and agitated. When we arrived back at the house, it was apparent something was wrong. The music was turned off and one guy was threatening everyone on the makeshift dance floor. Initially I took no notice and made my way for a can of beer. After opening the beer, I turned around to find the same guy coming at me. His name was Leonard Freidman. He had just fought for the South African heavyweight boxing title, losing to someone who would go on to fight for the world title. He was taking his failure out on anyone and everyone.

I hit him with my beer can and, mathematically, he couldn't have hit the ground faster. At this point I had no idea who he was, so the sudden accolades that came with that blow were as much a surprise to me, as was my breaking Leonard's jaw to him. The incident made me an overnight sensation amongst the rich kids in the northern suburbs. After that night, I was offered bouncing work at some nightclubs that had sprung up whilst I had been away. The following Monday night I was invited to take a look at a nightclub that had been opened in a five-star hotel. Kids with far more disposable income than me, were having a good time. The whole experience was something new to me. I was used to people abusing the liquor laws by drinking as much as they could and getting as stupid as they could as fast as they could. This club had a licence and the way people were acting was totally foreign to me.

I started university and a new job the next day.

Chapter 14

At the end of February 1991, I started attending lectures at the University of Witwatersrand and went, with other students, to my first meeting at the Department of Customs. I listened as the team debriefed us. Everyone had the same angle, namely to acquire information from wealthy black families. I couldn't help thinking we would do better if we actually had some wealthy black family members in the group, but said nothing.

My nights were taken up at the nightclub where I was working. I was the oldest in the group of bouncers working there, but by far the lightest, so I bought some steroids and went back to the gym. We had very few problems. It was more of a party than work. My hair by now was so long that I tied it up. This was a concern for some of the bouncers as, during the early nineties, it was not the norm to have long hair in those circles.

Then one night there was an incident. Members of a university rugby team had been admitted in dribs and drabs but they all ended up at the bar together. They were a toothache looking for a tooth. It's the kind of night that none of us looked forward too. Eventually, at the end when the bar was emptying, it all blew up. At some point in the fight, I was stabbed in the mouth with a broken beer bottle and lost all self-restraint. The result was that the entire team was ambulanced out of the club to hospital. That night effectively made me the head bouncer of the club. The word got out and, from then on, I was treated a little differently from the other bouncers. The others were all good guys. They just needed a leader. I now had a team of my own.

One evening, on early shift at the nightclub, I observed one of the barmen charging drunken patrons for a double, but only pouring a single and putting the difference straight into his pocket. This was amateur petty theft and got me thinking. Later that night, I pulled the bar staff into a small office at the door and explained how it would be better for us all to be on the same page. At first there was resistance but, after an argument with the head barman, I became angry and immediately had more co-operation. From that night on we started scamming the bar using a proper system. Instead of just over-charging inebriated customers, the plan was also to under-pour for a customer drinking hard liquor. Instead of putting the money straight into their pockets, the barmen would put it all into the till and take it out when cashing up. This made it less obvious and, as I explained that night, if it was obvious to me, it would be obvious to anyone observing. Every drink under-poured and over-charged would be matched by putting an orange peel into the sink next to the till. Before cashing up, the orange peels would be counted and the difference in the till readings and the amount of money in the till would be reconciled. This meant that a barman would only pocket the money once per shift, lessoning the risk of being caught. We would all take a cut from this new system and I was now in charge of the bar. We were all making extra money at the nightclub. The head barman was becoming more trusting and the entire staff had never been happier.

One night another group of bouncers came round and were totally hostile. They invited us to their club that Friday night after work and, like all bad decisions, it was easy to make. When we arrived we were initially treated very well with free drinks. It turned bad as soon as I went to the toilet. I was told by the bouncer to make way for a group of customers heading for the door. As soon as they went past me I moved forward and was hit in the jaw. I retaliated by assaulting the bouncer with the bottle of beer in my hand. He went down like a stone. After that, it all became very violent and, as everyone in the nightclub ran for the door, I was hit with a baseball bat. That night's events are hazy in my mind, as I was concussed, but we ended victorious. I was now put in charge of security at two venues.

This was the start of my night life, taking over venues all over the city and later the country. It wasn't something that I planned, but the outcome that night made me aware of how to advance it. Needless to say, the bar staff at the new club started to scam the bar the next weekend and we all started to make more money. It was a natural progression and would carry on for many years. By August 1991, I was running security for four nightclubs in the northern suburbs of Johannesburg. Although they were much smaller venues than the clubs in central Johannesburg, it was definitely where the disposable income was. The black bar staff and the bouncers were so loyal to me, that I could have opened my own venue at the time, but I suppose it was for the best that I didn't. The owners of the clubs must have realised their profits at the bar had decreased, yet the money at the door was getting so big that they turned a blind eye.

One evening, I was told about a new bouncer at a small venue near us. His name was Rob and he was the latest sensation in bouncing circles. I couldn't believe it would be the same guy I had gone into battle with, but it was hard not to see all the boxes being ticked. I went to see for myself and there he was, much heavier than I remembered, and looking a lot older. He had grown a goatee beard and still carried himself like a soldier. It was a reunion that, until Rob's death several years later, would catapult our lives forward at a pace hard to believe.

Rob had finished his five years in the army as an infantry captain and had recruited three of his former friends to form a crew of bouncers who were quickly gaining notoriety. That night he had my full attention. I was happy to see him, but was apprehensive as to how he would act towards me. The last thing I wanted was conflict. It wasn't so much my being intimidated. It was more my wanting an old comrade to be my friend. I succeeded in both that night. As the first fight broke out between some drunks, I watched as Rob did what he did best, direct traffic. When it was over I approached him and the smile on his face told me all would be well. I breathed a sigh of relief and we started drinking together.

The owner of the club had brought Rob in to keep us out. Rob had no idea I was the guy he was paid to keep at bay and now he did, we began to plot. It was a good feeling having someone like him around me again. We had shared time in Angola together and he was still in a military frame of mind, so I didn't care about him being in charge. That night we informed the nightclub owner that we were merging and his club would be exempt from controlled theft at the bar.

At university, I kept changing my tutorial times until I found the small group of Black Diamonds in the Commerce Department. They were not open to outside friendship of any kind, so I kept to myself at first. One afternoon, one of the black students was alone in the canteen and, as there were only a few places free, I took a chance and sat next to him. He was a friendly guy and I immediately liked him. More importantly, he liked me. That following evening, I handed his name into Peter with his student number and an accurate description of him.

His name was Steven. His father was a dentist with a practice in the South West Townships, situated south of Johannesburg. His family was living in luxury compared with most of his relatives. We met later that week in the canteen. He told me that it was his place in life to get an education and to uplift his family. He had many relatives living in hostels around Johannesburg working in the mines. I remember his passion to avoid the next generation of his family going underground. He was one of the nicest and most humble kids I had ever met. In fact, I liked and admired him so much that day, that I even felt concerned he shouldn't be a Military Intelligence nark. Unfortunately, his name was in and I had a task to complete.

As I became friendlier with Steven, he started to open up to me. His father was of the royal house of the Shangaan and had married his mother, a Zulu, whom he had met while studying in Johannesburg. Steven was being prepared to take on the future of both families. His father's family had many royal functions to attend, but his real concern was his mother's family. The tension of being the one who was to lead these two families was his paramount concern and his only motivation for education. I felt my life was pretty simple compared with his.

Peter was very interested in Steven. He was the perfect example of the demographic needed to understand the future of the new South Africa. It was very easy being friends with Steven. He was bright, enthusiastic and always in a good mood. We started to have the odd beer in the Commerce Bar and he changed his tutorial period for commercial law to correspond with mine. We were good friends by the time we sat our mid-year exams. By then I was truly sick of the deception and one afternoon I considered recruiting him. I asked Peter that week on his thoughts and he was horrified that I was about to compromise the entire game through emotion.

During the university holidays, Steven and three friends visited me at the nightclub. It was a brave decision by them, as the segregation of whites and blacks in the entertainment arena would be the last pillar to fall in the social agenda of South Africa. They pretty much kept to themselves and everybody soon realised they were my guests and left them alone. Looking back, that night could have gone horribly wrong in more ways than one. Luckily, it didn't and I was now in a truly social interaction with some Black Diamonds.

I spent most days at lectures, most nights at the nightclub and at least one day a week at the Department of Customs office in Pretoria. By now I was friends with the group of Shangaan students at the university. They all were living off the incomes of their parents and all had the same aspiration, namely uplifting their families. The Shangaan are a very special demographic in the South African landscape. Their history is clouded, but their pride was so obvious that I was totally intrigued by them. This was first generation wealth and their burden to keep up the momentum was pressing down on them. The first real obstacle they had after graduating high school was to graduate from a recognised university. I liked them and we grew closer and closer, month by month.

A couple of nights before my final economics exam, Peter paged me to meet him in Pretoria. He told me that one of the students I had been studying with had direct lineage to the royal house of Shangaan. I was to pursue this friendship with all haste before the exam period ended. I only had a couple of exams to go at that stage, but invited them all to my house for a night of cramming. Six of them turned up in one small car. It was hard to believe that royalty in any form would be cramped into one small, very cheap vehicle.

The next morning, we all wrote a commercial law exam and I knew we all had passed as, the night before, we had hit on all the right topics. We went out that afternoon and celebrated in the Commerce Bar. The relief I witnessed that day is hard to explain, but we were all now on the same page. Mike was the royal. He was a very large kid, but very quiet with strong cheekbones that made him handsome. He was one of four in line to the throne of nearly eight million South Africans and was nervous that he would fail in his coming future. Although he wasn't the oldest of his siblings, he was his grandfather's favourite and he knew that failure was not an option. I don't know why, but I felt sorry for him that day. I realised he was under immense pressure to conform and he was totally relieved we had all nailed the exam. I filed a report on Mike to Peter, who was not just pleased, but ecstatic when he received it. I don't think that, until that point, I had ever pleased him as much as I did that day.

The night after my last exam, Rob and I visited my old haunts in downtown Johannesburg. There were a lot of changes. In fact, I hardly recognised it. As the night wore on, I realised how lucky I was in making a living and moving forward. We were doing cocaine in the toilets of a nightclub, when, again, fate reared its ugly head. One of the drug dealers in the venue asked us why we weren't using his drugs. He could tell by the wrappings that they hadn't come from him. Rob hit him and we walked out laughing. About twenty minutes later I got hit with a knuckleduster. We were targeted and our opponents were serious. Rob pulled out his .45 service pistol and shot one of them in the arm. I responded by pulling out a .357 Magnum and shot one of my attackers in the chest. One of the things about a .357 Magnum round is that it always seems to leave someone dead. This time was no different. He was dead before he hit the ground.

My lip was sliced into a bad cut and the fact that I bear the scar reminds me every day how much blood I lost that night. We couldn't stop it from bleeding, so I decided to go to hospital. Later that night in the hospital, Rob and I were arrested for murder and attempted murder. The charges would alter Rob's future more than mine. We were locked up in Hillbrow Police Station. The cells were full of ANC supporters and I just wanted to go to sleep. I had been filled with local and ingested painkillers, I was drunk and the cocaine was wearing off quickly. More to the point, everything was starting to hurt.

The next day we were both charged with discharging a weapon in a built-up area and disturbing the peace and taken before a magistrate. We were both denied bail and sent to Diepkloof maximum security prison, near Johannesburg. My mouth was so swollen by this time that I was moved into the hospital section. Eventually, I was treated and the stitches that had been inserted on the night of our arrest were removed and the wound was drained. I was stitched up again and sent to another cell.

Later that week, Peter showed up. He was angrier that one of his missions had been interrupted, than the fact I had shot someone. He told me the murder charge would be reduced to culpable homicide, manslaughter, and the remainder would be dropped at my next court appearance. Peter never even mentioned Rob, so I asked. He shrugged and said he would only face a charge of discharging a weapon in a built-up area and receive a fine. He would be found guilty and never possess a licensed firearm again. I explained that Rob, being a decorated soldier, would surely make him an asset to the team. I could tell immediately that I was expressing what I was expected to come out with. They knew I would be less vulnerable with Rob. Peter told me he would see what he could do.

We were both released the following Monday. Rob had all charges against him dropped by the prosecuting authority and was discharged. My remaining charge was culpable homicide, committed in self-defence, and I was granted bail that was paid for and given a trial date. We were out of prison. Our weapons were given back to us and night life in Central Johannesburg would never be the same again.

At our first briefing, with Rob signed up to the team, one of the members told us that the North-West Johannesburg platinum mines were about to blow up due to the racial segregation of jobs. He was concerned. Separation by skin colour system was still prevalent in the mines and the backlash after the next elections would make it nearly impossible to gather personal motives and ideas from any black South African. More importantly, the migrant labour force in the mines, located on the platinum belt of South Africa, was never going to accept the changes that were coming. It seemed there would be a backlash from the miners themselves, or from the unions, to any new management positions created for black miners. Everybody was to focus on the mining industry in any way they could. Peter ended by putting it into perspective.

"Our mines are the most important industry to South Africa's future. The other industries will resist change for a longer period so, for a peaceful transition, we need to concentrate our efforts on the mind-set of the miners at all levels, black or white."

Rob and I were sent to a mining town called Rustenburg. There, we booked into an expensive lodge and using our customs identification and credit cards, we entered into a long-stay arrangement. We made friends with the staff at the lodge and settled in for the Christmas period.

After a few weeks of observation, Rob and I got bored with the same tactic and decided to take a different approach. We identified ourselves at the local police station in Rustenburg as investigators looking into the smuggling of explosives from the mines to neighbouring countries. Our credentials were checked and we were assigned as observers to a police task team who were investigating the escalation of violence in the hostels housing miners. The captain of the team was very intelligent. He had managed to graph violent crime in the area in a clever manner, demonstrating that a tribal faction crime wave that was on the increase. He had spent a long time cross-referencing crimes and convictions with specific factions over the previous five years and the results were plain to see. Civil unrest was increasing and it was organised. Rob and I went on a few sporadic raids with the unit and I was amazed, not by the amount of assault rifles found, but by the amount of rounds that were cached in the area. Someone was preparing for war and had been doing so for a while.

Rob and I had stumbled on what we hadn't being told and it was easy to understand the concern of the SADF. A lot of people were going to die and a lot of South African soldiers would be in the body count. By the end of the first week with that police task team, they had confiscated nearly ten thousand 7.62 39-millimetre rounds specifically for AK-47 assault rifles. We were about to experience Angola at our back door and nobody seemed too sure of what to do. Little did I know at the time that, within a year, I would be back in uniform and sporting a military regulation haircut.

Chapter 15

Just after Christmas 1991, Rob and I submitted independent reports to the Department of Customs. On 31 December, I was phoned by Peter before breakfast. He sounded strained and told me to get hold of Rob. We should prepare for a meeting at the Police Headquarters in Pretoria that afternoon. When I asked what it was about, he told me our reports were of concern to the SADF and they wanted to debrief us. By then, I had been promoted to major and Rob was a captain, middle management in the machine of the SADF, but for some reason we were about to explain our reports to the police executive. Driving with Rob to Pretoria, I believed that we were going to be questioned about the shootings in the nightclub. I was wrong.

We were both escorted to a room, shaped like an amphitheatre. It was about as intimidating an environment as either of us had experienced. We were led in and seated on a sort of stage. It started. Although it wasn't a court, it felt like a trial. Our names were read out and everybody opened a corresponding file. The silence that followed seemed to go on forever. The questions started with me. I was asked why I had infiltrated a police intelligence operation under false pretences. The operation was absolutely restricted and we had breached all protocols. I had never believed that the army and the police worked very closely together. That afternoon it was as though they weren't even on the same side. It lasted about forty-five minutes. We were questioned by more police generals than I thought could possibly be assembled in one room.

When I was asked to speak, I couldn't think of anything to say, so I kept quiet. This only made it worse and eventually I was ordered to speak. I couldn't believe our reports could have warranted this reaction, so I gave an oral account of our investigation. All I remember was feeling exposed and worried. It wasn't apparent what we had done wrong. We had been cleared to go on the raids with the police unit and had reported what we had seen with personal analysis. Obviously we were missing something. It all ended with a bang as our time ran out.

Peter was waiting for us when we left the room. He took us to a restaurant around the corner and told us that, in the eyes of the police, we had exceeded our orders but we shouldn't worry about it too much. He was very calm about the whole thing and I realised then we were just another item that day on the agenda at Police Headquarters. Peter told us that a police general wanted to have a private conversation with us and to wait in the restaurant at that table. Peter left and we ordered food. We both thought it best to remain sober and think clearly during the impending meeting.

The general arrived just before we finished our main course. He was a large man and very imposing in his blue dress uniform. He had been inducted into the army with Peter many years before and still worked closely with him. He told us we had breached a police operation and although the police executives were angry, their eyes had been opened to how easily it had been done. I wasn't that sure and we both kept quiet. He told us that, before we joined any future police operations, we would have to clear it with him. He gave us his business card with his private number and a paging code. The business card displayed his operational title; Special Operations Domestic. He left as fast as he had come in. I ordered a bottle of whisky and said,

"Fuck! This invitation was all a set up."

Rob asked me what I thought was going on.

"I think that some level of the army is selling the AK-47s brought back from the war to both sides of the factions and supplying them with reloaded ammunition. There must be police help, because nobody is being stopped, but I don't think the police are holding up their end of the bargain."

I'll never forget the look on his face when he realised I might be right. We discussed how successful the police had been in searching for weapons and how quickly they had found what they were looking for on the raids. I told him I thought the police were confiscating the weapons and then selling them back to whoever had the funds. It was a theory but I sensed the coming inevitable manipulation, because very soon I would be standing trial for the shooting. As much as I tried to see the angle that was coming, I mostly tried to forget about it all. Every evening I watched on the news as the violence escalated and the significance of the meeting at the Police Headquarters became increasingly relevant.

Within two weeks I met my legal team. It comprised a young, up-and-coming attorney, a very expensive advocate and a retired military judge. They had all the police documents and were very bullish that outcome would be a not guilty verdict. The drug dealer whom I had shot was a Nigerian national and had no permanent residence status in South Africa. The police had found the knuckle duster on his hand, an unlicensed firearm in his belt and almost two-hundred grams of cocaine in his pockets. That night, he had been about as illegal as he could have been. I felt much better after leaving their chambers that evening, but nothing is for sure in court. We were entering a plea of culpable homicide. Our strategy was self-defence and only one shot fired is a very reasonable ground. There were also photos from the hospital of my mouth showing a large amount of trauma and from the prison showing the inflammation. Those images were going to be crucial to my defence.

At the end of March 1992, my trial for the shooting in the club began. It started on a Friday morning, as winter was approaching. It was a cold morning. My bail had been revoked, so I was in a cell beneath the courtroom while the prosecution and my legal team started negotiations. Wearing a light suit, I was absolutely freezing. At midday, they were ready to start. The prosecution began by portraying me as a racist. My shooting of a black man in the public domain was motivated solely by his skin colour. If they only knew what we had done in Angola, I would have been troubled more. In fact, because most of the population of South Africa is black, if I had set out to shoot only whites, I would have waited my whole life to be in that position. I sat and listened to the argument and took notes, as I was instructed to do by my legal team. The court adjourned for the weekend after the prosecutor ended his introduction.

My lawyer applied for my bail to be reinstated before the court shut down. I wasn't holding my breath, but the retired military judge took over. He was very convincing and explained that I had certain requirements at the university to complete. In addition, I was working part-time for the Department of Customs, assisting a sensitive investigation of weapons being brought into South Africa from countries where there was an active movement to arm the domestic population in order to stall the date of the next elections. The judge was impressed by these arguments and granted me bail.

On Saturday morning, I was on the front page of every major newspaper in South Africa. The Department of Public Prosecutions had been unhappy with my bail being extended and had leaked the trial to the press. In one morning, I was elevated to being public enemy number one. Steven phoned me and asked me if he could come around that afternoon. When he arrived, he was with his oldest brother, who introduced himself as Innocent. As time passed, he was to become a very important person in my life in South Africa. In 1994, when Innocent joined the newly formed South African Defence Force (SANDF), the successor to the SADF, he became known as Bob, which is how I shall refer to him from now on. They explained to me that, after consulting their family, it had been decided Steven could give evidence as to my interactions with him and his Black Diamond friends during our first year at university. Bob, who was a member of MK, the ANC's military wing, was willing to vouch for his brother's testimony. Although I was grateful, I could see it all going wrong.

That afternoon, the three of us had a few beers and watched a local soccer derby on TV. Bob was a large guy, but his brain was the attraction. He knew everything that could possibly be known about the two teams. I realised that even the soccer teams in South Africa were very much part of tribal separation. Their supporters were divided by faction, political beliefs and leaders. Bob told me about his training in Russia. He had learnt from the best about psychological warfare. I couldn't help thinking that more of his time on a shooting range would have been time better spent. All we had done was shooting and training and we had won every conflict I had been in.

I decided not to say anything but to listen. After a few beers, Bob was warming up. He believed that the prosecution team were trying to discredit me because I had a history of arrests with the struggle. He got angrier when his team lost a very close soccer match and told me to "hold the line" as it would all work out in the end. I felt like a traitor that day, but was confused as to how much more bullshit I could put up with. Whose side was I on? The lines were becoming very blurred.

On Monday morning, I was back at the Supreme Court. One judge and two assessors would be listening and deliberating my future. My advocate opened with a brief statement and the prosecution started to do what they do best. Witness after witness came in and gave an account of what they had seen. There were no discrepancies in their accounts of the events that night, but I wasn't perturbed. We weren't going to be contesting the events that had taken place. Only motivation was in issue. My legal team spent little time cross-examining the prosecution witnesses. It established that none of them was in the toilet twenty minutes before the shooting. It was like listening to a poem. My legal team told the judge that they were not contesting my shooting of the deceased, but that the circumstances of the shooting would be, if the witnesses agreed that they were not in the toilets twenty minutes before the event. This process occupied three days and, on Wednesday evening, the court adjourned until the following Monday. The newspapers had lost interest and I was relegated to somewhere between pages three and five. On Monday morning, the retired military judge had told me not to worry about the reporters.

"This is South Africa. You won't be important for long."

On Thursday morning, I attended lectures at the university. After my first lecture, I went to the Commerce Bar and listened to the university radio. At first, I didn't think too much about it, but when the DJs changed, it was still all meek and mild. The DJ was a black student and he seemed to be very controlled in what he was saying. Strange, I thought. I decided to take some notes. Steven came in as I was writing. I think I was only doing it to take my mind off the trial. He sat down next to me and asked what I was doing. I told him that I thought the tone of the DJs had become very tame. After some thought he said,

"Dangerous times, Peter."

It struck me as strange that he would answer like that, but I wasn't interested. Steven said,

"My brother wants to meet you again."

My mind was elsewhere. I told him I wouldn't be coming to lectures any more until the trial was over. He went off and made a call. When he came back he asked if I would meet both of his older brothers at my flat the following night.

"Of course," I agreed.

When Steven and Bob arrived, I had food and drink ready. Steven introduced me to his other older brother, Daniel. After we had eaten we began to talk. At first we exchanged pleasantries. Daniel was quiet and only spoke when I addressed him. I liked all three of them a lot and the time passed quickly. As they left later that evening, Daniel told me that his uncle would be attending my trial. I didn't think much about it that night, but this meeting was going to change my path more than I could ever have imagined.

When I walked into the court on Monday morning, Steven's uncle stood out. He was dressed in jeans and a leather jacket, the uniform of an ANC veteran. He was the only black person there without a camera. He showed no recognition of me. He knew he would stand out and wanted everyone to notice him. When I sat in the dock, he sat right behind me and I felt strangely comfortable with him being there.

My defence team went to work and tore the prosecution apart. The backbone of the defence was an all-out attack on the version that had been presented thus far. I had a history of being an active part of the struggle. My advocate had subpoenaed a long list of activists who had been arrested with me. He began by calling a policeman I had assaulted while I was incarcerated a few years earlier with UDF members. The policeman changed the entire perspective of me in one afternoon. He answered all questions truthfully and admitted he had been in an altercation with a political prisoner in the cells and I had come to that prisoner's aid. The main point was that I was on the same charge sheet as those black prisoners and this sowed doubt about my racial motivation.

By the end of Monday, I had gone from being seen as a racist to the opposite. The newspaper reports adopted a different spin. It's amazing how quickly the Press will turn you from zero to hero. Although we weren't contesting the shooting, the motivation was being seriously commentated upon. That evening, I relaxed for the first time since the shooting and felt I was not only going to be vindicated as to why I had shot that dealer that night, but that I was not going to jail for it either. That whole week, my defence team called witness after witness who testified that I was not a racist. By Friday, my military counsel was convinced I would get off. I went home and went out.

On Tuesday of week three, the prosecution offered me a deal. They would drop the charges, if I pleaded guilty to discharging a firearm in a built-up area. I would receive a hefty fine and they would not ask that I be found unfit to possess a weapon. The retired military judge told me to take it, as I already had a criminal record and the army would pay the fine. The charges were changed and I pleaded guilty. The judge sentenced me to a fine of R100,000, to be paid within thirty days, or I would be re-arrested for contempt of court. I walked out of court that day feeling as though the weight of the world had been removed from my shoulders.

I started attending lectures at university again. I had missed a lot, but managed to catch up in time for the Easter exams. During the break after my exams, Steven left a message with my mom. When I phoned back, we chatted about the exams. He was confident he had done well, as was I. He said his uncle was in town and would like to meet me. In South Africa at that time, black adults meeting whites in their mid-twenties created all sorts of paranoia, so I wasn't surprised that he wanted to meet me in the flat at the bottom of my parent's house. I told him I would cook a barbeque for them the next day, when I would have the place to myself.

The next day, although Steven's uncle said little, he observed how close his nephew and I had become. Steven's uncle, whose name is Simon, had also received military training in Russia, but was less inclined to brag about it than the two brothers. He asked me about my time outside South Africa House and I was polite but vague. We actually had a good afternoon. It was all very cordial. I liked Simon. When he left, he asked for my parent's home phone number. It struck me he could have got it from Steven, yet he had decided to approach me outside his nephew's arena.

Later that week I attended a meeting at the Department of Customs. Peter was there and I briefed him on what had happened. He was delighted and asked me to attend a meeting the next day. That meeting would put me in the frontline of police and army operations domestically for the next twenty-four months. When I walked nonchalantly into an outside office the following day, I realised something was different. I was in a room with a purpose. Two lieutenant generals in full dress uniform were sitting at a desk. Peter was also in his dress uniform, looking very stern. My heart rose a couple of beats. At first, I hoped it had to with my trial, but that was soon dismissed as they got down to business.

My report the previous Christmas about the raids on the mines was the first order of business. I couldn't believe that a simple observation had made so many ripples in the pond. I remember feeling slightly nauseous as they went over it again. The meeting wasn't about what I knew. It was about what I didn't know. The SADF was indeed bringing weapons into South Africa and distributing them to the ANC's opposition, the Inkatha Freedom Party (IFP), thereby creating a split in the black vote and a wedge between the tribes, in order to destroy their policy of being united against white political parties. My fears were verified that afternoon. It wasn't a just case of certain generals making money. It was policy.

Simon was part of a future political voting base they hadn't yet tapped into and I was to be the conduit to drip feed them into the fight. They reminded me that they had looked after me during a few incidents. The whisky came out and, after a drink, I accepted.

I was to find a way of arming the Shangaan as soon as possible. Any help I needed would be given to me. Every step of this process would have to be cleared through Peter and under no circumstances was I to do anything without his express permission. That afternoon, the noose fell very tight around my neck. I was to start with Simon and expand the operation as soon as possible. All weapons would be made available to me and ammunition supplied as and when they wanted to turn up the heat. I would have access to a military range in the Northern Province of South Africa and was to give specific instructions on the weapons and the standard operation procedure of urban warfare. I would receive reading materials and be expected to pass military exams covering many new and diverse approaches to urban warfare.

The truth was I was already tainted. They had looked after me, so I couldn't see why I should have to hold any moral high ground. It was explained that the fight was inevitable anyway, even without my participation, but I could even out the percentages by helping this faction. From that moment, I was part of what became widely described for many years as "the third force". In hindsight, it's difficult to gauge how things would have turned out without my compliance that afternoon, but I try not to think about it too much.

Trading in weapons is the lowest form of action on any State agenda and you can rationalise it any way you want. If people are intent on fighting, then someone is going to supply them with the means to do so. A new government was about to be implemented in South Africa but first there would be a fight. I left that meeting, concerned about where my life was heading, yet it felt like a train that couldn't be stopped. I wrote my mid-year exams in June of 1992, after I had turned twenty-six. It had all started.

Chapter 16

I had no idea how to approach my new task, but they say that to start is to be halfway there, so I started. The military manuals were self-explanatory. I not only passed the exams I sat at Military Headquarters, but learnt lessons I would utilise for the rest of my time in South Africa. I was awarded the rank of major at the age of twenty-six. Looking back, rapid field promotions take place during times of unrest and South Africa was on fire.

In July 1992, I went back to a full program of lectures at the university and started to work five nights a week at the nightclubs. I had not attended enough tutorials at the university to qualify for writing my final exams, so attendance over the next few months would be crucial for putting it right. I attended every tutorial available. Steven was starting to panic about the end-of-year exams and he attended all the tutorials with me. I knew at some stage I would have to meet his family again with an agenda, but I suppose I tried to put that out of my mind. Luckily, things tend to fall into your lap and they did when Steven asked me to attend a wedding at his family house in Giyani. I accepted the invitation.

We drove up north together and he explained how his family had huge responsibilities there. He appeared to have a lot on his mind, but so did I. The next day the wedding was great. I was the only white person there but was made to feel so welcome that it seemed as if I were as black as they were.

It was after sunset when the shooting started. When the sound of an AK-47 is that close, you react. Everybody started to scatter. The fire was not a sustained attack. It was someone who felt in charge, because he had an assault rifle. Three of Steven's family were injured and the wedding was over. Simon was sitting at a table and looked defeated. I went over and sat down. After some silence he explained that the townships had become a war zone. It wasn't the casualty count he mostly cared about. It was the ability to respond. He had been in exile for most of his life in London and now he was in the middle of a fight between people he had trained with. Initially I felt sorry for him. It's a strange thing to watch a man coming to terms with the fact that the fight was no longer between whites and blacks. It was time for me to act. I told him I had access to people who traded in weapons. At first he said nothing. Then, after some thought, he told me that violent reaction was just what the people controlling the fight wanted. I had to agree and changed the subject. The wedding had fizzled out, when Steven eventually came back from the hospital. He wanted to go home and I agreed.

That night, driving back to Johannesburg, he was angry. I offered to arm him and he looked puzzled. I told him that some guys I worked with in the nightclubs had weapons they had brought back from the war. He told me he wouldn't know where to start with a firearm and that it was probably a bad idea. I told him I could access a shooting range. I would teach him. He asked me how much I would want to get him a weapon and I said,

"Nothing for you. You're my friend."

It was the ammunition that would cost money. I filed a report that weekend and the response was immediate. Peter gave me the coordinates to a farm in the Northern Province, a contact and more importantly one Russian and one Chinese AK-47 assault rifle. I was given spare magazines and ten thousand rounds of ammunition. That Saturday, Rob and I headed north to meet the owner of a game farm in the middle of cattle country. He had two camps about a kilometre from each other. One was a farm house and the other was a mass of tented accommodation. Most importantly for us, he had a full military specification firing range within his perimeter. The need to separate game from cattle was the cover for the nine-foot high electric fence.

The AK-47 is the mother of all self-cycling rifles. I'm sure the Israelis would beg to differ, but the truth is that the design of the moving parts on that weapon is replicated to this day. Rob and I were familiar with the weapon. We marvelled at its ability to fire as long as it was fed rounds. We shot the weapons on automatic for most of the morning, with no jams. By afternoon we began firing specific shots. We were a little rusty, but managed to reach our previous levels of competence within one magazine of thirty rounds.

We spent Saturday night with the owner of the farm. He was some twenty years older than us and, during the Bush War, had been a colonel at the Special Forces camp about fifty kilometres from a farm in Phalaborwa. He told us that anything we needed could still be accessed by him through that area. That night we got very drunk and he and Rob killed some wild pigs stupid enough to drink the water close by the bar. We stashed the weapons and what was left of the ammunition under a tree outside the tent and went home the following morning.

During lunch the following Monday, Steven came to sit with me as usual. I told him I had gained access to some assault rifles and ammunition. I think he thought I was joking. Eventually he admitted he had no working knowledge of firearms and felt very uncomfortable with the thought of owning one. He tried to make excuses for not taking delivery of them, but I was persistent. The range I was going to take him to was so close to where his family lived that he finally gave in. We planned to go to the farm the following weekend.

I filed a report and immediately received a message from Peter to meet him in Pretoria. When we met, I told him I would probably need more weapons soon and, after some thought, he asked me what I thought I would want. I asked for some service pistols and more ammunition. He told me a couple of firearm safes would be fitted in the house I was using. I could collect the keys from the house next door and it would be filled with what I needed, just as I had requested.

True to his word, that Friday, there were two safes in my main bedroom. In the rifle safe there were six more AK-47s with another ten thousand rounds. In the smaller safe there were ten Colt .45 M1911 service pistols with spare magazines and a thousand rounds. I loaded up the Toyota and went to meet Steven at my parents' house. As we drove north that afternoon, he seemed excited.

It's hard to forget that weekend. Rob arrived on Saturday morning while we were having breakfast and our lives as arms dealers began, not with a whimper, but with a bang. We started with the handguns. I broke one down and explained the workings of the pistol. Steven was a very bright kid and it was a painless process. Rob took over instruction and I began shooting. Steven was familiar with the sound of fire, so it was pretty simple making him confident with a side-arm. That afternoon we repeated the process and by the end of the day, we were all having fun. The next day, Steven invited his two brothers, Bob and Daniel, and Simon to the farm.

It always amazes me how quickly things snowball once they begin. I had bitten into this one and decided to hang on. I started a fire and whilst cooking breakfast for everyone, I asked,

"Who wants to go shooting?"

The relief was so apparent that we all relaxed. Bob, Daniel and Simon were a different kettle of fish. All three demonstrated breaking down an AK-47 with much glee. It was definitely not their first time. Although they were in a much more advanced mind-set with the hardware, they were lacking in rate of fire and how to work as an operational team. Rob had become an exceptional instructor in the last years of his military service and they were quick learners. After lunch, we ended the day by having fun. It was plain they had never enjoyed being on a shooting range before. That afternoon, we all bonded. If you can make practising anything fun, it becomes easier to teach. I have always had the ability to see the fun side to anything and Rob and I, with weapons, made a hell of a team. By the end of that day, all six of us shared common ground and I thought there was no time like the present to walk it on. I gave four AK-47s to Simon, along with all the ammunition that was left.

"When the first ones are free, be afraid," I remarked.

We all laughed, but they knew what I meant. The weekend ended in a blur. Rob went back to Potchefstroom and I to

Johannesburg, taking the pistols and the remaining AKs with me. On the way, I was stopped by the police at a roadblock and the Toyota was searched. The initial reaction to the quantity of weapons in the car was minimal. It was almost as though the police had come to terms with the fact that the country was being flooded with unlicensed weapons. I gave them my identification from the Department of Customs and they were happy for me to continue my journey. I realised then why we were using that identification. We were a front company for moving anything we wanted around the country.

I spent the next week working in nightclubs. It was all running smoothly until Saturday night. I didn't want trouble that night, but there was. Fighting broke out and I grabbed a jug of water from the bar top and hit the main antagonist, a member of the South African Narcotics Bureau, through the face with it. His skull cracked before he knew he'd been hit. He was not so tough when he hit the ground. In fact, he was immediately comatose. The rest of that fight is not important. We beat the hell out of the whole group. It was carnage. The managers of the nightclub were called into the police station and we were all named on the roster I had submitted at the beginning of the week. It was not what I needed. After my last court case, the last thing I wanted was another. I was given bail and reported to Peter the next evening. He was not even upset and told me to stop working in nightclubs and concentrate on the game in hand.

The following Sunday, I was in the newspapers again. As reporters do to create a story, I was made to look like a predator who couldn't stay out of trouble. As I read the article I wondered how many reporters had ever been in harm's way. At that time, I had no idea I was the subject of a team of reporters investigating the escalating violence in South Africa. As it turned out, when the victim of my assault regained consciousness, he refused to press charges. The case was discontinued, but the Press wouldn't let it go. I was hounded by a group of journalists and eventually agreed to meet one of them. He was a little older than I was and, although he believed he had a story, I said very little. He ran the story anyway and that morning I was featured in the editorial section of the largest selling Sunday newspaper in South Africa.

The next Sunday the reporter retracted his article and ran another from the point of view of the guy I had hit with the jug. He had admitted to being the main reason there had been any violence that night and I was vindicated. The reporter was Ken Oosterbroek and he would become famous as one of the four reporters writing on the escalating weapons-related violence in the townships of South Africa. They were known as the Bang-Bang Club, as they put their lives on the line to report a story. In the months before the General Election, they came closest to the truth about the civil war in South Africa.

Ken's overzealous reporting on that incident in the nightclub would give me the benefit of the doubt for the rest of his life. We became firm friends and spent many hours together debating. He never wrote another article with my name in it; nor published a photo of me again. One night in the future, I would leak him a story that he wouldn't write about on principal. On 18 April 1994, nine days before the first inclusive elections in South Africa, he was shot and killed by peacekeepers in the Thokoza Township about twenty-five kilometres east of Johannesburg. What a good guy and what a loss. But before that happened, Ken features again in this story.

Chapter 17

In October of 1992, I wrote my final second-year exams at the University of the Witwatersrand. Steven approached me after the exam and asked if I was willing to meet more of his family. I obviously was and told him to meet me at the farm in the Northern Province that weekend. He agreed and appeared grateful, as if he had been under pressure. I felt sorry for him. He was going to have to grow up quickly and there's no time like the present.

I went to the Department of Customs and told Peter I had been approached by Steven's family. Peter told me do him a favour and cut him out of the equation. I requisitioned more rifles, more ammunition and some training ordinance. The guns were on tap, but the ordinance was a special request. It was strange that assault rifles were on the menu but explosives with a charge slightly larger than a firecracker were a special request. That weekend, the safes in my house were filled and I knew I was going to be able to throw a party this time.

On Saturday morning, Bob, Daniel and Simon arrived at the farm. There was no Steven. I remember thinking how his family and Peter were on the same page. Had I thought about it more, I would have realised how much they were. That Saturday was very hot and Rob took it upon himself to be the range instructor. We were all exhausted by lunch but we were acting as a team and it was all going very well. I liked the three of them and after lunch, I decided to elevate the training. When Rob and I started to show them how to fire specific shots, we no longer seemed to be just gangsters. The questions started to flow and we were as forthcoming as we could be. Rob admitted to having been in the South African Defence Force for five years. He added,

"Thank God for that, or Peter wouldn't have a clue."

From that afternoon, that was how we played it. I was relegated to thug and Rob was the soldier. Because of the trials and the newspaper articles it was plausible.

On Saturday evening, I received money in exchange for weapons for the first time. Like all firsts, it was bitter sweet. We went to the gate just before sunset and let a new face in. He was part of Steven's family and wished to remain anonymous. He did for all the years I knew him. He paid me R1,000 for each AK-47, even paying me for the three AKs I had given his family the last time we were on the range. He paid me R500 for every 5,000 rounds used, including those used the previous time. We negotiated in private. In an unprofessional way, it was oddly professional. He refused my offer of a drink and, in all the years afterwards, I never offered him a drink again. He was very different from the others. It was all business. That evening we made a fire, cooked meat and drank whisky. I felt comfortable in their company and later that night I threw in three pistols with spare magazines. The next time I met the money-man, he paid me for them and asked me not to do it again. This was business and he didn't want the lines to become fuzzy. He told me they paid for everything in life and I would give him an exact account of everything I supplied. That was how I started to arm the very proud nation of the Shangaan. In less than eighteen months, one in every two assault rifles and almost all the ammunition that filtered into that area, passed through that farm. The business happened so quickly that day, yet it had taken nearly two years to begin.

I attended a meeting at the Customs Department with Peter. He had been promoted to major general, but there were no celebrations that evening and the mood was sombre. He handed me an order to report to Police Headquarters in Johannesburg at the end of the week. I would find my uniform in my house and should get a haircut. He told me the Defence Force was not getting the full picture from Police Intelligence. He wasn't sure if it was deliberate or if they were too busy to care. I was to take a first-hand look at the township violence and make a comprehensive report on what I saw. I had no idea what to expect in the coming days, but would act as though it was just another day.

I went home and spent the night at my designated house. The next morning my uniform arrived, with webbing and a brand-new side arm. The uniform was unwashed. I would have looked stupid in it, so I bought some bleach and let some of the brown from the uniform run into the bath-water. The boots were brand-new as well, which would be difficult to disguise whatever I did. I telephoned Rob and he told me he was being deployed with a police unit that weekend. I told him about the boots and he laughed.

"I think that will be the least of your worries."

After some teasing, he said he would bring me a pair of his to wear. It seems silly, but boots are an integral part of a uniform and if you haven't been in uniform for a while, it stands out when the boots aren't worn-in.

Resentfully, I shaved off my hair, but must admit that putting the crowns on my lapels denoting the rank of major made up for it. There were no name tags on my uniform and I thought that would be for the best. The next morning I reported for duty. My briefing was short. I was to be driven to Diepkloof Police Station in the South-Western Townships. From there, I would join a mobile police unit taking on the role of an observer. As I walked out of the office the colonel said,

"Major, you're only there to observe, is that clear? We want the army to know that we have no secrets, but we also don't need any help."

It was a strange end to the briefing. I turned around and saluted him. He then muttered in Afrikaans,

"*Ons ken mos vir jou, seun* (We know about you son)."

The police sergeant who drove me to Diepkloof was a huge man in his early forties. At first we were silent. Then, waiting in traffic, he burst out laughing.

"That's a very new uniform, Major."

Immediately I liked him and he started to chat. According to police intelligence, it was going to be a very active weekend. He was in a very good mood for someone driving into the type of war zone he was describing. We were laughing together in the Johannesburg mid-morning traffic. It's funny how some people bond together so quickly.

Later that day and over the entire weekend, I would encounter a very different type of policemen. They were all just that little bit more on the ball and I was about to find out why. After another briefing, which was more like a roll call, I jumped into the front passenger seat of the lead Kaspir, an armoured vehicle. Instead of the earth-brown colour I was used to, the vehicles were painted white with a blue stripe horizontally across the middle. I realised that getting into the lead vehicle had annoyed the police captain leading the patrol. It looked as though I were arrogant and was a bad start. Although I was the ranking officer, I was younger than nearly everybody in the police unit. It wasn't the cleverest of decisions, but it was done and I made a mental note to swop places the first time the convoy came to a halt.

The operating procedure of the unit was vastly different to what I had experienced in the army. They were in constant contact with each other. The radio was hardly ever silent. When we stopped at a huge depot to fill the tanks with fuel, I jumped out, approached the captain and asked him if we could swop places. He smiled and nodded. I had made an ally. We deployed to Inhlazane Train Station. There, the four vehicles stopped on high ground, each separated from the other by about fifty metres. It was executed with an expertise that comes with doing it over and over again.

I exited the vehicle via a hatch in the roof and took a look. Below me was an absolute war zone. Boulders in the roads and even some concrete blocks had been moved into the area to stop civilian vehicles from entering or leaving. They would not stop the police vehicles, but would definitely slow them down.

Friday afternoon was mostly quiet as we observed the residents of South-Western Townships. It is impossible to know how many people resided in the township, but it's best said that it's a lot more than you would think possible. It became chaotic in the late afternoon, like watching ants. That night, the captain came to my vehicle. I was thankful I had made the concession to him earlier, as he now took me into his confidence. He told me we were staying for the entire weekend. All ablutions were to be done as close to the vehicles as possible and preferably the passing of stool would be done at night. We would change positions before sunrise every morning for hygiene purposes and stay mobile.

That night, the sound of drunken revelry was set against a background of music, played from different locations. It seemed as though there was no cohesion, yet you could feel it was a normal behavioural pattern. I slept a little, but the nervous tension in the vehicle made long periods of sleep impossible.

It began at 10h00 the next morning. There were two distinct groups. The ANC supporters were congregated in one area and the IFP, comprising migrant Zulus, were about a kilometre away. The IFP group grew much quicker than the ANC faction and by midday there must have been at least 2,000 IFP members in the streets. They were very organised and all were wearing something red; a T-shirt or vest, but mostly red headbands, to distinguish themselves from the opposition. It was an obvious uniform of sorts. The number of ANC supporters also swelled as the afternoon wore on.

It was late afternoon before the first phase began. At first the two factions slowly drew nearer to each other. Then, at a distance of about 100 metres apart, both sides stopped. It was obvious this was not the first time they had done this. They spent what seemed like an eternity shouting abuse and insults at each other. I was joined on the roof of our vehicle by the staff sergeant. I offered him my binoculars and he declined. He smiled in a way that suggested he was resigned to something happening he had seen many times before.

Then the next phase began. Women, some bare-breasted, but all wearing red, joined together at the front of the IFP lines and hurled abuse at the ANC. The staff sergeant shouted into the vehicle,

"*Hier gat hulle* (Here they go)."

He chambered a round into his R1 7.62 assault rifle, smiling as I looked at him. A rifle was passed to me from inside the vehicle.

Then the two tribes went to war. The IFP started shooting first. Single shots at first, then short bursts. At that range, it was impossible to miss a large crowd. They probably weren't all killing shots, but people were dropping. Then small-arms fire came suddenly out of a window to the left of the IFP crowd and some of them went down. I was absorbed by the whole thing. Then it became stranger. A police armoured vehicle stopped between the two groups. A policeman popped his upper body out of the top and raked the house to the left with an assault rifle. My initial thoughts were that the police were acting like referees in an eccentric game. Shooting from the house was as if the person responsible had committed a foul, for which the penalty was death. I couldn't help thinking that you had to be very stupid or over-confident or both to commit a foul in this game.

No ambulances were coming to the aid of the wounded and no choppers were flying them to hospital. If they were lucky, some of the wounded, as well as the dead, were carried off the field of combat by their arms and legs. Mostly they were left where they lay. I estimate around 100 shots were fired that afternoon. As night drew in, the crowds dispersed and I thought it was over. Far from it. Saturday night in that part of the South-Western Townships was the real killing time. Under cover of darkness, the sounds of shots and people screaming continued until the early hours of the morning. The shooting had been like a well-rehearsed play, performed in front of an audience that had seen it all before.

On Sunday morning, everyone had taken up position around what could only be described as strong-holds. The whole thing was crude but effective. The amount of hatred it takes to wage pitched battles like that, was something I needed to see. By lunchtime on the Sunday, the captain came over to us. All he said was,

"Have you seen enough? Show's over for the time being."

He addressed me in Afrikaans, but it wouldn't be possible to translate it correctly. I knew what he meant. I had been given a grand-stand view of a weekend in South Africa's townships. The Press had arrived and I couldn't help thinking that, although most middle class white South Africans thought they were aware of what was going on so close to their cosy suburbs, panic would have been the order of the day if they had known what was really happening. I realised how important censorship was.

I was driven back to my own vehicle. When I arrived at my house, I was so tired that I went to sleep. There was nothing I had witnessed that weekend that could possibly make a difference. It was barbaric and pointless and yet, to the participants, it must have seemed worth dying for.

Chapter 18

I was depressed by what I had seen that weekend, so the night after I returned, I went out and was offered free cocaine. At the time, I didn't realise this was how the drug dealers worked. I would later term gratuitous drugs as tax.

I felt there was something I was missing. It wasn't the selling of weapons in the now obvious civil war raging in South Africa that had got to me. I felt no moral obligation to stop the flow of weapons into the townships. If anything, I felt it more of a duty to increase the flow of weapons to my new friends. Even if I stopped doing it, the fighting would not have stopped and my friends would have been more vulnerable while seeking out a new arms-dealer. If I dropped out, there would be four more like me, ready to jump up in my place. The operation I had joined was already nearly twenty-four months old and, like a runaway train, there was no stopping it. At some stage during that week, the missing pieces dropped into place. What I had heard was more important than what I had seen. The small-arms fire had been a fruit salad of sounds, but the assault rifles were specifically two sounds. They were the same calibre bullet, but had a different length of round. The ANC were using AK-47s and Inkatha were using the same weapons we had used in the war. In fact, it had sounded like an Angolan killing field. I suddenly knew why I was so disturbed. It had brought back suppressed memories.

How could I utilise this knowledge better? I had stumbled upon it and there were a lot of people who knew much more than they were telling me. Sometime during the next weekend, I wrote a report. I should have learnt by that stage that fucking up a good story with facts could only lead to more problems, but I hadn't, and I wrote exactly what I thought. I drove to Pretoria the next day and submitted it. I received a response that afternoon. I was to meet Peter at Police Headquarters that evening. Again, I was subjected to a lot of questions from policemen. I just verified my analysis of the report and didn't make any friends. I answered the questions that evening as guardedly as I could. It became apparent that nobody wanted the truth. That day, I decided I would never give a personal opinion again, not in writing anyway. The bottom line was pretty simple to state. We were all involved with distributing weapons to both sides. We were obviously creating havoc, but it was apparent from the weapons fired, that one side was being given the advantage. The whole episode left me tired and surrounded by confusion. When I walked out, Peter was there and we went for something to eat. I told him that shooting the messenger was not the answer. That day he listened to me for the first time. We decided to change our approach.

It was important to supply different weapons to both sides. It would disguise the fact that they were being armed by us, leaving less of a fingerprint. If it was apparent to me, then we had to believe it was apparent to everybody who sooner or later was going to start watching. We needed to diversify the weapons we were filtering into the fight. Not only to disguise intent, but to make it less obvious that both sides were being supplied with different ammunition. This would become more important in the event that, at a later stage, we had to fight them. Making each side more dependent on more than one specific round of ammunition would also give us a better hold on the buyers by withholding rounds at will. He agreed.

We decided to implement this new strategy in the Northern Province. That weekend, fifty Vector R1 assault rifles were transported to the farm and locked up safely in a newly-built armoury. When Rob and I opened the safe, we had enough weapons and ammunition to start a small war. We couldn't wait to use the same type of rifles we had been issued by the army all those years ago. We started shooting and both felt a little let down. Although the rifles were the same, the R1 assault rifles had standard sights on them and there is only so much rapid fire shooting up the back wall of a range you can do before becoming bored. With one hand, the past moves you forward. With the other, it holds you back.

After firing some shots, we had our first rifle jam. It was a defect in the ammunition and the rifle would need to go to an armourer to be fixed. The retired colonel told me he could fix it in his outbuilding. Neither Rob nor I believed him, but we were happy to let him have a go. Just before lunch, he came back with the rifle and fired a couple of magazines through it. We were impressed. When a round jams in the chamber, sometimes you can bully it back out, but if the round actually locks into the barrel, it's called a squid. When this happens, you need to have somebody who knows what he's doing, so as not to destroy any of the rifling, the grooves down the barrel that make the weapon accurate. He had removed the squid round from the opening of the barrel, cleaned the working parts and brought it back in under an hour. He told us he had been an armourer in his previous life. Now he was just a caretaker of somebody else's property. That evening, he revealed that, with the right equipment, he could do almost anything with weapons. He had certainly caught our attention. Driving home, I told Rob I intended requisitioning a metal workshop for him on the farm, as he was wasted just doing maintenance. Rob replied something like,

"Good luck."

I met Peter at his earliest available time. I told him about the weekend and added that we could teach some guys sniper shooting. If he really wanted to make either side any better, systematically killing the leaders of the other faction would be the most efficient way to do it. If we could increase the distance of the contact, one side would immediately have the advantage. Even though welding 'scopes onto the dust covers of certain rifles would increase their accuracy, they would still be less effective than the rifles we used in Angola. This meant I could make one side more dangerous, without making them better than the SADF. He eventually agreed that it was worth thinking about and told me not to put it into a report.

A few days before I was to attend my final year at university, I was told a workshop would be built on the farm and I would receive a list of the machines needed for the retired colonel to make it all happen. I went on my own to the farm to deliver the news. The retired colonel was ecstatic. It was as though I had given him a new lease of life. We spent an evening together, when he gave me a display of all the weapons he had accumulated during his years with differing units. His knowledge of almost every firearm on the planet was outstanding. That night started a friendship that would last until his death. Like many men whom I would trust, he died from a severe heart attack in his late sixties.

By March 1993, we had a basic training camp on the farm, with an armoury and a fully equipped metal and carpentry workshop. The retired colonel proudly told me we could make almost anything out there. I laughed. The Military Intelligence budget had been well and truly raped.

I was seeing less and less of Steven, seemingly by design from his family, but that March I met Simon in a nearby town. I told him if he got twelve guys together, then we would do something different. He was over the moon and we made plans for the following weekend.

The retired colonel had set up cameras at the gate that were movement-activated. He had them delivered under the pretence of controlling the predators on his farm. He told me that if we were going to train people, we had to keep records of them. I disagreed and asked him to take the cameras down. If we wanted these people to trust and relax around us, we would have to rely on memory and not on cameras they might discover. I also believed in some kind of honour amongst rogues. He was not convinced, but promised to remove them.

The range was being used for what it was initially designed, namely sighting-in weapons before a hunt, but now it was training hunters for two very different purposes. The following weekend, we had fifteen men on the range; twelve new guys, Steven's uncle and his two older brothers. I let Rob run the training, with the enthusiastic retired colonel as his second-in-command. These new guys were being taught from scratch and spent all morning being lectured on weapons, calibres and basic firing methods.

After lunch, the fun started. The new guys were very enthusiastic and each one was assigned a different weapon. By the end of the first shooting session, they had become familiar with their weapons. The amazing thing is how enthusiasm can be all that's needed to override inexperience.

The same weekend, I was paid in cash by the money-man for fifteen modified Vector R1 assault rifles with 3,000 rounds. The next day he bought fifty Chinese AK-47s with 5,000 rounds. The following week, Rob and I took the retired colonel to a five-star game park for a big evening meal and a night in luxury accommodation. The next morning, the retired colonel asked me if I would request to have our sleeping accommodation on the farm upgraded to the same standards. I won't recount the details of how it happened, but by 13 June 1993, my twenty-seventh birthday, the retired colonel was running a five-star game farm.

Then came the fall-out. For every action, there is an equal and opposite reaction. In August 1993, there was a shooting incident in the Northern Province that made national newspaper headlines. It was different to what had been taking place until then in the area. It was reported that an ANC faction had opened fire on a wedding, using snipers to start it off. I don't think it surprised me much. In fact, I remember thinking how this new tactic being brought into the game would have terrified the other side. At the time, I wasn't bothered politically about which side I was helping. Supplying both sides was the objective, so it didn't matter. I was proud we had taught them so well. I didn't even waste a second wondering which of our pupils were involved. I knew they had done a good job. In fact, the tactics used that day had done such a good job, that it caused concern right across the board.

That following week our budget was made larger. The retired colonel was also on a run and had convinced the builders to build a swimming pool in the accommodation area. Looking back, we had become a luxury hunting farm, covering a very sensitive operation.

One night, I ran into Ken Osterbroek again at a bar in the Johannesburg northern suburbs. He was with two other members of the now famous Bang-Bang Club. One of them,

133

Greg, had been awarded the Pulitzer Prize for a graphic photograph of a man being set on fire. He had photographed the exact time of the man's death, delivered by a traditional weapon called a panga. They were all very drunk and a pain in the security staff's neck. I decided to intervene and walked over. Greg didn't recognise me, because I had cut my hair and I must have made some opaque reference about the Bang-Bang Club, because he threw a punch at me. He was an exceptional photographer, but not as skilled at fighting. I held on to him and spoke. When he had calmed down, I took them all to one of my nightclubs. There I received the full impact of his opinion on the civil unrest in the townships of South Africa. By that stage, Greg was a man tortured by his mission to tell the world what was happening in South Africa. However, he was in a better state of mind than the friend with him called Kevin. Kevin had become unstable and was unpleasant to be around. They were being hounded by the security police and had become paranoid and distrustful. Greg saw me as just a thug that night. Eventually, Ken said to me,

"Schools out, bru (a South African colloquialism for brother). Let's drink."

I got very drunk with them. The dynamics of the team were apparent. They had been working in the townships around Johannesburg and were absolutely determined to get to the bottom of the arms dealing that was fuelling the civil war. I watched them get angrier all night long and I remember Ken sounding strangely naïve. Although he was very close to the truth, he couldn't see the forest for the trees. It made me uncomfortable to listen to his theory on the number of snipers involved. It's funny how you can come to see how your work has affected others. I filed a report about my progress that week, including my interaction with them. At my next meeting at the Customs Department, Peter was there. When he asked me about the Bang-Bang Club, I told him it seemed to me that the sniper's specific shots were being perpetrated in more than one Province. I knew I was right when he brushed me off, telling me I was being looked after and should keep moving. That next week I sold another fifty AK-47s to my friends.

The retired colonel came round for supper and told me he had secured a budget for the purchase of many different new animals to be hunted on the farm. He was delighted with the new lease of life given to him and he knew I was his ticket. I couldn't help but be happy for him. His life was simple and that's all he wanted.

By August 1993, I was taking weekly orders for weapons. We were asked to do another training day and I made it clear we would only be training with standard weapons for a while. By then, Bob had got himself in real deep with the distribution of firearms and was trying to fulfil promises he had made. I gave in and we trained another twelve men in specific shots. We had the weapons adapted on the farm. It was like a cottage industry of how to kill. We were vertically integrating the whole process and eventually made a package deal for them to stay on the farm for a night. The whole process had become like something out of a movie.

In the first week in September 1993, it all fell apart. Three people were shot in different parts of the Northern Province at about the same time of the day. It made the police and Press in the area take note and both became nervous. Not only were there obvious specific shots taking place. They were co-ordinated as well. I was called in and we were shut down. I told Peter it was stupid to punish me for my success. He thought for a while and told me it would all blow over. I was not to go to the farm until further notice.

Chapter 19

On 10 April 1993, Chris Hani was assassinated outside his home in Dawn Park, a racially-mixed suburb of Boksburg, only a few kilometres from my parents' home. He was the General Secretary of the South African Communist Party and the chief of staff of MK, the armed wing of the ANC. He was shot in the head and back as he got out of his car by a Polish far-right anti-communist immigrant called Janusz Walus. Walus was arrested and, soon after the shooting, Clive Derby-Lewis, a senior South African Conservative Party MP and shadow Minister for Economic affairs, was arrested for complicity in Hani's murder. Both were convicted and sentenced to death. However, when the death penalty was abolished in South Africa, they had not yet been executed and their sentences were commuted to life imprisonment.

Chris Hani was regarded by many as the first black President of South Africa. He had been one of the first black South Africans to campaign as an active soldier in the Zimbabwean War of Liberation and, by 1982, he had become sufficiently prominent to become the target of several assassination attempts. Following the un-banning of the ANC in 1990, Chris Hani had returned to South Africa.

Historically the assassination is seen as a turning point with serious tensions following. The two sides, namely the minority white government and the ANC, were galvanised into action over negotiating transition. A few months later, a date was set for the first democratic elections. They were to take place on 27 April 1994, just over a year after Chris Hani had been shot.

Once the date of the elections had been set, the impact on my life was huge. We were told at the Department of Customs that all meetings were now monthly and I was to shut down the house I had been given. I felt I had done my duty by that time and was thankful it was over. Now natural progression would be the order of the day. I started to concentrate on my final exams and worked the odd night at one of the nightclubs.

In October 1993, I wrote my final exams at university. I knew I had passed every exam as soon as I had written them, but it's still a stressful time. Rob came back home to Johannesburg after finishing his exams and we decided to visit Peter in Port Elizabeth.

He wasn't home, but had left word with his wife for us to wait for him. We settled into his bar and got stuck into his whisky. By the time he eventually arrived, Rob and I were drunk. Then the three of us got drunk and Peter told us we were only under contract to Military Intelligence until the elections. We would both be promoted and retired within months of the result of the elections being verified. He asked us what we were going to do afterwards and we explained how we had recently taken over a group of bouncers. We didn't mention exactly how we had taken them over, but by the end, we were in charge of most major venues in Johannesburg night-life. It was the direction we felt our future was going. He told us we were welcome to live in the flat at the top of his garden for as long as we wanted. We decided to stay a while. Rob would only have to be back in Potchefstroom by the end of February and we both wanted to see how the city had changed.

And how Port Elizabeth had changed! There were now running battles in the city centre between the police and the trade unions. It was absolutely the worst advertisement for reconciliation in any South African city. The way Port Elizabeth had urbanised along the coast with no real development plan had caused multiple townships to be established too close together. The crime level in the suburbs had spiralled exponentially out of control, while the police were busy keeping the peace between the warring political parties.

We lay by the pool and drank a seemingly endless supply of whisky. I started to think for the first time about life without military identification as my safety net. It seemed to have its ups but it actually made me feel vulnerable. Then my future took care of itself.

The two of us were having lunch at a restaurant on the beach. We had parked our vehicle on the main road and while we were eating, a young black guy broke the window and tried to hot wire our car. Rob jumped over the banister and shot him twice in quick succession. It wasn't the cleverest thing he had ever done, but it happened so fast that I only reacted after Rob had killed the thief. There was a full restaurant of people who had witnessed the shooting, but it looked like Rob's first shot had broken the window. The judge would later state that Rob's actions were specific and deliberate. I don't think Rob could have been more specific and deliberate if he had written the script himself.

It was a time of political upheaval and racial tension and when the police arrived they seemed resigned to the fact that they must arrest us. That evening, when Peter came for us, he was not even angry, which should have rung warning bells. The next morning, Rob and I appeared in front of a magistrate on charges of murder. We were given bail and went back to Peter. That night, Peter told us that, after the elections, the offices we used to report to would be occupied by the same people with different titles. If we signed up for a further five years, we were assured a favourable outcome in the trial. He had used the same inducement every time and every time we had gone for it. We signed on for another five years with Military Intelligence and went to sleep.

Rob and I decided to spend New Year's Eve at Peter's flat. He had been newly promoted to major general and had planned a party. As we were both back in the fold for the next five years, we were put on the invitation list. It was to be held in the veteran's hall at the local chapter of the Memorable Order of Tin Hats, a South African veterans association founded in 1927.

1994 began that night and by the end of it, I was on first name terms with three lieutenant generals and Rob had made firm friends with their colonels and chief of staff. It was a night well spent. Two days later the military got the next five years of our lives after one appearance in court. Rob would not go back to university on a military subsidy, but would join me at Military Headquarters in Pretoria. I had already graduated from the University of the Witwatersrand. We would be in uniform and present ourselves as suitable officers of the SADF. In essence, we were to shave, get a haircut, clean and press our uniforms and report for duty. I was twenty-seven and a decorated major in an operational army, serving in the same uniform and using the same weapons. The only difference was that this time it would be on home soil instead of in Angola.

The following Monday morning, I met Rob in the Military Headquarters parking lot in Pretoria. He looked a little sheepish and I remember him saluting me with much glee. We were only kids, but had a very strong sense of not knowing what might come at us next. We were deployed to a combined task-force made up of the South African Police Force and the SADF. We were just observers for the army, expected to file independent reports to Military Headquarters in Pretoria on anything we deemed relevant. It was a very loose order. If we missed anything, it would be on our heads and if we reported something nobody wanted to know, it would likewise be on our heads. This was nothing new in operational procedure.

The first briefing was also nothing new. We were told how Inkatha, representing most of the nation of Zulu people, was not only refusing to contest the upcoming elections, but was going to boycott them. This was fighting talk and if there is one part of African culture that has always been underestimated, it's the fight in the man, not the man in the fight. The colonel of the task-force told us it was his job to keep control, not to keep the peace. I understood his predicament and sympathised. By now, both Rob and I were not just on his side. We were under his command. As we left the briefing, I looked at Rob. He smiled. This would be much more fun for him, than going back to his last year at university. We had no idea that we were about to observe just how South Africa was getting a feel for the impending democracy.

We started in the early hours of the next morning. I was not used to the type of policemen we were with. They were battle hardened and focussed. I was the ranking officer in the convoy, yet from my previous experience of a police armoured column, I didn't make the same mistake as I had before. I told Rob to get into the front of the third vehicle and I took over the second. This left the captain in charge to take the point of the convoy. This turned out to be a good decision, as this captain had the absolute respect of his men. We were the new guys and I wanted the whole process to run smoothly, which it did from that morning.

We spent the next few days becoming part of the unit. They were good together and when everyone started talking to each other, Rob and I relaxed. The experience was nothing new for either of us. Running battles between the ANC and Inkatha were pretty much random urban warfare. People were dying on both sides but I don't think this was by design but more as a consequence. The white government was no longer seen as the enemy. It had become the umpire in a very dangerous political game.

The police captain, Rob and I decided to collaborate over our reports. All three of us felt it was the best way to go forward with the least amount of fall-out. We agreed to keep them as short as possible and to compare notes before we submitted them. I told them I felt as though I was cheating at an exam. We all laughed and the ice was broken. The reports would seem contrived, yet we all agreed that a difference of opinion would not be in the interest of any of us, let alone the analysts who had to deal with the information. We formed a good bond in that first week, but the events of the weekend would leave all of us a little on edge.

On the last weekend of January 1994, I witnessed a truly South African event. It was something no military machine had seen in nearly 100 years. On Thursday morning, we took up position outside an area known as Stanger in KwaZulu-Natal, in 2006 renamed KwaDukuza, making camp on a rural farm. From the high ground of our first camp, Rob and I spent most of our time looking at the Indian Ocean. It all seemed so peaceful. It was very hot, sticky and the humidity was unbearable. The entire personnel from our vehicle sat in their shorts, eating lunch and being very loud. It was so different to my last experience in a rural environment, where we had been in harm's way. That afternoon the police captain took Rob and me for a short briefing. He told us there was going to be a funeral in the area that weekend. The deceased was a prominent member of a large clan of Zulus, who ruled the emotions of the people in the area. Nobody knew what to expect but Police Intelligence had predicted trouble.

That evening, the entire police unit lit cooking fires. The valley below was completely surrounded by glows on the high ground above. Rob commented it was lucky we hadn't used these tactics in Angola, as we would never have fired our rifles. I remember thinking that was exactly the point. It was a form of a signal to whoever was watching that we were there. There was nothing covert about the plan.

The next morning, we witnessed a bus convoy moving across the landscape. At the point where the road went inland, an army contingent had taken up position. The earth-brown colour of the vehicles and uniforms left nobody in any doubt that the army was there. It was both clever and stupid. When the busses started to arrive, although the police were logging the number of them, it was impossible to work out how many people were in them. They were crammed to over-capacity with men from the area, ordered by their tribal chiefs to muster that weekend. They were all wearing at least one piece of red clothing. I had seen this before. This was a gang on the move and a very large one at that.

On Saturday morning, I saw something that again everybody in the area would remember until they died. The Inkatha members had changed into tribal clothing of skins, shields and tribal weapons. They formed in ranks known as "Impis" with one "Induna" in front of each. It was a sight to behold. We couldn't tell how many were present, as we could only see those at the front of each formation. I do remember, however, that there were enough men assembled to make the earth tremble when they stamped in unison. The whole experience was as though I had been transported back 200 years in South African history. It was a show of absolute power that lasted all morning. Every so often, a small group would break off and disappear behind our line of sight. This would be followed by the police radios going crazy, as they tried to track the movements of the splinter groups.

While I was watching the spectacle, Rob had lost interest in a sight that looked like something out of a historical film. He nudged me and, with a smile on his face, he said,

"Look at things to come."

The real thing about that day was that the Zulus were not only well drilled, but they were extremely well disciplined. Driving back to Johannesburg the next week, Rob said to me,

"The soldiers with us were afraid."

I agreed. It was the first time I had seen so many white men in uniform appearing so afraid. I knew from previous experience that it was an observation to be left out of my report. This would be the first time the messenger would not be in the firing line. I wrote a very short report. It was well received and I heard no more about it.

The next weekend we were back in uniform in the township of Tokosa, east of Johannesburg. This was something totally different and it was by no means just a show of force. There were peacekeepers cowering underneath their vehicles while urban guerrilla warfare was taking place all around them. It was chaotic and there were no real lines in the running battles. I felt nothing other than despair that the approaching elections would be anything close to being free and fair.

At the end of the month, Rob and I were summoned to a meeting at the Department of Customs, where we were re-introduced to Sean. It was a pleasant surprise and I was glad the new game I was about to play was with the two people I had been in contact with in Angola. Sean was sitting in the main office. He had a more pressing problem than our last brush with the law. Sean was now a lieutenant colonel and was working an operation in the north east of South Africa. The violence had been getting increasingly worse in the country, making peaceful elections look as though they could never happen. What Rob and I had witnessed in the previous two weeks had left both of us with serious doubt too.

It seemed the main problem wasn't ethnicity, or even political parties, but a fight for position after the elections. There were ancient family feuds with old wounds needing a lot of work to patch. We were told there were enough positions to keep everybody happy, yet they would all have to work together so as not to bring the infighting of the clans into the different offices. The worry was that infighting would cause a deadlock and the civil service is usually deadlocked enough, without historic hostilities making things worse. It would be a full-time job for us. Sean knew I had been part of an operation to distribute weapons in the North East and wanted me to open communications with my clients again. We needed to know if any co-operation between us, my clients and any rival clans could help the elections to be presented to the rest of the world as free and fair. He believed that negotiations could smooth over the transition period, known as "sharing the pie", with as little jealousy as possible. We needed to understand which problems could be bridged and which should be avoided during the initial distribution of the local gravy train.

The three of us went to supper on Sean's credit card and got drunk. Later that night, while swilling whisky neat from a bottle at one of our newly acquired nightclubs, Sean took me aside and asked me what I needed. I wanted to use the farm, from where I had been distributing the weapons and where we had been training clients. Sean agreed it would be the best place to use, as everybody would feel more comfortable in familiar surroundings. He told me he would have an answer by Monday morning. It was good to be working with him again. Sean and I shared secrets from the war in Angola. He trusted my ability to work on my feet and I trusted him to make the right approach to the relevant people. He wished me luck and reminded me,

"I put you two together and, apart from the odd court case, it's been a good decision."

By Monday night, Rob and I had been granted full access to the farm and were told to report to new offices in the North East. When we arrived at the farm, the retired colonel was very pleased to see us. Either that, or he was relieved to be involved with something again. It felt good to be back with him and he proudly showed me how many weapons he had modified. I explained that we were about to play Band-Aid for the foreseeable future. We would be patching up wounds, as opposed to teaching how to create them. He seemed disappointed at first, but decided to stay. I felt he wanted to help me in any way he could.

Within the first week, we met Simon and his two nephews. When we eventually came to the real reason for my returning, Simon asked me who I represented, what my position was and, more importantly, what did I want? I took a chance and told him my rank and my unit. His initial response was to smile. He told me he had always known my friends supplying the weapons had to be soldiers and not criminals. It was a massive risk exposing myself that day but, over the coming years, I would work for him in many countries in Africa.

Simon told me that afternoon that he would feel more comfortable if we all wore our uniforms around him and anyone he would be bringing to the farm in the future. I agreed and we had our uniforms sent up. I sent a message to Sean requesting twenty-four operators from the Special Forces base, together with a medic and a signalman and all equipment they would need. They arrived later that week and I asked Rob to create a roster to secure the perimeter around our camp. A medical tent was pitched and a communication point created on the highest ground within the perimeter. We were now ready. We had generals from many different regiments coming and meeting Simon and his nephews. Within ten days, things became more active. The only feedback I had access to, were the communications that left the farm. It was obvious that meetings were going on all around the country, yet it was impossible to tell how successful they were. We were being excluded more and more as the days went by and so I kept myself pretty much to myself.

I tried not to observe the different ranks of the military, incumbent politicians and ANC representatives who came to the farm over the next month, but I do know that some were the royal families-in-waiting. Although the IFP did not engage in the negotiation process to take part in the 1994 elections, at the last minute, after a great deal of local and international pressure, they decided to participate.

The first fully inclusive general elections, in which citizens of all races took part, were held on 27 April 1994. They were conducted under the direction of the Independent Electoral Commission and marked the culmination of a four-year process that ended apartheid. Millions queued in lines over a three-day voting period. Strangely, they were the most peaceful three days that I could remember in South Africa. The result was that the ANC formed a Government of National Unity with the National Party and the IFP. Its first act was to elect Nelson Mandela as President, making him the country's first black Chief Executive. Throughout the elections, at the farm we were ordered to remain on stand-by.

Chapter 20

There was nothing to do over the next week and we ran a very loose ship on the farm. All was quiet and there was nothing to report. Sean rang me. He was in a great mood, probably because everything had run so smoothly over the last couple of weeks. The conversation was light and I enjoyed his sense of humour. He told me it was all beginning and that I was expected to keep the flow of information between the military and the newly elected local government going until a new plan was brought into play. Meanwhile, I was to keep the farm secure as it was going to host many local politicians and he didn't want any fuck-ups. He asked me what I needed to get the job done. I asked him for twelve more men from the Special Forces base, with as many black operators as possible, including, ideally, a black sergeant, and a .50 calibre rifle. He laughed and told me to stand by. A week later, I was introduced to our glorified guards. We had a new white staff sergeant and a newly promoted black sergeant. He would later become the first sergeant-major of the Special Forces and my friend for the whole of the rest of my time in Africa. We also had ten more Special Forces operators, four of whom were black. I requested a larger perimeter and left the organisation of details to Rob. As well as all this, builders came in and put up some further luxury accommodation. They built an industrial-size kitchen with a walk-in fridge and even a splash pool in the rocks outside the recreation area. We were well and truly open for business. So began Phase Two of what, tongue in cheek, I named Operation School Fees.

Rob posted two soldiers at the front gate with an armed guard detail running convoys from the gate to the hunting lodge. Outside the area where the meetings took place, things were very informal. We were never included in the meetings. Over those days, there was a constant stream of arrivals; politicians, both black and white, and military personnel in full dress uniform. Eventually the volume of people living and negotiating at the farm dwindled to a few meetings a week. I guessed the schooling had become less important and the new political faces had decided they were ready to govern.

In what can only be described as the fruit salad that comes with change, by July 1994, the SADF had become the South African National Defence Force (SANDF), an amalgamation of the SADF, the MK, the Pan Africanist Congress's Azanian Liberation Army and the Self-Protection Units of the IFP. When Bob arrived he was now a colonel in the SANDF and my new boss. It felt kind of strange but not unexpected. He wanted us to be in uniform at all times while on duty and to be out of sight while we were off. My role had been reduced to glorified butler.

One day, Bob came to see me and asked me if I wanted to travel overseas with him. I jumped at the chance as I was bored. I was told to choose three of my team and send a travel requisition to Military Headquarters Pretoria. I asked where we were going.

He smiled.

"Haiti."

I applied for Rob, the new black sergeant and one of the Special Forces operators to be re-assigned to Bob's office in northern South Africa. Within a couple of days, I received confirmation of my transfer. I told Rob we had been re-assigned and I would need him to disband the rest of his team back to their base and brief the two that we were keeping. As usual, he was happy to keep moving and I remember thinking how lucky I was to have him taking care of the operational details. He arranged the changing of the operation in one afternoon and we spent that night drinking and shooting with two new guys at the now empty farm. The four of us had become very relaxed in each other's company. Although they were from Special Forces, I was still in charge. I jokingly told them that if I could shoot like them, we wouldn't need them. I briefed the team that day on my standard operational plan. We were all new to what we were doing but would conduct ourselves as if we were old hands. We would observe, saying as little as possible unless we were alone.

The next day Bob arrived, with one of his nephews, and we all drove down to Johannesburg. From there, after we had declared our weapons to the pilot, we flew to Havana, the capital of Cuba. I don't remember much about Cuba from that first visit. We were driven to a five-star luxury hotel and, the next morning, choppered to an airfield at Guantanamo Bay, the American part of Cuba. There we interacted with U.S. soldiers, mostly attached to Navy and Marine forces. We spent a week on the base, after which, with twelve members of a Navy Seal team, we flew to a landing strip in Port-de-Paix, just north of Haiti's capital, Port-au-Prince. The Seal team were carrying a lot of equipment and I think the six of us felt a bit silly with our civilian bags and 9mm pistols. Bob made conversation with the Seal team leader and, after we landed, they handed out sunglasses to all of us. We were driven to a small hotel in the town and although it was very basic, the food was great and the skeletal staff friendly.

Recorded Western history of Haiti began on 5 December 1492, when the European navigator, Christopher Columbus, happened upon a large island in the region of the western Atlantic Ocean, later named the Caribbean. By the time we arrived at the beginning of September 1994, Haiti was in a state of transition that made the South African elections look like a walk in the park.

We spent most afternoons in the lounge downstairs, the four of us sitting at a table just out of earshot of Bob and his nephew. Bob had an endless stream of meetings every afternoon. Some of his hosts were repeats, but mostly, they seemed to be meet and greet exercises. Everyone who came into the hotel had their own security team, but it was all very cordial.

One week, a meeting between Bob and a face that we had seen more times than anybody else ended abruptly. We were told to pack up and be ready to leave that evening. The same night, we flew to Miami and, after Bob produced his ID at the check-in station, the six of us boarded first class on the next flight to Jan Smuts Airport, Johannesburg. I couldn't help thinking how fast these new ANC guys were learning. Not in how to gain information, but how to use the state-owned industries to help expedite process.

On arrival at Johannesburg, we were greeted by a contingent of ANC operatives and shown to three white Mercedes Benz cars. All were new and top of the range. I was given the keys to one and told to go back to the farm and await further orders. The four of us were happy at the way things had gone and we drove the 450 kilometres to the farm in absolute luxury. We had been in the Caribbean for less than sixteen days, but we knew that whatever had gone on there had been successful.

The following day, Bob arrived at the farm with an entourage. He looked relieved and was in a great mood. He told me that the communication area was to be re-activated and I was to make sure it was again secured. I asked for more soldiers and they arrived that afternoon. We were obviously high on the list of priorities. Rob again took on the role of timetable master and chief guard. I, on the other hand, had nothing to do but help with the logistics that went with our newly built kitchen. I decided to get it running like any nightclub.

In October 1994, the rains came early and everything turned to mud overnight. The trees became green and full of wild-life. One morning, Bob came down from his quarters and asked me to have breakfast with him alone. Of course, he wasn't really asking, but we had become friends and I don't think he had become altogether comfortable in his new role as my boss. After we had finished eating and making small talk, he came to the point.

"Can you take some weapons into Mozambique for me?"

Bob told me he wanted the rifles modified with telescopic sights and fired on the farm before I took them across the border. I was a little taken aback but not totally surprised. Now I knew why I was being retained. He emphasised that the entire operation was restricted to the highest level. I was under no circumstances to divulge the nature of my brief. The whole operation was not "on the books". I was to handle the planning myself and anything I wanted would be given to me. The entire operation was to be completed within one week of my receiving the weapons. I agreed and he left to get his gear from his quarters.

I requisitioned three white Toyota Land Cruisers and four new South African passports. I decided we needed new identification with no history of our recent trip to Cuba, Haiti and, more importantly, the United States of America. I also requisitioned five AK-47s, 5,000 rounds of ammunition, new clothing and a credit card. The rifles we were going to transport were delivered in the last week of October 1994. They had been modified, with 'scopes welded onto their dust covers. We fired them all the next day.

Rob had plotted a path through the northern region into Mozambique via an area known as Crooks Corner. It wasn't anything clever, more a choice of something familiar. He had crossed this way before, while serving in the SADF. I was in the lead vehicle with our black member. He was Shangaan. If we were stopped, I would do the talking on the South African side of the border and he would take over, once we were inside Mozambique.

I had drawn nearly R50,000 on my credit card over the previous ten days. This was how Africa worked. A smile and a handful of bank notes were worth as much as a smile and a gun. We had both and I intended to get those weapons across the border one way or another. I won't go into too much detail of that trip, because I was arrested years later on a weapons trafficking charge that was thrown out of court as vague and lacking detail as to time and place. It's enough to say we buried the weapons at a location just south of Maputo. We had made sure we had the exact coordinates of the cache and we headed for Maputo in good spirits. We buried our personal weapons just outside the city and went for a night out in the capital of Mozambique.

The fact that we hadn't used any cash to bribe any officials until that point meant we were loaded. It's difficult to explain the poverty in Mozambique, coupled with the affluence of very few. With the wad of cash divided between the four of us, we were able to sample anything Maputo had to offer. Rob took me to a restaurant on the beach where we gorged ourselves on seafood and steak. Later we booked into a luxurious hotel.

After three days, we sobered up and went down to our vehicle. It had been broken into. All the equipment we had left was gone, including the commercial and military radios. When we went to the other vehicles, where we had left our personal weapons, they had also been broken into. At that point, it would have taken a lot more than that to dampen our spirits, so we laughed, recovered our AKs, and drove slowly back to the farm via a slightly different route. We logged the AKs into the armoury. The other two members of our team took the Land Cruisers and went home.

The same evening, Rob and I drove back to Johannesburg in the Mercedes, handed the coordinates where we had left the weapons over to Bob and went home. The next day, with the money left over, I bought a motorbike for each of us and we rode them down to Durban.

All in all, for us it was a successful year all round. It even looked as though South Africa had a bright future ahead. 1994 was a year of great promise for many people in South Africa. We had no idea what was in the near future, so, that Christmas, we basked in the fact we were not facing any criminal charges.

Chapter 21

In January 1995, I was paged and told to report the next morning to the Department of Public Works in Johannesburg. Bob was at the offices and was in a great mood. He told me the transfer of weapons had been successful and I needed to assemble my team for a return trip to Haiti. The following afternoon, we would be flying via Miami to the capital of Haiti, Port-au-Prince. Our trip had all been arranged and I was to collect him just after lunch from the same offices. This was different from the first trip, as this time I had been given some vague schedule as opposed to flying blindly. We were obviously being trusted more and slowly being introduced into Bob's circle. At the time I was happy that I could give the other three guys some sort of idea of what we were doing. Although we had felt like little blind mice on the first trip, we were now being given at least a smell of the cheese. I couldn't help but wonder how much trial and error the first trip had been for everybody.

On the flight to Miami, I was given a file on the brief political history of Haiti over the past couple of decades. As I read it on that plane, it would be a lie to say I cared. I only read the file, because knowledge is power and I was obviously expected to know and utilise the information that had been given to me.

From 1986 to early 1988, Haiti was ruled by a provisional military government. Although a new constitution was ratified in 1987, the elections that followed in November of that year were cancelled after troops massacred a group of voters on Election Day. The next attempt at elections in 1988 saw a turnout of four percent. The result was that Leslie Manigat became President of Haiti for three months, until he too was ousted by the military. Further instability ensued, with several massacres. In the presidential election of December 1990, Jean-Bertrand Aristide, a Roman Catholic priest, won sixty-seven percent of the votes. I couldn't help thinking that my time at a Catholic school might be why I was part of this operation, but I put that to the back of my mind and struggled to concentrate. International observers had deemed the elections largely free and fair. It was a country running a parallel course with South Africa, but a more complex one, as it was always known who would win our first inclusive elections in South Africa. In Haiti it had been influenced by many external factors.

Aristide's radical populist policies and the violence of his band of supporters alarmed many of the country's élite and, in September 1991, he was overthrown by a military *coup d'état*. Then, in July 1994, the United Nations Security Council passed resolution 940, authorising member states to facilitate the departure of Haiti's military leadership and to use all necessary means to restore Haiti's constitutionally elected government to power. In mid-September 1994, as U.S. troops prepared to enter Haiti by force, the military leaders stepped down, opening the way for a new election and the restoration of constitutional rule. In October 1994, Aristide returned from exile to Haiti. Although it seemed to me to be another example of international manipulation, it was obvious that Aristide was the latest blue-eyed boy. At that point I had no idea why we were going back. My view was that all this political manoeuvring had nothing to do with South Africa. I was to be proved wrong.

The trip from Miami to Port-au-Prince was uneventful. We landed in Haiti in the early hours of the morning, booked into a small hotel near the presidential palace and slept. The next morning, we laid eyes on Aristide for the first time. In the hotel, we took up two positions behind Bob. Rob and I were to his left and the other two members of our team to Bob's right. Then, when Aristide walked into the hotel with his security detail, I struggled to remain nonchalant. His security detail was armed with assault rifles with 'scopes welded onto the dust covers that was the fingerprint of our farm in South Africa. They were the very same weapons we had transported into Mozambique a few months earlier.

The four of us remained calm and when the meeting moved to a private room behind the kitchen, I motioned for the two other guys to stay seated where they were. Rob and I followed Bob towards the kitchen. At the doorway to the kitchen, there was a bit of a confrontation between Rob and me on the one hand and members of Aristide's security detail on the other. Bob called me over and asked me what had happened. I told him and added that, if I had realised we would have ever been under direct threat from our own weapons, I would have filed down the firing pins, before the weapons had left the farm. He burst out laughing and asked me how I knew. I reminded him I had been supplying him with weapons and that the last batch was altered in the same way. He had asked us to modify them and as I had no information as to what they were to be used for, we had used the same modifications under the impression they were to be used by the same people.

Bob told me to keep Rob calm while he took the sting out of the confrontation. I agreed and, after a few minutes, Aristide's security team leader and I were summoned into a room at the back and told to calm down. There were more important things to worry about than conflict between our security details. It was like being in the headmaster's study all over again, but this time I realised there was a lot more riding on us all being friends. We were both relieved for the rest of the afternoon and told to make friends at the bar. On my way out, I sent one of the two guys who I had left at the table to go and back Rob up in the kitchen. I took up a position at the bar where I could see my last team member.

It was a few minutes before Aristide's security team leader came to the bar. I found out later that evening that he had given stern instructions to his team and, from then on, the whole mood was relaxed. It was difficult at first as I don't speak French, but we were both cut from the same cloth and, with alcohol, it became easier. We became friends that day and I'm sure we would have remained friends, but for the fact that, in 1996, he was killed in an incident in Haiti, so we would never find out.

Chapter 22

A couple of days later, we flew home. Bob told me to keep the team in Johannesburg and to find some temporary employment while we waited. I used my credit card to pay twelve months of rent for four different townhouses. They were all in the same complex, situated in a suburb about thirty kilometres east of the offices of the Department of Public Works in Central Johannesburg.

So, for my team it was back to working in nightclubs again for the foreseeable future. We divided our shifts between the eight biggest venues, where we provided security. I decided that initially it would be best if we rotated the shifts amongst the four of us, so we would work different venues every night. We would compare notes every lunch-time and take it from there. The first change I noticed was the free flow of cocaine that was taking place in each of the eight nightclubs. After three weeks, we took on another eight venues and rotated around them. Same sort of observations, but in varying degrees. It depended on the disposable income of the parents and the type of work the kids were doing. In the more affluent northern suburbs of Johannesburg, it was as though everyone in the nightclubs, including bouncers and bar staff, were high on the "white lady". It didn't make much difference to me, as everybody appeared happy and relaxed. It seemed it was a cure for South Africa's violent nightlife and we decided to let sleeping dogs lie.

The four of us continued to attend meetings once a week at the offices of Military Intelligence. On each occasion, we would have a sort of huddle with the other teams. Everybody appeared to be reserved about their projects and information. It was a boring time. In June 1995, a week or so before my twenty-ninth birthday, Bob attended one of the meetings. He rotated the teams in and out of his office at an alarming pace. We knew something was up. I think we were all relieved, not just for having something to do, but because inactivity can create paranoia about your future. It was just over a year before I was looking to leave this arm of the military, but I admit I was concerned about my relevance to its operations and, hence, my future.

When we were called in, the meeting was brief. I was to turn the farm into a hunting lodge, which would make it relevant to everyone in the neighbourhood. All funds being requisitioned for this smoke screen had to be justified. When it was necessary to be there, we were to book the farm as a hunting party. As the hunting season was during the winter, we were to move quickly.

When the four of us left for the Northern Province the next day, we already had a plan. When we arrived, we found the farm gate was locked with different locks and the farm looked as though it had been abandoned. I phoned the farmhouse from a public telephone in the town and, much to my relief, my old friend the retired Special Forces colonel answered. He was very happy to see me and once I told him we were going to try and make the farm a commercially viable business, he was over the moon. That night, we all got drunk together and reduced our plan to writing.

Firstly, we would need to create the illusion that some form of conservation was taking place. Secondly, we would have to attend an auction to purchase the game we needed. The retired colonel brushed off step one and two as being easy, provided we could secure the budget. I left the micro planning to him and to Rob. When I woke the next morning, they had been awake all night, concocting a costing list for me to send in.

To this day, the semantics of a military budget are beyond my comprehension. It seems that if you are at the top of the list of operators, you will be given almost anything, so it's best to ask for a lot more than you need and wait for an answer. Nothing new in that. This way, you are not only allocated a budget close to what you thought you needed, but the ratio of what you are given to what you have asked for pretty much tells you how far you are up the ladder of importance.

Everything I requested was approved. We were given a budget to buy animals and two extra Land Cruisers, which would be delivered, converted for game viewing. I asked for an array of hunting rifles with ammunition and a large fuel tank to be installed next to the farmhouse. Finally, I wanted a fencing expert to check out the perimeter fencing and have any necessary repairs done. We were given all of it. I concluded that anything that happened on that farm in the near future was very important to at least one person on the procurement committee. More importantly, the committee was active on a regular basis. I had everything I needed in less than three weeks

We had the fences repaired, attended game auctions every weekend and started to explore the farm for the first time. We surveyed the perimeter and made a crude map with the man-made water reserves plotted, and a note on how they were supplied from the central water reserve. There were three boreholes that would supply the main reservoir on high ground that distributed water to different watering holes by force of gravity. It was a slick operation and the animals started to arrive.

By the time the rains arrived that year, we were ready for business. The farm was in a near perfect condition. When the hunting season was over, we decided to advertise tourist game drives in both local and international hunting magazines. The response was immediate and, by November 1995, we were up and running. I compiled a report and took it to our offices in Johannesburg. The following day I received a page and was ordered to meet Bob that evening at a restaurant in the northern suburbs of Johannesburg. The meeting would supply the final piece in the puzzle of what we were up to.

This time I was not asked, but ordered to take another shipment of weapons into Mozambique. We were to book into a game lodge that was having an auction for game just south of the capital, Maputo. We would take the weapons and bury them on the way to the lodge, page the coordinates to Bob and await further instructions. No modifications were to be made to the weapons. They were to be transported in the boxes we received them in. That weekend we did as we were ordered. The auction went well. The black member of our team was well and truly knowledgeable about wildlife and we bid for and bought three giraffes, six Kudu females, one of which was pregnant, and a massive Kudu bull.

That night during supper I was paged by Bob. When I returned his call, he told me to expect a list of coordinates on my pager the next day. I was to recover and transport back into South Africa everything we found at that location. The following morning I received a page as promised. We packed up and plotted a course on the map we had with us. The coordinates led us to a location about five kilometres north of the lodge.

It was all fun and laughter reversing our game plan until we dug up the bounty that had been left for us. There were twenty-five bags filled with white powder and, as I opened the container and saw the bags, I was in no doubt as to what they contained. In one weekend, we had been elevated from gun-running to trafficking narcotics across international borders. We weren't surprised. That evening, Rob and I drove with the cocaine to the farm in South Africa. We stashed the load under my tent and waited.

Bob arrived a few days later and, although nothing was said, he asked to have a private conversation with me. The two of us went on a game drive to see our newly purchased giraffes in their new environment. At first we made small talk, but eventually the subject of cocaine came up. I let him speak as I needed to know what our orders were. If we were going to be doing this run on a regular basis, I needed to put a better system in place. He told me it was an approved operation. I explained I couldn't have cared less what the motives were, I only wanted to fine-tune the operation, as we were at risk of being caught. Bob agreed. He asked me what I wanted to change. It was not the means we were using to transfer information that worried me. It was that it didn't take a rocket scientist to work out that we were transmitting latitude and longitude coordinates on open lines. Again, he agreed, but he moved the goalposts, asking me if I could help him distribute the cocaine. I should have seen that request coming. It was one of those moments when a relationship moves to a higher level of trust. I told him to give me a week to put a plan together. The relief on his face was obvious. That afternoon the two of us watched the giraffes move around like the prehistoric creatures they resembled. I drank whisky and Bob chain-smoked the day away.

Over the next couple of days, I put our new problem to my team. We needed a better way to transfer coordinates via our pagers. If we were going to be taking weapons into Mozambique illegally and then crossing back into South Africa with cocaine, we needed to fine-tune our communications. We came up with a solution. There are only ten numbers from 0 to 9 that can be used before they repeat each other, so we needed a code to transfer the numbers in sets of coordinates giving precise lines of latitude and longitude. Our solution was to use words with ten letters that did not repeat. The first word we used was Washington. The number 0 was assigned to the letter W, the number 1 was assigned to the letter A and so forth. Only the person who had the code-word could work out the exact location of the weapons that were being left in Mozambique and we would use the same method for the coordinates of the cocaine. Whatever happened after that was not something I wanted to think about. Without gloating, we came up with a system that would be used for the next twelve years by both the military and everyone else I did business with. It is probably still used to this day and although most are aware of it, the procedure is still impossible to breach. I couldn't have cared less as to the purpose of the weapons. I was more focussed on getting on with everything with as little hassle as possible. I pitched the plan to Bob at our next meeting and he was sold on the idea. As long as only three people had the word that we were using, any mistakes would be easy to track down. I didn't want to be caught or ripped off.

Now it was time to address the second problem. How were we going to flood twenty-five kilograms of cocaine into South Africa without making waves? I knew it would be impossible not to make ripples, but we did not need to make waves. We decided upon the nightclub scene as the entry point. Although there was a lot of cocaine being distributed in Johannesburg, we had very little knowledge of the amounts and, more importantly, of the purity. It sounds simple when you watch television on drug deals, but the reality is very different. To move twenty-five kilograms of cocaine is no easy task for beginners.

I requested a meeting with the Nigerians in Hillbrow and did my first major drug deal. I told them I had twenty-five kilograms of cocaine to sell and, after they stopped laughing, they realised I was serious. I was offered R100,000 per kilogram after it was tested by them. Our driver came up with a sample and the deal was done. I sold twenty-five kilograms of cocaine to them that night for R2½million. It all ran smoothly. Now R2½million might not sound like a lot of money in today's terms (about £133,000 or US$180,000), but to us it was a fortune. It was paid in cash and I realised we could have done better.

I took the money to our next meeting and Bob was happy. I was given R100,000 in cash and was promised our first code-word would be used from that moment on. He told me our operation was going to be up-graded. We would be sending more weapons per delivery and bringing back twenty-five kilograms of cocaine. I didn't express my concerns that evening, because I believed we would be able to overcome any problems. It wasn't the transportation either way that caused me concern. It was the distribution of the drugs. I would be cutting into someone else's profit, which could only lead to confrontation.

I spent the next few days with Rob, visiting nightclubs around Johannesburg. We went to any new venue that was popular and, without doubt, the cocaine was flowing. Every night we were offered lines in the toilets or an office, if one was available. We decided to open one of the packages we had stashed in my house and take it out with us. The first night we did this, we tried it for ourselves before we left to go out. At that time, we were both amateurs when it came to any real knowledge about cocaine. Although neither of us were first-time users, we were not in-the-know when it came to quality. The cocaine we had brought back from Mozambique was the purest we had ever sampled.

At some stage during the evening, we concluded we had hit the mother lode. Looking back, it was partly the realisation that every time we had used it before, we had been duped into doing cocaine that was heavily cut; and partly to do with the fact that we were as high as we were ever going to get in our lives again. They say you will always chase the feeling you felt the first time you do really good cocaine, but the fact of the matter is that, once you access good cocaine, it's a gradual process until dependency. I remember a song by Guns and Roses which went, "I used to do a little, but a little got too little, so a little got more and more." In about twenty hours, the two of us used nearly four grams from one of the packets. It might not seem a lot to regular cocaine users, but that night set the bar for things to come. From then onwards, Rob and I made nearly all our decisions on cocaine.

I approached Bob with our dilemma and my solution. I wanted him to introduce me to a newly appointed political person, preferably a police general in the office of South African Police Intelligence. It was a long shot but, to my surprise, within the week a meeting was arranged on the farm. He was a young man, a little older than me, slight of build and dressed immaculately. My first thought was how white his teeth were and I soon realised how intelligent he was. He got straight down to business.

"What can I do for you? I'm all ears," he said.

I had never heard that expression before. It was such a text-book intelligence line. I told him my concerns. He said very little at first, then started probing me on the different personalities involved in the Johannesburg nightclub scene. I told him that, if we regulated the nightclub security industry, it would take the sting out of fighting for control. He thought about that for a few moments. He never missed a beat. I was relieved when he told me he would have to take instructions and would meet me again the following week. I decided to remain on the farm until he came back.

The following weekend, the police intelligence general arrived with two advisors. I was told to submit a game plan to be considered for implementation. It all seemed vague and wasn't the answer I had been hoping for, but beggars can't be choosers. I gave him the model. It was very simple. We were to hold meetings with all the major nightclub security groups and register their bouncers under a non-governmental organisation. We would create a data base of everyone deriving an income from security work in a nightclub and, by that means, gain control over them.

We even had a name for this collection of bouncers. We called it the Security Officers Board. A very fancy name for a very blunt instrument. After hearing me out, I waited patiently for an answer. It seemed like an eternity before he asked,

"You seem to have a plan. What do you need me for?"

I knew then how new he was at being a policeman. I replied,

"To cover us from unnecessary investigation, while we implement the plan."

My plan was approved within a couple of hours. Any incidents arising from its implementation that could be helped, would be. I now had an office in Military Intelligence and one in Police Intelligence, providing me with cover. I didn't think we could have had more protection without causing official jealousy.

So it began. Most venues were easy to convince. We started off with the soft ones and, as they capitulated, our plan got bigger. During the first weeks of December, I was starting to be pressured by Bob to turn the cocaine I possessed into money. Then came Christmas Eve, 1995. We weren't in any position by then to distribute that amount through our new concept, so I asked for a meeting with the Nigerians in one of our nightclubs. We invited them around for a Christmas Eve party at a nightclub called Pharaoh's. It was a stupid decision, as the nightclub was situated in a very conservative suburb of

Johannesburg. If you fuel a fire with drunken white South Africans celebrating a festival and they believe they are being invaded by armed Nigerians, it can be a recipe for disaster.

Twelve Nigerians arrived at Pharaoh's that night, heavily armed. They were not feeling safe outside their comfort zone. I don't remember how it all fell apart, but it did. Upon their arrival I remember a commotion at the entrance. It was all a blur after that. The result was that in the ensuing confrontation twelve Nigerians were shot. Two survived the initial shooting. Rob shot them both in the head. As he put it,

"To put them out of their misery."

What should have been a profitable Christmas Eve for everyone, turned into a bloodbath. An undercover policeman made a statement that Rob had walked up to one of the two who were still breathing and, just before he killed him, had bent down, looked into his eyes and said,

"Merry Christmas, mother-fucker."

That night, every Nigerian present was shot and killed. The exact sequence of events will be forever debated by the people who witnessed it. The leader of the group had been shot through the head and what was left of his brains had been sprayed onto the guy standing behind him. At some point he too had been shot. It was a gruesome sight, a dead body covered with his leader's brains. To say the least, this incident caused concern to all. The strangest thing about the aftermath was that, although ambulances arrived to scrape the bodies off the floor, there wasn't a single policeman at the scene. There was a lot of screaming, but no police sirens.

There was an innocent girl in the front of the queue, who had been shot in the arm and shoulder. I can still remember her screams. The paramedics gave her morphine and she went quiet. In fact, it was the quietest I ever remember a nightclub to be. The music had been turned off, the shooting had ceased and the screaming had ended. It was very peaceful to be at that bar that Christmas Eve, but I felt very little Christmas spirit. As I drank straight whisky at the downstairs bar, listening to the aftermath of that night, I didn't expect to be free from a cell in the near future.

The funny thing was, if there is anything funny about twelve men being killed, that a point had been made. There were new sheriffs in town and it was the onset of a very violent struggle for a very lucrative business. The void we created that night was ultimately the beginning of things to come. Standing around the carnage was nothing new to anyone in my team, but the feeling of being at war was as sweet as it had felt during my operational time in Angola. We had killed twelve men in one shooting incident that had very little to do with the colour of our skin, but more to do with the training and experience we had. That night I felt very little remorse, only a strange feeling of guilt. We had caused an incident that could have been avoided with better planning, but maybe it was the inevitable consequence of the path we were following. I can't help but feel that, had we had been given more time, things would have worked out differently.

Chapter 23

In the early hours of Christmas Day 1995 following the killing of the Nigerians, Pharaoh's was closed and we were sitting inside waiting for the hammer to fall. Nothing happened. Eventually, we split up and went home, Rob and I to our complex, where I woke the other two guys. I sent one of them to my townhouse to empty the safe of money and weapons and to get some cocaine from the open parcel. On 26 December 1995, I woke, filled with trepidation and anxiety. I believed we were in real trouble this time and, with our track record, there was no way we were going to convince any authority that it had not been our intention to have a bloodbath in a nightclub. There was very little media coverage, but we believed it was the calm before the storm.

I remember 29 December 1995 like it was yesterday. I got a page from Bob to meet him at the Department of Housing. I was going to have to answer to somebody and Bob was by far my best option. I wasn't convinced we were off the hook for the débacle that later would be referred to as "The Christmas Eve Massacre". I arrived early and Bob was already there, calm and in a better mood than I expected. He showed me a coroner's report. The twelve Nigerians all had powder burns on their hands and forearms which showed that each had shot a firearm within 20 minutes of their deaths. I said nothing and waited. Bob told me that the bottom line was that these twelve Nigerian, and hence non-South African, citizens had been armed and had been firing the weapons in a built-up area. There was to be an investigation into how the deceased had obtained their weapons and ammunition. The girl who had been hit in the shoulder had made a statement that described the twelve men as looking for trouble. In her opinion, once the shooting began, the security staff had no way of saving her life other than by using the force they had done, which she deemed acceptable. She believed that everybody who had been in the queue outside had been in grave danger from those heavily armed men. She ended by adding that she was truly grateful to those who had come to her rescue.

Although we were being let off the hook, it was surreal. I was shown a statement from the South African Police that had been given to the Press earlier that morning. It exonerated all the security staff working that night and even elevated us to hero status for doing our job in the face of a large group of drug dealers who were trying to intimidate a nightclub into allowing them to sell their drugs. Now Bob expected me to secure the market those twelve guys had been running, filtering the profits in a direction that was deemed to be of national importance. I felt relieved. I couldn't have cared less about which coffers I was supposed to fill. I just wanted to go home and get some sleep.

By New Year's Eve, we had effectively cut off the supply of nearly all the drugs that made up the Johannesburg nightlife. We had become dealers overnight and it was a comedy of errors. As soon as we put out the word that we had a supply of cocaine, our complex became busier than anywhere else in the city. We had queues of people at our complex gate. It was insane. We moved twenty kilograms of cocaine in one afternoon. We sold it in the form we had received it and they were camping outside for repeat purchases. The amount was not so much a surprise to us as the amount that we could charge by selling it in smaller quantities. By 2 January 1996, we had effectively filled the vacuum that had been created only just over a week before and we had just over R4million in the houses we were renting.

I paged Bob on the morning of 3 January. I received an immediate response and was told to report at the Department of Housing that evening. Upon arrival, there were security changes to the building that had taken place in the last few days. It was on near lock-down. Rob was refused entry and I was told I could not take any weapons past the door. I had R4million in a couple of carrier bags the security didn't even bother with. The bags looked like what they were. Bags stuffed with loads of money in small denominations. I was escorted into Bob's new office. It was very small and had no windows. He was seated behind his new desk, on the phone. He motioned to me to sit down. As I waited for him to finish his call, I noticed a few grey hairs at his temples. I wondered how many of them I had caused.

Bob was very matter of fact with me that day. He addressed me as "Major" and told me that, from now on, this would be his permanent office. As of that day I was to make an appointment to see the Director whenever I wanted to see him. Although it seemed very cloak and dagger, I felt a strange sense of comfort with this new way of meeting him.

He told me the four in my team were now employees of the Department of Housing. I was to collect new ID cards from the new security company downstairs, submit new banking details for the four of us to his outer office and collect new expense credit cards on our way out. He was very business-like and it was almost a boss-employee relationship he was instilling that day. It didn't make any difference to me. At least they were changing some of the past procedures and that had to be a good thing.

Then he asked me, in a very matter of fact kind of way,

"What do you know about the private military contracting company, Executive Outcomes?"

I thought for a minute, before I told him what I knew. Following the conclusion of the South African Border Wars in Angola and Namibia, the SADF faced deep cuts to its personnel. It was decided that certain Special Forces units would be dismantled. Executive Outcomes had been established in 1989 by a former lieutenant colonel of the SADF, together with an Irishman from Dublin, who had been in charge of the Western European deployment of a very dubious section of South African Military Intelligence. Its purpose was to provide specialised covert training to Special Forces members. The company was known for its ability to provide features of a highly trained modern army to less sophisticated governments. Executive Outcomes had initially trained, and

169

later had fought on behalf of, the Angolan Government against UNITA.

In March 1995, Executive Outcomes had contained an insurrection of guerrillas known as the Revolutionary United Front in Sierra Leone, regaining control of the diamond fields and forcing a negotiated peace. Characteristic of one of the first private military outfits, since its formation, Executive Outcomes had been involved militarily in more than Angola and Sierra Leone. In September 1993, Executive Outcomes had been registered in the United Kingdom by a former Special Air Services major, Simon Mann, and perhaps another. Although I had heard many differing stories over the years from drunken bragging mouths, it was difficult to know who had worked for them and who hadn't.

What Bob said next took me totally by surprise.

"I have the number of a recruiter that I want you to phone. They have a contract in Haiti next month to escort some families in Aristide's inner circle out of Port-au-Prince. You are going along as an observer."

Elections had just taken place in Haiti and a new president, René Préval, was to be inaugurated on 7 February. Paranoia was running high amongst some of the financially elite on the island, because René Préval had been an aide to Aristide. Some of the families wanted to leave Haiti and South Africa was prepared to grant them asylum. Bob told me that Executive Outcomes were going to transport them to Angola and, from there, to Pretoria. It was a purely logistical operation, in which I was to direct the traffic. The proposal took me by surprise, as I felt my hands were full with the implementation of the Security Officers Board.

Bob must have seen the concern in my face, because he added,

"This will only take a week. I want you and Rob. You're to be my eyes and ears from the time you leave Johannesburg until you return."

I looked him in disbelief. I asked,

"You want me to spy on your spies?"

It was getting worse and worse. It seemed ridiculous. I was to infiltrate a very dangerous group of guys and travel with them to a country that was going through political upheaval known to most as a civil war of disobedience. It could easily turn into a one-way trip.

He laughed as he realised how I had misinterpreted his orders.

"No, Peter. I want you to join what is a mostly observer group and brief me on your return."

I breathed a sigh of relief as he further explained,

"Just keep out of trouble and bring me back an interpretation of what you see."

I didn't feel any better with that clarification and thought about the next three and a half years, when I was still going to be at the beck and call of these seemingly ridiculous orders. When I told Rob about the plan, he wasn't happy. We drove home in silence, Rob in a foul mood.

After breakfast I phoned the number that I was given. Bob was right. Everything had been taken care of. The two of us were to fly to Windhoek in Namibia and would be contacted on our arrival at the airport. We were to take only one set of clothes, as everything we would need would be supplied to us.

Upon arrival at Windhoek International Airport we were met by a Sergeant Visser. He was heavily overweight and was probably the least patient man I had ever met. We were ushered through to the subsidiary runway and boarded a small King Air passenger jet. We flew out over the sea and then circled the runway at Cabo Ledo, Angola, once, before coming in to land. I remember the landing was very poor, because the runway was filled with weeds and cracks. Cabo Ledo had been a Cuban military base during the Bush War, from which MiG fighters had been launched to attack South African targets. Executive Outcomes were now officially operating from the home of the old enemy and being paid handsomely to boot. I don't think I resented them. The irony was totally lost on me. We were escorted by two men wearing Forces Armada Angolan (FAA) camouflage fatigues and transported to the Sixteenth Regiment

Commando Base, where we were given three bottles of whisky and shown to a room that was as unwelcoming as the two pseudo FAA operators. We were told we would receive our orders in the morning and they left.

Rob looked at me and made the same point about Angolans he had met eight years before, when we had first been in Angola together.

"They're still fucking cowboys, Peter."

During that first operation with Executive Outcomes, we spent a week pretty much left to our own devices, provided we stayed within the perimeter of the barracks. During the whole week, the families were flown from Port-au-Prince to Luanda. They were extracted out of Haiti like clockwork, which was the sum total of my report when I returned to South Africa. My first operation as a private military contractor was the most boring I had ever been on. The only thing that made it in any way worthwhile was the US$150,000 that I was paid at the end. I never saw the list of names that were flown out and can only presume they spent a lot of money to get preferential treatment, both in Haiti and then in relocating to South Africa. I never heard a single shot fired, but was intrigued by the amount of money people would pay for their safety. After speaking to Rob the morning we returned, I took his advice and wrote my report which I filed the next morning.

A few days later, I was called into the Housing Department offices. Bob told me that neither Rob nor I would be retained beyond the end of our contracts in April 1999 and we were free to feather our nests for the future. He was really pleasant and I felt as though I had been written off as a loose end. As he walked me out of his office, he added,

"Just keep up the good work for us until you leave."

Then came a night that once again changed the dynamic of my life. It started off as just another night, but soon turned everything upside down. I was invited to an opening of a nightclub in a north-western suburb of Johannesburg called Across the Border. The concept of this venue was unique in two ways. The entire space had access to a bar which snaked around the walls and, using two different colours, was split into two equal sections. One side was selling beer imported from the United States and the other side was selling beer imported from Mexico. It might not seem innovative to people who haven't grown up under a cultural boycott, but to the South African youth it was as new as finding a needle in a haystack. I made an instant connection with the owner and we became friends.

Over the next couple of months it became almost impossible to get access to the bar of this new phenomenon. People were being herded around the entrance and made beer runs in small groups to the bar. It was madness. The success of this drinking hole made a mockery of the space available. The profit margin from selling cheap imported beer at exorbitant prices was the future. This niche market created profits only seen in the narcotics trade. I spent a lot of time in the office doing cocaine, as did most of the well-known gangsters of Johannesburg. From the first night the office of Across the Border was known as the meeting place for Murder Incorporated, South Africa.

As fate would have it, the owner died of a cocaine overdose. There was very little police intervention and the coroner's report disclosed that he had succumbed to a cardiac arrest due to increased heart rate induced by cocaine and associated with very little liquid or food. He was the first person I knew, who had died due to his body not being able to absorb the amount of drugs his brain and wallet could handle. I attended his funeral with an old friend, Dave Levinson. Dave was a strange man. He had made it through the selection process to receive a Special Operators badge in One Reconnaissance Regiment. The selection was brutal and he was known for being brutal. He was built like a bodybuilder and had competed and won titles in that sport. I had worked with him in a few different nightclubs over the years and had seen in him a propensity for violence that made people around him very nervous. He was my friend and I didn't care what people thought and nor did he.

I don't remember much about how it happened, but by the end of the funeral Dave had negotiated the sale of Across the Border and all the beer licences into his name. I left the funeral with a small share of what was about to become the largest retail outlet of imported beer in South Africa. During the drive home, neither of us understood how that afternoon would change our lives. By the beginning of winter 1996, Dave and I had transferred the shares of the company that housed the nightclub into our names. We registered it as Chillers and it would launch the next two evolutions of Johannesburg nightlife; and ultimately the entire focus of South African nightlife.

We opened Chillers on a Thursday without too much publicity, because we didn't need any. What surprised us was the amount of beer sold that first night. We had so much space that it seemed impossible for us to completely fill the place. We were wrong. By the second weekend, we had a queue of at least 100 people from opening time until just before midnight. It was the most popular drinking hole up to, and until the millennium. Dave and I had tapped into what could only be likened to a gold mine. The problem with success is that there will always be somebody who will try to tap into the money. It happened within the first month of us opening.

The police I had seen neither hide nor hair of for many months suddenly reared their ugly heads. It turned out that the previous owner had been paying a hefty part of his profits to the local SANAB. We didn't see it coming, as surprisingly they had kept it quiet. The police waited to see if we would succeed and once we started to show promise, they came to negotiate the new deal with us. Looking back, it wasn't so much the amount of money they wanted per week to let us trade that annoyed us, it was the arrogance of their approach. We were shown the original liquor license of the premises and it was torn up in front of us. We were told that if a payment wasn't made that afternoon, we would be raided and shut down that evening. I think the smugness of what they saw as a checkmate was the final nail in the coffin.

I went to see Bob immediately after meeting them. Bob was intrigued and a counter-plan was devised. The operation was put together in hours. We marked the notes we were to pay to the police unit and, when their courier turned up just before opening time, all hell broke loose. Taking account of how little time we had to plan, the débacle that took place was not that bad. So far as I was aware, Military Intelligence were about to lock horns with the old ways of the South African Police Force for the first time. As the policeman left the building with the bag of money grasped firmly in his hand, three black policemen tried to effect an arrest. It would have been funny, if hadn't been so serious. This white policeman had never had to answer to a black man before and his actions displayed everything that was about to go wrong in the new South Africa.

Chaos ensued as he resisted arrest and very nearly managed to break free. It was an absolute nightmare that made both sides look like bungling idiots, but somehow it ended with four bleeding policemen in our car park. One of them was in handcuffs and a substantial amount of money had been picked up by the spectators outside the building. I watched it all from the top of the stairs leading to the entrance and despaired at the circus I had witnessed. The end result was little more than we were embarking upon confrontation with a South African Police Force that was not only designed to fail, but would fail in a spectacular fashion as new recruits would view policing as a secondary function to making money. That night we had our victory and, although it was a spectacle of incompetence from all sides, the comedy of errors was a sign of things to come.

As it turned out there is nothing like a spectacle to get people talking and that night proved it true. As word spread about what had transpired, Chillers became the place to be. The income that was about to be generated was to become a platform that would subsidise the control of the next phase of world trending, namely ecstasy and rave clubs. After that night, we changed our operations and applied for a legitimate liquor licence. Bob rushed a licence through his contacts. We had so much floor space, that we installed an industrial kitchen and created a dedicated seating area for a restaurant.

A few weeks later, in June 1996, I turned thirty and it seemed the world was my oyster. I was spending one night a month attending briefings at the Department of Housing. Although I was still receiving a nominal income from Military Intelligence and still had their credit cards for expenses, I was actually being used as a glorified delivery boy. Once a month I would collect a large consignment of cocaine and a few weeks later, I would drop off an even larger amount of money and attend a briefing, all on the same night. I was being let go slowly and it was working for everyone.

Chapter 24

I first came across the Hells Angels in 1996. Until then, I had known nothing about them. Rob had opened a new nightclub, called Global Explosion. An incident had occurred, when a Hells Angel had been slapped around at the front door by Rob's disciplined platoon of bouncers. Later the same night, I went to see Rob at Global Explosion. While we were sitting in his office, the head bouncer ushered in an oldish looking man wearing Hells Angel clothes, called "colours". His name was TK and he told us he was the president of the West Rand Charter of the Hells Angels, South Africa. We were wary and chatted. After a while, TK phoned a number. When TK started his phone conversation by giving a coded number, things started falling into place. He was working for someone, and I can still remember the look on Rob's face as we started to piece the puzzle together. Rob was getting angry and I think I was as well. The two of us were very close to beating the hell out of our first Hells Angel by the time he put the phone down.

Within the hour, Rob received a phone call on the same number TK had used from an office of the National Intelligence Agency (NIA), the successor outfit to BOSS. The caller was a former colleague from Rob's days in Angola. The operator asked Rob to let TK go, and we would all walk away from this nightmare and that was an order. Rob, true to usual form, put the phone down and slapped TK around the face. He shouted at TK that the Hells Angels must be a front company for a state organ and he should leave before he changed his mind As much as Rob was outraged that a state operator had come into his nightclub, I was intrigued and, as TK scampered out of what was now an empty building, I shouted,

"Keep in touch, bud."

Were the Hells Angels working for the NIA? Or was it just a few of them who had sold out? I had to go on my rounds. By now I was late for the cash to be put into safety deposit boxes in the nightclubs for which I had taken responsibility, but the next day I intended to find out exactly what I didn't know. As I left,

Rob snarled,

"They just a bunch of pricks."

If he had known we would both be wearing their colours within two years, he might have been a little bit more forgiving.

The following Monday, I requested a meeting with Bob. He was happy to see me. I wanted to know about Hells Angels South Africa and, to begin with, about an old man who had an exit strategy that began with his state number being the beginning of a distress phone call? Who and at what level were the Angels paying the NIA off? I had to know. I was obsessed with it. Another flaw in my personality that would backfire later over my life decisions. So who were they paying, how much and why were they being given this kind of comfort? That afternoon I had my answer. I read a file on Hells Angels South Africa and was amazed. The biker community predominantly comprised retired or serving traffic policemen, normal policemen and the odd drunk biker enthusiast. There was very little information on TK, which seemed odd. I went back to Bob and asked him specifically to look into padding out the information. I remember his words that day.

"You should be looking at what you're going to do for retirement, rather than messing with police intelligence."

Looking back, I should have taken his advice, but I didn't.

The only serious incident in the biker world had happened a few years before, when a Hells Angels internal problem had lead to a shooting at their clubhouse in Hillbrow. Some had been sentenced for manslaughter. Others had been given shorter sentences for inflicting grievous bodily harm and discharging a weapon in a built-up area. That was not what I was looking for. I wanted more information. By the end of that week, I had a lot more. The Hells Angels in South Africa had approached the World Body in the early 1990s and, after being vetted, they had prospected for the World Organisation. They had received full colours in 1994 and now they were expected, as it was put, to "show some class".

Prospecting had separated the Hells Angels in South Africa into two groups. Those who wanted to go through the motions and those who didn't. Joe, the then-president of the Hells Angels South Africa, had left with most of his old guard and formed The Satan Saints Motorcycle Cub, leaving the remaining members to go prospecting. I was about to relive the latter part of the 1980s again. A different war and different outcomes. It was probably inevitable that I was going to be used again for what I knew, and to find out what I didn't know.

During the week following the TK episode, life carried on as normal. I was totally absorbed making the nightclubs successful and churning out money.

Chapter 25

My first encounter with someone called Mac Evil was during a fight in Durban. One of our bouncer friends, Billy, was in a nightclub in Durban as we tried to expand our influence. One night when a person purporting to be a Hells Angel from Amsterdam pulled out a sword to threaten him, Billy pulled out a gun and shot him in the head. Billy won that conflict, but the politics of that incident would begin the dance.

The same night, Rob and I drove to Durban to give Billy moral support. Life had become crazy again, but we weren't going to back down. Billy was absolutely unconcerned that he had killed a Hells Angel from Holland and both Rob and I agreed. In South Africa, taking a sword to a gunfight was always going to end in tragedy. There appeared to be no backlash from Billy shooting a Hells Angel. The authorities had no interest as, under South African law at that time, the shooting was legal. Billy had retaliated to an immediate threat to his life with maximum force.

Billy, Rob and I went to a nightclub in Durban. The Red Dog was a large venue. It was hot and full of customers. We were at the venue looking for someone, who Billy wanted to talk to. One of the owners of the nightclub met us at the front door and took us through the bar and the kitchen into the heart of the venue. As we entered the main downstairs area, we were suddenly backed into the crowd and it took off. Rob bumped into a table and, without noticing that a drink had been knocked over, he carried on moving through the people around him. But this wasn't just any drink. It belonged to a member of Durban's Security Police. He was not by himself either. The whole unit was present and was already in a bad mood and drunk.

As the drink hit the floor, Rob had already passed the table where they were sitting. He was unaware of what he had done and kept moving. The policeman stood up to make physical contact with Rob. As I passed the table, I hit him with everything I had and it all started to go wrong. I felt an impact and my mind went blank. As I landed my first punch, someone who was used to contact reacted. I was being hit from every direction and all I could do was to stay on my feet. In fact, this is where they were failing. Instead of letting two of the unit work me over, they were getting in each other's way.

Rob and Billy did an about-turn and entered the fray. As quickly as everything goes black in your brain, so just as quickly your senses return. Suddenly everything came back to me and now we were on. This fight continued until we had the last of them outside the front door. We had won and we had damaged this group of policemen, but, as they were taken away by ambulance, I had no idea that we had started a feud that would be the first of many.

While I was kicking someone outside the front door, a bouncer, who was much stronger than I had previously encountered, took hold of me and started to shout in my face. Although strong, he wasn't too clued up on violence and he paid dearly for that. I head-butted him and his nose burst. As he bled all over me, he let me go. The Durban bouncers had formed a pact to respond in unison to any of them being assaulted in any of their venues. Without knowing it, I had breached their pact. We walked away. I had sustained a hairline fracture from the crown of my head to my jaw and felt light headed. I would later learn I had been pistol whipped by the unit commander whom we had fought. All over a spilt drink.

Later that evening, as we were sitting in Billy's apartment, he received a call. He was told we should either leave Durban, or come back to the nightclub for a fight. Lo and behold, all the bouncers had indeed got together. Durban bouncers were getting tired of groups of holidaymakers coming in groups to their city and causing trouble. Because the bouncers were usually outnumbered, they had come up with this new approach. The three of us went to my car, where we had stored our weapons. We went back to the nightclub armed. I had a CZ-92 9mm submachine carbine, a Czechoslovakian weapon which was relatively reliable. My Beretta 9mm pistol was on my hip. Billy had a Vector 9mm pistol with two spare magazines, Rob had a pump action shotgun with a shoulder belt filled with shells and he also carried a .45 mm Colt 1911 pistol. We felt pretty confident.

At the same time, the Johannesburg Hells Angels were having a meeting at their Durban prospect clubhouse. This new policy about nightclub security had been explained to the Johannesburg Hells Angels president, so as soon as our incident had become news, he wanted to see it for himself. It's surprising how fast things travel in Durban. At that time, an old friend of mine, Rocky, was prospecting for the Hells Angels. He was a large man who had unsuccessfully plied a trade as a professional boxer, but had made a career of sparring as a professional. He made a good living out of nightclub security and was the last person I expected to run into that night. We were good friends and I was surprised to see him when the three of us went back. Rocky, as I found out later, had been giving his opinion of me to the Hells Angels, as he knew me better than anyone else who was present that evening.

When we got to the corner of the street leading to the club, we realised how many bouncers had turned up. The Hells Angels were also there, watching with interest. The bouncer could never have believed we would come back to the nightclub, just as we could never have believed how many of them would arrive. To tell the truth I was pretty apprehensive as to how this scenario would turn out, but, as we walked up the street, there was no turning back for this collection of bouncers from all the nightclubs and bars in Durban.

They were divided groups of security personnel, but had a plan they had all agreed. That was as far as their planning had gone. There was no second phase to their plan. That night, they had gathered to show their solidarity with the plan. I can remember thinking, 'Shit', but it was too late for either side to back down. Rob muttered under his breath,

"When this starts, just open fire above their heads."

The best that we could hope for was that there was no contingency plan for our action and it was pretty doubtful there would be one. At that time, gun-play was much more a regular reaction in Johannesburg than in Durban.

Each group was wearing its nightclub colours and the groups were definitely not as united as they initially appeared. Their formation showed flaws in attitude. They were not soldiers and I suppose the fact that South Africa had ceased conscription eight years previously worked in our favour. I decide to take the initiative. I knew Rob was very close to opening fire, because he was liable to shoot first, having nothing but disdain for anybody who hadn't served in the SADF. I think everyone was looking for a way out of what was a loose, loose situation. There was no real command structure amongst them and I saw an advantage. I looked for a leader to start a negotiation with, but they were fragmented in a way I could have only hoped for. Theirs was a very badly planned show of strength.

I singled out the bouncer whom I had head-butted. He was still covered in blood and was easy to spot. We were the only two guys who had blood all over our clothing. I yelled at him,

"You and I are the reason for this, nobody else. Let's keep this between the two of us. No need for this to turn into everybody's problem."

I immediately sensed relief amongst the other bouncers. There was a way out without someone losing face. This guy was bigger than I was and must have been well-known. He was in no position to turn this challenge down, without the wrath of everyone there and everyone knew that the incident could turn into a shooting. The Hells Angels were watching from the side and the bouncer had nowhere to go.

I thought better of showing signs of retreat, so I kept shouting at him as I was coming up the road towards the nightclub. Everybody could see a way out and the tide had turned. The bouncer was on the spot. He was carrying the entire situation on his shoulders. Everybody else was looking for a way out with their pride intact and by now everybody had seen how heavily armed we were. I carried on shouting at this bouncer to clean his face and stop making things worse. He was in his very early twenties and must have realised that everything depended on what he did next.

To my surprise, from my right, another voice joined in, a voice of reason which was strangely calm, rational and unthreatening for a flashpoint situation. He said,

"You're flogging a dead horse, Peter. Can I speak to you?"

I looked over. Standing there was a guy wearing Hells Angels colours. His hands were showing, palms facing me. He appeared genuine and was taking control of a very serious moment. This impressed me. With the benefit of hindsight, Mac Evil's timing was perfect, as nobody had foreseen this set of events taking place. The Durban bouncers hadn't expected us to return, so they had no real plan if we came back. However, the three of us were in trouble as well. All in all, it was a bad situation that could have sparked into anything at any time. The fact that a third party, who until then had been there to observe, stepped in had de-escalated the situation. Everybody there saw the way out. I took it.

This was my first interaction with Michael Hall, aka Mac Evil. As he and I spoke, things started to defuse. You could feel the tension and adrenalin drain away and when the bouncers started to leave almost thankfully, it became less dramatic. I watched Rob slowly calm down. He was still in conflict mode, but was improving every minute. As spectators started to leave, Mac Evil and I spoke for some fifteen minutes. Only then did I realise how many there were. Outside the venue were not only patrons from the club, but the staff as well, waiting for the situation to explode. They had probably not considered how much danger everybody present was in. Rob walked over to me as I was talking to Mac Evil. He was still very worked-up. Rob wanted to leave before the police got it together and arrived on the scene.

I had met an officer in the Hells Angels whom I respected. In the summer of 1996, we met again. By then, I was so caught up in my own world that I had almost forgotten about the night in Durban. My phone rang in the car. It displayed a number I didn't recognise. For whatever reason, I answered. It was Mac Evil. I had given him my cell phone number at some stage during our short conversation. I don't think I ever expected him to call me.

"What are you doing?" he asked.

"The usual," I replied. "Driving from club to club, checking the cash and fixing the problems that go with my life."

He then asked if I wanted to pick him up, as he had nothing going on.

"I'm at the Johannesburg Hells Angels clubhouse," he told me. "I'll keep you company."

This seemed a good idea to me that night. For some strange reason, I welcomed a new approach to the evening. He gave me the address of the Hells Angels clubhouse and I turned around. I have no idea why I did, but I guess it was good timing on his behalf.

It was the first time I had ever been inside a motorcycle clubhouse. The house was a dump, but I was impressed with the amount of memorabilia on the walls, including photos of members from all over the world. However, overall I was disappointed by my first impression of a Hells Angels clubhouse. I kept my opinion to myself and was introduced to the whole charter of the Johannesburg Hells Angels. They all seemed warm, but I had a strange feeling it was contrived to gain them an advantage. I kept mostly to myself and felt like the stranger I was. Eventually enough was enough. It felt like a staged production and I told Mac Evil I had to get on with my night. He grabbed his colours and followed me to my car. It was the beginning of a long association between us.

Chapter 26

In November 1996, I took a call from a man called Brett Cleaver. I had met him during my time in Angola and again in Haiti. Now he worked for Executive Outcomes and wanted to meet me. I hadn't seen him since the Haiti operation and wanted to meet him as well.

When we met that night, Brett Cleaver was excited. He had been offered a contract to secure Luanda Airport in Angola for a company called De Beers. Brett wanted weapons training for the guys he wanted to use. I don't know what he knew and I didn't care. I had the weapons and the training facility at the farm. He offered me R150,000 to facilitate a training base and I accepted. It was like old times.

That weekend I drove with Rob to the farm. It was doing well as a hunting lodge and the old retired colonel was in great spirits. As it was the beginning of the southern hemisphere summer and hunting only takes place during the winter, he was very happy to open the armoury and start a new training regime. Brett Cleaver arrived later that week with twelve hardened, ex-Special Forces Operators. They all drank heavily during the week, but, to my surprise, they were ready every day for training in the Lowveld sunshine. I decided that De Beers was getting the most belligerent security detail I had ever witnessed. I was paid in cash and was very happy at the outcome. Rob arrived at the end of the week and, observing the training they were doing, he shook his head.

"They're still fucking cowboys, Peter."

When I returned to Johannesburg, Brett Cleaver phoned me. He asked if I would come and see him at a nightclub called 70s, where he was working as manager. We met and, as I walked into the nightclub, I remembered how much I hated binge drinkers in public. The venue was aptly named, as they played retro music and sold copious amounts of alcohol. It looked pretty much like I remembered nightclubbing to have been ten years earlier. It was a recipe for violent behaviour and was in great need of security. My first thought when Brett

Cleaver had phoned me, was that he was looking for security staff.

In Brett Cleaver's office, I was given a bottle of whisky while I waited. Brett Cleaver came in and was very happy to see me. We made small talk for a while and then he started. He told me that the administration officer they had been using at the airport in Luanda had been diagnosed with lung cancer and was retiring. He asked me if I wanted to work for a three-month stint in Angola while Executive Outcomes found a replacement for him.

Going back to Angola was the last thing on my mind, yet it did sound appealing. I was becoming bored with the day-to-day monotony of nightclubs. I was feeding Police Intelligence and Military Intelligence edited reports of the nightclub scene, but mostly I was in a rut. The Security Officers Board would work whether I turned up or not and I needed something else. I sat back and listened.

Executive Outcomes was securing diamonds for the De Beers Group in Angola and shipping them out via Luanda Airport. All that I would be expected to do was run a standard rotation of the security staff at the airport, as well as making sure the inventory checked out. He was asking me to make the inventory, ensure all shipments were counted and cross-reference the parcels with the incoming accounts. It seemed simple enough and Brett Cleaver offered me US$100,000 for three months' work.

I knew very little about the De Beers operation, so I asked him. He was very informed and answered my question thoroughly. He told me that the earth hides its diamonds well so they take years looking for them. The hunt takes major investment and advanced technologies coupled with know-how. He smiled at me and said,

"They know how, bud."

He told me they were providing security for the staff during the reconnaissance and discovery phases. They kept the staff safe in a hostile environment during the early exploration stages, but he was very quick to add that they made the most money on contracts securing soil samples for further analysis. He said,

"Don't worry too much about what's in the boxes, bud. Just make sure they don't go missing."

I left, telling him I would let him know within forty-eight hours. I called to see Bob and told him about the offer. He answered immediately.

"Make hay while the sun shines, Peter. But you must still send us reports on what you're doing."

I think, looking back, he had known about the job offer before I had. I phoned Brett Cleaver the next day and asked,

"When do I start?"

The decision made, I couldn't wait to get out of the cities and hardly went out. Brett Cleaver called me with the coordinates of a training farm just north of the Lesotho border, fed by a town called Ficksburg. I was happy to go somewhere I had never been before.

I boarded a DC10 from Ficksburg to Luanda and went back to Angola. I suppose I was apprehensive, but felt more confident than I had done when I had been deployed there ten years earlier. I remembered how I'd felt, crossing the border from South West Africa then. Strangely enough, it felt the same that day. Once again, I was going into the unknown. On arrival, I was not impressed by the infrastructure of the airport. It was small and looked pretty depressing, much like any other African airport. I remember thinking how many South Africans, both black and white, had died in Angola, fighting to take control of this very backward country. I put those thoughts behind me and kept moving.

The next three months were uneventful. The United Nations Security Council had voted the previous month to impose sanctions on UNITA and, by Resolution 1127, it had prohibited UNITA leaders from travelling abroad. All UNITA embassies had been closed in Europe and UNITA-controlled areas had been declared no fly zones. While I was there, no UNITA members tried to leave Angola via the airport.

I had to tag three bodies of black South Africans during my time there. One had been riddled with bullets and I was told he had been stealing from a dig-site up north. I tagged him, "Died of natural causes". The other two had contracted malaria and died of dehydration. They were also tagged, "Died of natural causes".

We discovered on a flight from Cuba a shipment of cocaine on its way to South Africa. I told the guy to be more careful and put him on a military flight to Pretoria. I logged all metal trunks and checked the locks for my paymasters. Most of the time, I was bored. My biggest problem was keeping the Angolan staff sober.

I returned to Johannesburg and went to see Bob with reports of my time in Angola. I had been thorough with my information, making sketches of the layout and operations of the airport. Bob was happy to see me and hardly looked at my report. He told me that Executive Outcomes were not happy with my replacement and they wanted to me to go back. I thought it better not to point out that it seemed strange that a private military contracted company were being so open with him. The answer was obvious. They were feeding information to his office at every turn. So, I resigned myself to another three months.

In mid-January 1998, I deployed from Lanseria Airport back to Luanda Airport. The guy I relieved had only been there for three weeks but he had made enemies in the airport and was in harm's way. The Angolan staff was very happy to see me. In fact, I would have never believed I would be made that welcome in that country. I moved a bed back into my old office, put on fatigues and got drunk with a copy of *The Washington Post*.

The next morning, I started the routine again. Again, if I rack my brains, I don't think there was too much excitement in the first few days. Within the first week, I received a call from a London agent. I was to welcome two De Beers directors that weekend. They would expect me to be on duty when they arrived on Saturday afternoon. I was to brief them on the procedure I was implementing. Great! That night I phoned Brett Cleaver and asked him what plans I should make. He laughed and told me to book the presidential suite for myself and the two diplomatic suites for the directors at the Hotel Presidente, Luanda. He said that would do just fine and to stay calm and not expect too much interest in my operation. He explained it was just a holiday and an all-expenses-paid experience for them. We made some small talk. Before I ended the call Brett Cleaver added,

"Keep them safe, bud."

I decided to check out the hotel. I took a vehicle into Luanda. The Hotel Presidente was a pleasant surprise. It had been constructed in the 1960s, but had been renovated five years ago. It had two pools and a beautiful view of the sea and harbour. As I walked into the reception, I started to relax. The entire hotel was perfect for VIPs. I sat in the bar and watched the new Angola go by. Somebody had spent a fortune on this little piece of paradise.

Eventually I was approached and told that only residents or their guests were allowed to drink at the bar. Just when you think you have left Africa for a short space of time, the third world regulations come back at you. I asked to see the manager and was given a dirty look. After playing cat and mouse with a junior manager, I tried to book the presidential suite and one of the diplomatic suites. At first, I was treated with caution, but once I produced my Lloyds credit card, I was taken to the manager's office. I booked the rooms that afternoon with an open-ended departure time. I left my credit card with the desk and went upstairs. The view from the penthouse suite was spectacular. In fact, the whole place was breathtaking. From one seated position, you could see the whole harbour and the twin pools cut into the rocks beside the ocean. I ordered food and a bottle of the most expensive whisky from room service and settled down.

When the two directors arrived that weekend, I was surprised by how young they were; only a few years older than I was. I spent a week in the diplomatic suite below them and we all became good friends. We lay by the pool most days and I listened to them dealing with their business before getting very drunk and ordering top-end prostitutes. I couldn't help thinking that not only was I getting paid for this experience, but I was in Angola and not expected to shoot anybody.

During that week they had many visitors, but the most important person I met was a man named Brett Kebble. I knew he had been involved in the sale of Johannesburg Consolidated Investments' gold assets to Mzi Khumalo in 1995. We got on well and he was so impressed with me that he insisted that my job description was a mercenary. I tried to explain I was only a glorified security guard, but he would have none of it. When Brett Kebble left to go back to the airport, I drove with him and walked him through the departure red tape. He gave me his business card and told me he would be grateful if I would contact him when I was back home. He insisted on giving me one of the watches he carried around with him and I protested very little. He seemed such a romantic. The watch was an eighteen carat gold Rolex Submariner.

The following week, the directors flew back to England. All in all, it had been a pretty boring time and, halfway through April, I was relieved and went back to Johannesburg. Rob eventually came to see me and I told him about my experience at the hotel. He laughed. When I told him about my meeting with Brett Kebble and showed him the watch he became all serious. When it came to money, Rob was always serious. He eventually talked me into giving Brett Kebble a call. I left a message with Kebble's personal assistant and forgot all about it. That afternoon, to my surprise, Brett Kebble phoned me back. He was genuinely happy that I had called and invited me to his house that evening for dinner. I asked him if I could bring a friend and he was delighted.

Rob said,

"I'll walk him through any airport he wants for a gold Rolex."

By this stage, Brett Kebble was running a series of mining companies, the biggest being Johannesburg Consolidated

Investments and Randgold & Exploration. These companies were entrenched in South Africa and had been around for well over a hundred years. They had been set up by entrepreneurs, still referred to as the Randlords, who had established the gold mining industries in Witwatersrand, South Africa. Brett Kebble's house was something to behold and, as we were let in, I don't think either of us were quite prepared for it. I had seen opulence before, but never anywhere that had every detail so meticulously taken care of.

We started the evening on the patio and every part of it was like living in a film. The butler was on time at every turn. The food was exotic and arrived in many differing choices. After supper we sat and chatted and there were at least thirty different cheeses, with at least ten different sorts of biscuits. Brett Kebble was a most gracious host and, as I drove home with Rob, we were both slightly drunk on whisky and this man's personality.

Rob muttered,

"I wonder what he wants from us."

Chapter 27

South Africa's second non-racial general elections were due to be held on 2 June 1999. The incumbent president, Nelson Mandela, declined to run for a second term and things became somewhat messy in the ANC. It was decided that the deputy president, Thabo Mbeki, would head the electoral list for the party. That wasn't the problem. The problem was the jostling for position, as the names and numbers ran to an infinite number of party members, further down the list. As happens in Africa, some politicians were having accidents and some were being shot at. Some were even being killed.

In 1994, South Africa had become an internationally acclaimed democracy when Nelson Mandela was elected president. He inherited a treasury that was almost empty, but his main problem was the security cluster. The different ministries concerned were not only fragmented but hardly worked at all. I had first-hand knowledge of how little was actually done. Prior to 1995, South Africa had been divided into different, self-governing territories and development regions. Each had its own policing agency, bringing the total number of policing agencies in the country to eleven. Ranking structures, different uniforms and conditions of service had been established under differing legislation. On the adoption of the interim constitution in 1994, these regions and territories were integrated into a united South Africa. The new constitution established a single organ, called The National Police Services. To say that the wheels came off is an understatement.

After the 1999 election, I was offered retirement from the military. I took it immediately and was told I would leave as a lieutenant colonel with a full military pension. I got offered a one-off payment as a settlement and took it with both hands. Looking back it wasn't a very clever thing to do, as I received more from a three-month tour in Angola than I did from fifteen years of pension from the military, but, at that point I wanted to cut all ties.

I started prospecting for the Hells Angels and, one night, I called Mac Evil. He asked me if I would collect him from the clubhouse before I went out that night. He sounded desperate and, reluctantly, I agreed. Mac Evil pressed me on exactly which clubs I would be visiting. I told him I would be going to as many clubs as possible. We began at a hotel complex, where a friend of mine ran security and we settled in. At the end of the first batch of cocaine, I ordered more to be brought. Mac Evil was becoming jumpy. At first, I considered he was bored with me holding meetings in a hotel, but it became apparent there was something on his mind. By midnight, I had settled into the night and was in no rush. I was going to leave everything to the last minute. Eventually Mac Evil had enough of my procrastination and wanted to leave to go on my rounds. I pulled him aside and asked,

"What's up?"

He insisted we should leave as soon as possible and go to a certain club. It felt as though I was being set up, but I wanted to see exactly what was on the menu. As soon as the two of us walked into the nightclub Mac Evil insisted on visiting, the bouncers were waiting at the door for me. They told me they had let a Hells Angel in on my guest-list earlier and he had told them he was waiting for me. Although this was strange I wasn't too worried. I asked them if they thought he was alone. I was told that although the Hells Angel was wearing South African colours, he had a strong English accent. Inside the nightclub, Mac Evil was in earnest conversation with a very large Hells Angel at the bar. I scanned the nightclub for any other Hells Angel members, but couldn't see any. All I was thinking was, 'This guy must be confident.' I went into the back office and beckoned the bouncers over. I told him to watch the door until the Angels showed exactly how many of them were there. The Hells Angel followed me into the office and, with a very strong London accent, he shouted at me,

"I've been waiting three hours for you to get here and you just walk past me!"

There were at least three bouncers standing behind him. I told him to sit down if he wanted to talk to me. I think it was then he realised he was on his own in the office. He sat next to me and I saw his colours for the first time. Hells Angels have the logo, "Red and white has got to be right". I had seen it on stickers. Their colours were red writing on a white background, as were the flashes stitched onto the front of their vests. This member was wearing a flash on the right-hand side of his vest. It was black wording on a white background and it read, Filthy Few. I had no idea what it meant. He told me he wanted to talk business.

We had a drink together. He told me he went by the name of H and we shook hands. I invited him to my house. Mac Evil seemed relieved when we walked out of the office. I told H we would have to become friends before we spoke about doing business. He agreed. I was all ears as he got into my car and I drove them both to my house. That night we snorted a lot of cocaine and, much as Mac Evil was relieved, I was happy because H was a good guy. We had a few laughs, drank a lot of whisky and got to know each other. As the sun was rising, I phoned a bouncer to collect the two of them and take them to the Johannesburg clubhouse.

I saw less and less of Mac Evil, and more and more of H. If truth be told, I was not looking for any kind of grooming from the Hells Angels. It seemed a natural course of events was taking place. In about October, H told me he had been asked by a Dutch Hells Angel living in Johannesburg, to set up a meeting between the three of us. Again I didn't see grooming coming. I had no idea what I was going to do after the coming elections. I knew I was going to retire from the military. I wasn't interested in meeting any new Hells Angels. I was only looking at the nightclubs being successful.

As luck would have it, I was assigned to a rota for the protection of a politician. I was the only white male on the detail and I hated every moment of it. The other guys were suspicious of me and hardly ever spoke in English. I felt at a loose end and knew I needed something more. When H asked me again, I gave in and told him I would meet the Dutch Angel that weekend.

We met at an upmarket restaurant in the North East Suburbs of Johannesburg. I had had a bad day sitting around the local ANC offices. When the two of them walked into the restaurant, neither was wearing colours, but it was obvious who was in charge. I was introduced to Charles. He wasn't very tall, but was huge in muscle mass. He had reddish blond hair, cut very short. He took control of the meeting and as I was tired, I let him run with whatever was going on. Charles would become my friend that night, and although we would have differing ways of reading some situations, we would remain friends right up to the night he was shot by a police hit-squad.

On Christmas Eve 1998, Charles asked me if I was interested in joining the Hells Angels. It seemed like a good idea, but I thought it best to speak to Rob before I gave him an answer. I enjoyed his company that night, because he gave me more insight into his past than he had done before. He made the Hells Angels seem like a very romantic proposition and I decided to take the offer seriously. On New Years Eve 1998, I spoke to Rob. His night club had just gone under and he was at a crossroads, much as I was. As I began to pitch the proposition to him, he stopped me and asked,

"What's in it for us?"

He had a point. He said he wasn't about to swop one uniform for another without a carrot, adding,

"They need us more than we need them."

It was a hard argument to win, so I asked him if he wanted to meet Charles.

"Let's just get through tonight, and talk about it in the morning."

He was right and I dropped the topic. It amazes me how vividly I remember every New Year's Eve. They were always filled with some sort of incident, and seeing in 1999 was no different. By midnight, every part-time drinker was drunk. They sang a song that not many South Africans know the words to and all hell broke loose. By the morning, I had broken two bones in my right hand and had a huge headache. There was no more conversation about the Hells Angels proposition until 3 January, when Rob and I went out to see my mom. It was her birthday and we were invited to lunch.

Later, as we were driving home, Rob suddenly said,

"Let's go and see your new friend, Charles."

I phoned Charles and turned the car around. It was the beginning of the next chapter of our lives. Rob and Charles hit it off immediately. Although I had expected some form of a dance between the two of them, there was none. I saw Charles in a totally different light that evening. He was charm itself. I sat in awe as the two of them agreed on almost everything. When I realised they were cut from the same cloth. I wondered what life was going to be like with the two of them around.

On 3 February 1999, Rob and I were inducted into H's charter, which had been formed only a few days before. HAMC Nomads South Africa was made up of H, Charles, Kevin, Lucky, Dave and Jason. We officially became prospects. There were no induction ceremonies and it all happened without any real change to either of our lives. We attended a meeting every Tuesday at Dave's house, where little was expected of us. With hindsight, that was not a good thing. Anything that comes too easy cannot always be good.

We needed a clubhouse and the solution was easy. Jason, Kevin, Rob and I bought a small hotel in the eastern suburbs of Johannesburg. We turned it into a whorehouse and filled it with women. We converted the downstairs bar into a strip club and the restaurant into our meeting room. The hotel was a dive, but it did have one redeeming feature, namely its own parking area. The whole operation was pretty slick. We made enough money to pay the bills and, apart from our initial investment, we managed to make a small profit every month. We had taken in all the long-term residents, but when one of the rooms became available, I renovated it and its ensuite bathroom and made myself comfortable.

At our weekly meetings at the Department of Housing, both Rob and I were staying off the radar as much as we could.

In April 1999, this came to an end. On the night of my thirty-third birthday, 13 June 1999, I was informed that Rob and I were expected to visit the Dutch Hells Angels in Holland. That night, Paul De Vries, the sergeant at arms of HAMC Nomads Holland, met us at a hotel. Paul was in his early fifties and was in excellent physical shape. Paul had spent much of his life, either running from the law or in prison. In my experience, long-term prisoners age well, as they have little better to do inside, other than to stay in shape. His head was shaven and his colours bore the flash, Filthy Few. That night, Charles reached into the boot of the vehicle he'd arrived in and put on his colours. He was a Dutch Nomad and his colours also bore the flash, Filthy Few. We were a truly cosmopolitan group that night; one Hells Angel from England, two Dutch Hells Angels and Rob and I.

Earlier the same week, I had been invited to the opening of a Blues nightclub in northern Johannesburg. I had declined the offer as it was my birthday and I didn't want to go out. This little gathering changed all that. As soon as I brought up the invitation, Paul jumped at it. He told me he had learnt to play the harmonica in prison and always carried it with him. He loved the Blues and wanted to go, so the five of us jumped into my car and went to the opening. We were given a table at the front of the stage and so began my friendship with Paul.

Years earlier, my parents had bought me a guitar and I had taken lessons. Although I could hold onto simple chords, I was never any good. That night was the only real payback I would ever receive from those afternoons of practice. As we were getting drunk, Paul asked me to find out if they would let him play with the band. I thought about it and told him that not only would I get him on stage, but I would join him on guitar.

We joined the band and it kept the rhythm simple. I strummed away at very basic chords and Paul and I had a great session, much to the delight of our table. I even think the other patrons were enjoying our obvious discomfort at being on stage. As the set ended, Paul asked the band leader on the drums if he could do a solo on his harmonica. The band agreed.

It was hard to forget. Paul showed off his harmonica skills and the whole nightclub went silent. This was not a riff. He was really skilful. As we walked off the stage, he was grinning from ear to ear. He told me,

"That's twenty-seven months in solitary confinement."

I burst out laughing.

The next day the HAMC Nomad South African charter met at the hotel. Rob and I were treated like members and we were invited into the meeting. Paul was introduced to the other South African members. It was decided that Rob and I would travel to Holland with Paul. That would take care of the travel rule that the Hells Angels have, before gaining full membership.

Three of us flew on a direct flight from Johannesburg International Airport to Schiphol, Amsterdam. We were met by the Vice President of the HAMC Nomads Holland and drove down to Sittard. Sittard had been developed by the German Wehrmacht during the Second World War as an almost entire town of houses for soldiers. That was still apparent as, although the houses built to house German officers and non-commissioned officers were pretty plain, they looked comfortable and neat. It was a huge improvement on some of the council estates I had seen in England.

Paul, we found out, was a gypsy by birth and very definitely by culture. He was the perfect example of a nomad and that afternoon our travels began. We were dropped off at one of his houses. It was occupied by his wife, who made us a lunch and told us she would appreciate us keeping Paul safe. I remember Rob pointing out that he was hoping Paul would keep us safe. We both nodded and, as we left, I wondered what she had meant.

Rob and I were left at a farm just south of Sittard and although there was a very pleasant house, it was nothing like we expected about this visit. Paul had issued us with pistols before he left and, as we sat there that night, we couldn't help but think what was going on. I didn't care as it would have been stupid to arm us if something underhand were to happen. We went outside and shot the weapons to ensure they worked.

After a week of meeting other charter members in Holland, we flew back to Johannesburg and, on 3 July, Hells Angels Nomads South Africa held a vote on my full membership to the club. Jason, of all people, no-voted Rob and me. His reasoning was that we had never ridden together. Although the three of us had motorcycles, we had actually never been together on a ride with the charter. The Nomad charter rule was that we had to own a Harley Davidson motorcycle. The concept that we were the fat wallet gang was now instilled. I had never in my life wanted to own a Harley Davidson, but decided to go with the flow. The Hells Angels World rules dictate that the minimum requirements to be a full member are to be twenty-one and own a motorcycle with an engine capacity above 750cc. Each charter could amend the rules above the bar and the Nomads South Africa had raised the bar.

I bought a Harley Davidson and had it painted in pearl white with the European Filthy Few Death Head sprayed onto the petrol tank. Rob had his new Harley Davidson sprayed grey, with the South African Nomads Death Head image on the petrol tank.

One cold July day, we rode with the Hells Angels South Africa on a national run. As prospects, we had to ride behind the members, which was strangely humiliating. We didn't go too far, as a fight broke out at a petrol station and by the time the police arrived there was blood everywhere. Four guys in a car heading south had decided to nudge a member's motorcycle. The driver of the car had totally misjudged the impact and although it was an old bike, the member was not amused. I witnessed the entire incident and thought the reaction was justified. Those four guys will probably remember that morning forever as the worst mistake they had ever made. They bear the scars to prove it. While I watched the fight Rob came up behind me and observed,

"I never can be more surprised by the stupidity of men."

Charles spoke to Kevin, who was the Nomad charter president, and it was decided the Nomad charter had fulfilled the riding rules. What I remember most vividly about that day was that Charles had changed his colours. He now wore a bottom rocker that was no longer Holland but South Africa.

The following Thursday night Charles proposed a motion to award us full colour membership.

Chapter 28

Brett Kebble had left me a message. When I phoned him, he asked me to dine with him and a friend on Friday night. I agreed and put it out of my head. I needed to get back overseeing the nightclubs in which I had a financial interest. I went out that evening in my colours and immediately ran into a problem. The Hells Angels South Africa was a long way from being a respected outfit and it seemed as though I was a magnet for trouble. By the time I got to Chillers in the early hours of the morning, I had had enough of the remarks about what I was wearing. I was drunk and belligerent and ended the night with my new colours covered in blood and a broken hand. By the time I got to Brett Kebble's house on Friday night, it was swollen beyond recognition. When I was trying to lock my car-door, my hand had almost ceased to work. Brett came out and was very concerned. He phoned an orthopaedic surgeon who arrived within the hour. It all seemed over the top at the time, but I had agreed to see the orthopod the next day and he left.

Throughout dinner, as I was being probed by the other guest on my knowledge of differing topics, Brett remained quiet. He asked me what I knew about the country of Sudan sometime during dessert. I knew very little about Sudan apart from the geography of the country.

"It's where camel meets donkey," I answered, meaning it's where in Africa Christians start overlapping territorially with Arabs. He thought about my answer for a brief moment and burst out laughing. That line had just got me a job. From that moment, I was in. I eventually got tired of the questioning. My hand was hurting and the questions were giving me a headache. After dinner, Brett Kebble walked outside to the veranda for cheese and biscuits. I followed him outside, leaving the other man at the table. Brett looked relieved as he said,

"That's an important man, Peter."

I was given a file on Sudan and spent the rest of the night reading it in Brett's study. My hand was the size of a big balloon and I was in absolute agony. Most people don't realise that, even if you win fights, your hands can be damaged in the process.

Sudan was involved in its second civil war. It's just as well someone was counting. This conflict had started in 1983 between the central Sudanese Government and the Sudan People's Liberation Army (SPLA). The whole thing was a continuation of what was called The First Sudanese Civil War. If my hand hadn't been hurting so much, I would have laughed at the much used oxymoron, civil war, to describe the state of African countries.

The problem was not tribal but religious and seemed to be nasty. As in all conflicts, there had to have been a trigger. In the case of Sudan, it hadn't been diamonds, but oil. At first, after being given semi-independence from Britain, Islamic fundamentalists in the north had granted relative autonomy to the non-Islamic people in the Southern Sudan Autonomous Region. However, in 1983 the whole of Sudan had been declared an Islamic state, abolishing the Southern Sudan Autonomous Region. The SPLA had been formed and the inevitable conflict had ensued.

The man who had been seated at the dining-room table finally came outside and introduced himself to me. He was a member of the Board of British Petroleum (BP) and came straight to the point. He wanted me to join a South African Military Intelligence convoy that was to be driven from Cairo through the Sudan to Cape Town. I sat and listened. On the way, I was to establish contact with as many of the people he wanted me to as possible and arrange for them to be flown to London. He would pay my usual fee upfront and I would receive the same amount for every tribal leader from the Southern Provinces that I managed to persuade into a board-room in London. He gave me another file, containing details of the people BP was asking me to contact. I was going to agree. I knew that even before I was told what I was to do. I just said,

"Yes."

He told me I would be met at Khartoum International Airport on 15 November 1999. That left a little under two and a half months for my hand to heal. The money would be in my account by the morning. It was. I went to sleep that night with my hand really bothering me. The next day I went to see the orthopaedic surgeon who, after looking at X-rays, told me I needed surgery. My hand would be out of action for three weeks. He strongly recommended surgery and told me he would bill Brett Kebble as he had been instructed. He would pin my hand first thing that Monday morning and I would be discharged from hospital the same afternoon. I agreed. My hand was badly damaged and, as I intended to do whatever they wanted me to do in the Sudan, I was going to need it well. After the pins were removed, my hand quickly recovered and, more importantly, there was no more pain.

I flew into Khartoum, Sudan, via Harare, Zimbabwe. It was hot and my nose was the first sense to kick in. Immediately I hated it. There was no alcohol for sale in the airport and I was the only white man in the international arrivals lounge. I would be earning my money this trip. I was toying with an evening meal in the international arrivals lounge, when a voice I hadn't heard for many years, said,

"Hey, bud, let's get something good to eat."

It was Sean. I couldn't have been happier to see him. When I told him I was waiting for someone, he laughed and said,

"I'm that someone. Let's leave."

It all seemed too well orchestrated, but, by then, I had realised that the machine driving my life was way larger than I could control. Sean's convoy had taken over a small hotel just north of Khartoum. I was booked in and immediately took a cold shower. However, I couldn't shake the smell from my nostrils. I was going to hate this country.

The next morning, I met the team I was joining. Sean introduced me as his friend. Because Sean was in charge, I was greeted warmly. This was one rolling intelligence-gathering circus. It was so opaque as to be clever. There were guys on motorbikes, who took the point of the convoy, followed by Land Cruisers. They were legitimised under the auspices of being on a tour from Cape to Cairo. I was introduced to the people paying for the whole thing. There was everyone from European royalty to new rich industrialists. I asked Sean if they were all observers.

He smiled and replied,

"We cover their safety, but they provide us with cover. These people are bored. They have slept with everything, eaten everything, drunk everything and been everywhere. We're their last chance of excitement."

It made sense and, as I climbed into the lead Land Cruiser, although I had thought I'd seen it all, this was something else. We made our way slowly down to Juba in the south. Some days, when Sean suspected we were being observed, we acted like tourists. I had written down my directions in a form of code on the inside of a packet of cigarettes, but it turned out to be unnecessary, as Sean was fully aware of whom I needed to see in Sudan. It was all very slick and Sean was as proficient as he had been the first time he had led me into battle. The whole affair was a walk in the park. Every tribal leader whom I met in southern Sudan had already been to meetings in London. They knew the drill and I was like a glorified alarm clock. I set up meetings, times and travel for nine out of the ten names on my list. The tenth name on the list had died the week before, but his eldest son was willing to represent the tribe as their new leader. We even managed to secure the release of three hostages from one tribe. Mission accomplished.

I received a message from London congratulating me and was told to stay with the convoy until it crossed into South Africa. Sean told me it would take a month to get back and I had better not eat too much. I was happy to stay with them. They were good guys and I was now on holiday.

The guys on the bikes were hardly ever around long enough for me to get to know them. They left in the early hours of the morning and went to sleep very early at night. The rest of the convoy moved at a more sedate pace. Some nights, after supper with amazing quality food, I would have the odd conversation with the four bikers. When they realised I was a Hells Angel, as biking enthusiasts, they made friends with me.

One morning, as we were going through Kenya, I was woken at what seemed like a ridiculous hour. They had taken one of the spare bikes from a support vehicle and wanted me to ride with them. I had a huge hangover and put up some resistance. They told me it was an off day. We were going into a game reserve and I would have some fun if I came along. After protesting for a few more minutes, the youngest told me he had always wanted to ride with a Hells Angel. For a group of ex-Special Forces soldiers to be this persistent, I realised the impact of the Hells Angels on bikers from every walk of life.

They brought out a pair of leathers and boots and, as I put them on, I saw they were all shirtless. When I walked to the bike chosen for me, I saw an assault rifle strapped on the back of the frame. I smiled and checked their bikes. They were all carrying the same weapons. I was given a webbing belt with spare ammunition and some gloves. They were pleased with themselves and smiled the whole day. Then, as I was checking the assault rifle, which was a very new M14 .223 calibre, the oldest of the four came over with a radio. It had an earpiece attached to it. All he said was,

"As soon as we leave, I'm in charge Peter."

The youngest said,

"This is how we roll."

I had begun to like him since we had begun talking and that morning I understood why. He was so full of life. As the sun rose, they quickened pace. They were much better than me on the bikes and the jibes started to come. When we stopped for breakfast and I took in the beautiful landscape of Kenya's protected area, I was quite tired.

I spent the New Year's Eve that saw in the millennium of 2000 in a nightclub in Lusaka, the capital of Zambia. There was no conflict at all between anybody there. I was thankful for the peaceful environment. I couldn't remember my last peaceful New Year's Eve.

We crossed the Limpopo River back into South Africa in the third week of January. I had totally lost track of the dates by that time and understood why people were willing to pay for this experience. Sean arranged for one of the vehicles to take me to the farm. It had been a while since I had last been there and it showed. The next day I took one of the farm vehicles into town and hired some staff to clear up the house and garden. I then went to the bank and when I saw my bank balance, I couldn't believe it. I had been paid in full. I guess everyone had turned up in London on time. I was now very rich. I had nearly US$3million in my account and the bank manager came out to greet me. At that time, all I could think of was how much I loved Brett Kebble. I phoned him that day to thank him but he was not in the office.

With the money, I decided to build a house.

Chapter 29

In the early hours of 17 June 2000, there was banging on the garage door of my newly-built house in Johannesburg. I went out feeling that my head was about to explode. There were two Hells Angels prospects at my front door. They told me that Rob had crashed his Ford Mustang convertible on the main ring road that circumvents Johannesburg. I asked how bad it was and they both shrugged. I told them to hang on while I put some clothes on.

We arrived at the hospital at the same time as the paramedics were trying to stabilise Rob in the ambulance. Rob had driven off the highway and the first person at the scene had been a tow-truck driver, who was also a Hells Angel. Rob's body showed very little physical damage and it looked as though he was in a peaceful sleep. He was taken to the casualty department and I was told to wait outside in the foyer. Hells Angel members and police started to arrive at the hospital in droves. The senior ranking police officer was a very young captain, who told me he would appreciate my keeping everyone calm while we waited. I was not in the mood for requests, but he was right. It wasn't the place to be showing emotion.

The police contingent took position at one side of the foyer and I persuaded the Hells Angels to gather on the other side. When Charles arrived, he handed me a large packet of cocaine and told me his car was outside, unlocked. I don't know what I was thinking, but I did my first line on a table in the hospital in front of the police. There was no reaction.

Later, as the sun was rising, a doctor came and spoke to me. Rob was bleeding inside his skull and they needed to operate. If the pressure wasn't released, Rob would die. I told him I had power of attorney over Rob and to go ahead.

After the operation, Rob was put into an induced coma. Two of Rob's sisters arrived at the hospital and, vultures that they were, the first questions they asked were about his finances. That was the last thing I thought they were going to say to me. After it sunk in that they were only there to watch him die and claim all his assets, I left. The next thing I did was to visit a very prominent Johannesburg loan shark and secure a loan for R500,000 in Rob's name. That was the first asset his sisters would inherit.

In June 2000, I flew to Heathrow with my dad to attend the remarriage of my sister. I spent several months in England, meeting Hells Angels there and having problems with the police and the courts. In December 2000, following a hearing at Islington Crown Court, where I was fined £7,500 on various charges, I flew back to Johannesburg and was met by my dad. The next day, I phoned the nurse on duty at Johannesburg Hospital and told her I would be there before 15h00. She agreed to allow me a special visit that afternoon. The next call I made was to the office of Brett Kebble. Although I only asked if I could leave a message, I was put through to him immediately. He asked me to dinner at his house that evening. I told him I had other plans, but promised to be available in the New Year. Then I phoned Warren Schurtal, a Hells Angel prospect, and told him I wanted him to come with me to see Rob at the clinic. When Warren arrived at my townhouse, he seemed agitated, but I brushed him off. I should have listened to his concerns, as he was trying to warn me about what I was going to see.

That afternoon, I saw Rob for the first time in nearly six months. He was being kept in an induced coma. His body was emaciated. I don't know why I hadn't prepared myself for the sight of Rob lying in that bed, but I hadn't. It was the first and last time I cried in public. For at least half an hour I sat next to what can be best described as the prone body of a man whom I truly loved. We left the hospital in silence. I don't think, before that day, I had ever felt that sad. There was a flood of emotions going through me; anger, sadness, anxiety and, most of all, paranoia. I had no idea how life would be without Rob and I didn't want to find out.

I was sent by Brett Kebble on a mission to Liberia. Nothing much happened whilst I was there and, after a week or so, I returned to Johannesburg. I decided to attend my Hells Angels church and turned up at the hotel. Church is the name given to Hells Angel meetings. Every member of the charter was in attendance, and there were members from Durban and one from Cape Town. In the Nomad charter this was unusual. Even more unusual was the fact that an American member was in attendance. His name was Dean Michael Hall, aka Jethro. Although I had met him briefly at the Hells Angels Johannesburg clubhouse a few weeks earlier, I hadn't paid much attention to him. Tonight was going to be different. Jethro was a very large man. His presence was imposing, with long brown hair and a massive set of shoulders. He was wearing his colours with a bottom rocker on his back denoting that he was a member from California. His front flashes told me he was the vice president of the Orange County charter. The sergeant at arms of the Hells Angels Orange County charter had died in a motorcycle accident and Jethro was distraught.

He would not be attending the funeral because of charges against him back home and it weighed heavily on him. I told him I would go to California and represent South Africa at his funeral. I asked Warren to arrange my flights and buy me a video camera. I would record the whole time I was there. Everyone agreed and I realised I was about to get onto yet another aeroplane to yet another destination. I've heard it said that, if you want to make someone useless, then keep them busy with travel and multiple focuses. The trip was not what I wanted to do, but I would do it to keep busy.

When I arrived at Los Angeles International Airport, I met the Hells Angels Orange County members. One called Adam, aka Atom, was not a large man but he wore the flash displaying that he was Filthy Few. He was using the car of the wife of the president of Hells Angels Orange County and she was with him. They waited while I changed into fresh clothes in the parking lot at the airport and then drove me to their clubhouse.

Later that evening, Atom told me the arrangements he had made. The rest of the charter was on the road and we would hook up with them at the house of the parents of the dead member. Later, the member's best friend from school would collect us from Sioux City airport in Iowa.

Our first flight was to Salt Lake City, Utah. I was stopped at the check-in, searched and taken into a room and asked some basic questions. At that stage of the journey, I thought it was just bad luck and went with the flow. I was legitimately going to a funeral and truthfully answered the questions I could. To most of them, I honestly had no answer. I had no idea which town was my final destination, nor the name of the person who was to collect me at Sioux City. Eventually I was allowed through and boarded the plane.

After we landed, there was a six-hour drive through snow and ice to a small town in North Dakota. I was very cold and tired. When we arrived at the dead member's family house, his parents were very grateful that I had travelled from South Africa to attend the funeral. They made me a meal and gave me a thick pair of socks, advising me it was too cold to stand by a grave in the thin military-style boots I was wearing.

The day of the funeral was the coldest I had ever experienced. Afterwards, I drove with the Hells Angels Orange County charter to Minneapolis airport in Minnesota. The weather got worse by the hour and, by the time we had returned the hire car at the airport, I was cold, tired and hungry. Our flight was delayed by a blizzard, so we waited in one of the departure lounges. There we were met by the Hells Angels Minneapolis charter at the airport and all hell broke loose. We were surrounded by a tactical FBI team and ordered to lie on the floor with our palms showing. One by one, we were taken to different offices in the terminal. I was so tired of being harassed by this time, that all I could think about was going home. I was questioned extensively for about an hour. The agents refused to believe I had come all that way from South Africa just for a funeral. I was carrying US$10,000 I had been given at the funeral, a donation from a Hells Angels defence fund to take back to South Africa for Jethro. They focussed the entire interrogation around that money. I lost interest and went quiet.

The interrogation process was below the standard you might expect from a United States federal agency. They threatened me with everything from a beating to isolation in a cell. I had been trained in the dark art of interrogation at the tender age of seventeen and I was not at all impressed. They seemed to be fishing in the dark and the time on their warrant must have been running out. It all seemed desperate. What they couldn't come to terms with was that I had no ulterior motive. In fact, the FBI intervention made the whole situation worse, if that were at all possible. I realised I must be bleeping on some United States federal radar.

Eventually, I was escorted onto the plane I had been waiting for. The weather was terrible and I remember thinking how impressed I was with anyone who chose to live in that climate. The entire Hells Angels Orange County charter was on board. Atom smiled as I was having my handcuffs removed.

The next day, Atom drove me to Los Angeles International Airport. I boarded the plane without incident, put my hand luggage above my seat and sat down. There was a woman with two small children in the seats next to mine and I thought nothing else could go wrong. I was wrong. As soon as I buckled my seatbelt, three men shoved guns and identification into my face. I would later discover that, as soon as you show an intention to fly, in my case by buckling my seatbelt, you could not only be charged with possession any contraband in your luggage, but with its transportation across international borders.

I had just come for a funeral. I couldn't believe the Federal Government of the United States were this badly informed or this desperate. I was handcuffed, led off the plane, stripped and searched. They went for the US$10,000 and my passport. The money was in exactly the same denominations as it had been when I had been questioned about it in Minnesota. This time I was told I was being charged with conspiracy to smuggle crystal meth across international borders. It would have been funny if it hadn't been so serious. Those charges carried a minimum prison sentence of ten years and a maximum of life.

To smuggle crystal meth into the United States would be like smuggling sand into a desert. I hoped I would be going up in front of a liberal and knowledgeable judge.

Although I was not formally charged, I was informed I was being held until a federal undercover operation was finalised. I would be taken by United States federal marshals to Boston. All I could think was, 'Great, another domestic flight and another American airport.' I would discover I was wrong. I went to sleep that night in a clean and sanitised cell, feeling very sorry that I had returned to the United States as a Hells Angel.

I spent the next five weeks being driven by three US marshals via Washington to Boston. We travelled slowly and made very little progress each day. I was handcuffed to the same man and put into the local county jail every night in whatever town where they decided to spend the night. I had to wear a bright orange boiler suit. I was issued with a fresh one every morning. The only excitement I remember was that the marshal I was handcuffed to, was being continually paged by his wife. I felt sorry for him as he used payphones in little towns to phone her every day while I listened, handcuffed to him.

At the end of it all, I was given back my passport and the money, taken to Logan International Airport, Boston and flown to Heathrow in handcuffs with the federal marshals sitting next to me on the plane. When we landed, I was handed over to British Customs and Excise officials. My handcuffs were taken off and I was told that a flight had been arranged to fly me to Johannesburg. I was happy to be going home.

Chapter 30

I turned thirty-five on 13 June 2001. Four days later, Rob died. The machines were switched off. The process was called changing his state of medical assistance from active to passive care. Rob died within twenty-four hours of the decision by the clinic. It was a nightmare I had known was coming, but there is no way to prepare yourself for it. Rob Reynolds died, lying asleep in bed, not the optimum way for a warrior to go.

After Rob's funeral, I made a Hells Angels trip to Europe. Then I returned to South Africa, and as soon as I landed at Johannesburg International Airport, I phoned my dad to collect me. Bob had left me a message every day for the last three days to phone him as soon as possible. I knew I was going to receive some bad news and wanted to get it over with, so I phoned him at his office. Bob asked if I could meet him that evening and when I told him I had just landed in South Africa, he said,

"This is urgent, Peter."

I told him I would go home, have a shower, change my clothes and see him later that evening. As I got into my dad's car, I knew there was something wrong with the conversation I had just had. My first words to my dad were,

"I think I'm in shit."

I arrived at the Department of Housing. The security company assigned to the building had been changed and although they were going through the motions, they had been taught in their manuals there were flaws in their systems. I was on the Visitors' List and it all ran pretty smoothly. I was addressed as "Colonel" by the ranking officer in charge of the security detail.

Bob had a new office on the top floor of the building and I was shown into a reception room. When Bob came out to show me into his office he looked terrible. His hair had almost turned white and he had lost more weight than was healthy. His clothes were hanging on his body and he was a shadow of his former self. I knew I wasn't responsible for his demise, but had added to it. Bob told me the United States Federal Bureau of

Investigation had delivered an indictment against me to the South African Embassy in Washington and was about to start an extradition process. He poured two large whiskies and said,

"What are you thinking these days? You were never this stupid before."

I thought it was best to hear him out, before I said anything.

"We can't let you be taken as you have a lot of sensitive information on operations that are ongoing."

I was in total agreement.

"We have an exit strategy for you, Peter."

I breathed a sigh of relief. There was always a way out, but what was it?

"There's someone using one of the offices in this building who would like to talk to you. Listen to her and we can help you."

I knew what that meant. Agree to her terms and I wouldn't have to go back to the United States in handcuffs. I answered,

"Of course."

Bob made a call. A woman came into his office and introduced herself as Marion Sparg. She was pretty and composed. She told me that the information she was about to give me was by no means restricted and I could turn her offer down at any stage. She added,

"I really need you to think, before you give me an answer."

She handed me a file and said she would be back in an hour. This world hadn't changed and I wasn't surprised. The file was titled, *The Scorpions, The Directorate of Special Operations*. The Scorpions was a multidisciplinary agency that investigated and prosecuted organised crime and corruption in South Africa. It had been established under the banner of the National Prosecuting Authority of South Africa. I knew that whatever was coming next was not going to be my idea of a future. Prosecution conducted investigations were almost always emotionally led when choosing targets. So now, South Africa had its own FBI. I felt the noose tighten once again. When

Marion and Bob came back into the office, I used a tried and tested approach to what was coming next. I kept quiet.

I was told I would be exempt from extradition to any country if I signed up. I would be expected to retrain and pass exams. I would be given a state salary and an expense account, authorised by a verified accounting department. I switched off at that point. At the end I just said,

"Yes."

It was the same shit, but with different names on the office doors.

When Marion left, Bob poured me a stiff whisky and groomed me for more bad news. He told me that, before I did anything for Marion, there was something I had to do for him. By that stage of the evening, I had resigned myself to this inevitability. I was to go back to Angola to represent his office on operations that were to take place at the end of the year. He patted me on the back as he walked me out of his office and told me I would receive my orders from Marion the following Monday evening. As I drove home, I wondered how the Hells Angels South Africa would react to my missing church because I was attending a briefing for yet another new intelligence agency. I went to sleep that night in a state of anxiety. A conflict of interest was bound to arise at some point in the future.

The following Monday evening, I attended my first meeting at the Head Office of the South African National Prosecuting Authority in Pretoria. Marion walked me to her office and I was given ID. Although I hadn't posed for a photo, the picture of me was very recent. I realised it had been taken the previous week by a surveillance camera at the Department of Housing. I wasn't sure whether to be paranoid or impressed. Marion told me she had requested certain disciplines to be added to my training in Phalaborwa and we would take it from there. Marion was a really pleasant woman and her mind was electric. She would be the first woman I would take orders from and I had no complaints. I asked a few questions and she had the answers to hand immediately. As I was leaving, Marion said,

"Don't worry. We don't have the Hells Angels on our radar. We have much bigger fish to fry."

Aged thirty-five, I reported to the Special Forces base. I couldn't believe I was going back into the world of military training. I spent the next five weeks attending sessions, dedicated to special operations and counter insurgency. Thankfully, the physical side of it was not that high and, as I was never going to wear the badge of a dagger that denoted a Special Forces operator, I was treated kindly. In fact, I hoped I would never have to put on a military uniform again.

On 6 September 2001, I went home to Johannesburg. The following Monday, I attended my first briefing at the Department of Housing since I had signed myself back over to the South African State. I was told I was going to Angola by the end of November. I would be transported to Cassinga in Southern Angola, where I would receive orders and equipment on arrival. All I knew about Cassinga was that there had been a controversial South African airborne attack on SWAPO there in 1978. There were claims from SWAPO that Cassinga was a refugee camp at the time and it had been a massacre of civilians, rather than a highly successful military operation. What I did know, was that the records of that operation were declassified after the election in 1994 and all they disclosed was photographic evidence of a mass grave.

Sarcastically, my thought was, 'I can't wait.'

I was to write daily reports on everything I witnessed and would be expected to compile a comprehensive report after three months. I couldn't believe that whatever was going on in Cassinga would take three months, but it was better than going back to the nightmare that the United States called a penal system.

Bob may have felt a little guilty that he was manipulating my situation in his favour, but if he did, it didn't last long. Bob asked me if I wanted to see my results and evaluations from the five weeks in Phalaborwa. I told him jokingly that, if I had known I was going to be operational, I would have failed on purpose. He burst out laughing and, pouring me a whisky, he added,

"That's not really in your nature is it? We're banking on that in this operation."

It didn't make me feel much better, but I knew I had no choice.

At the end of November 2001, I flew from Lanseria Airport, Johannesburg, to Windhoek, Namibia, where I was met at the airport and put on a Cessna to Rundu on the Angolan border. When we approached Rundu, it looked as if time had stood still since the previous occasion I had seen it from the air. As we circled, I got a bird's eye view of the hospital and the memories of the night with the nun came flooding back. It felt as though I had come home. After we landed, I was taken to a lodge situated just outside the town. I only had one change of clothing and took a long shower and cleaned up for dinner. As I was putting on my clothes, there was a knock on the door. It was Sean. I should have guessed. He was in his usual good mood as he walked in and sat on my bed.

"So, you had problems in the States, bud? You shouldn't be running drugs across international borders." He burst out laughing and added, "Unless you're doing it for us."

I smiled and replied,

"Let's go and eat and you can tell me what's going on."

I was relieved to be in his detail again. Over dinner and a bottle of whisky, Sean filled me in.

"We are rolling in a convoy from Cassinga with the Angolan Special Forces on what is supposed to be a good-will mission. As most of the rural towns we're going to target have very little idea of what is going on in their country, we are going to supply them with their opinion."

I couldn't wait to find out what their opinion was but wouldn't give Sean the satisfaction of my asking. He eventually told me that the message was simply that the Angolan Civil War was over. Sean was having fun drip-feeding me with the information, so I listened and said very little. When he asked me what I thought, all I could say was,

"But it isn't over."

He told me,

"That's the beauty of this operation. It will be over by the time we leave."

By now, an American cell was looking a lot more attractive than it had earlier that morning. As he left that evening, he said,

"You'll be filled in on the rest tomorrow at the base. I'll fetch you in the morning."

I ordered a bottle of whisky and took it to my room.

The next day we flew by chopper to Cassinga. When I saw the Casspir armoured vehicles below I looked at Sean, shrugged and remarked,

"Hard vehicles? Really?"

My head was pounding from the helicopter engines. Having a hangover didn't help. When we landed the first thing I noticed was that the Casspirs had Red Cross insignias on their sides. I had to laugh. Sean was the same Sean who had taught me operational camouflage when we were kids. I liked being in his company and knew that whatever we were about to do, he would have planned it better than anyone else.

We spent the following three months driving through Angola with the Angolan Special Forces, gathering intelligence from small villages. It was all pretty routine and I made comprehensive notes for my report. During the trip I engraved a face on the dashboard of my Casspir and have the photos to this day as a reminder of those months.

On 22 February 2002, Jonas Savimbi, the leader and founder of UNITA, was killed in a battle with Angolan troops along riverbanks in the Angolan province of Moxico, his birthplace. In the fire fight, Savimbi sustained fifteen gunshot wounds to his head, upper body and legs. He died immediately. The Angolan Civil War was over. On 27 February 2002, I flew home to Johannesburg. Another Christmas and another New Year had been spent away from home.

When I submitted my report of what I had seen in Angola, Bob was in a great mood. I think he was happier to see me than he had been in a long time. He didn't even open the report I had painstakingly compiled, but asked me just one question.

"What does Angola need right now?"

The answer was simple and I summed it up in one word.

"Peace."

Bob said that a meeting had been arranged with Marion for the next day. He told me to meet her and report to him as soon as the meeting was over. It didn't sound much like there was a lot of trust between the two agencies, but I supposed that was the nature of the game. I decided to do as I was told and let it all unfold.

After a long-winded process of filling in a security register and making my sidearm safe, I was escorted to Marion's office. She was on the phone and pointed to the chair in front of her desk. When she finished, she told me we would start in a briefing room a few doors away. I couldn't have cared less about where I was going to be given the assignment, but she added,

"This way, I'm not obliged to answer the phone."

I smiled and shrugged.

The briefing was that I would be given a large house in the northern suburbs of Johannesburg, designed around the previous owner's catering to entertain his guests. It had a large garden and pool. I was told an architect had been appointed who was both trustworthy and part of the team. I was to create a new and up-market approach to selling prostitution. Prostitution was still illegal in South Africa, but the little den of iniquity I was about to operate obviously wasn't high on the prosecution list. I was told that all building and operational expenses would be taken care of. She expected me to be creative.

"We need something that is new, Peter. Do something that attracts the right people."

She told me the whole house would be put under surveillance from day one. After she had finished talking, I asked,

"So, are we going to make a movie?" She nodded. "Who's it for and who'll be starring in it?"

She thought for a second or two and said,

"It's for us and the stars will be anyone and everyone that you can attract as clients."

I voiced my concerns about the presence of cameras and microphones.

"The installers will have a road map of our production and might even be able to gather their own intelligence by hacking their own system."

"Leave that to me," was all she said and I was satisfied by her honesty. I told her I would do my best and left.

Bob didn't seem surprised when I told him later that morning at his office. He ordered some coffee and, after painstakingly pouring two cups, he remarked,

"You realise that you're going to be running a parallel operation for us as well?"

Him saying that made me feel a lot better. The office of Military Intelligence had been my safety net for many years. I felt more at home with their ways than learning about how prosecutors believed operations should be done. A few months earlier, the retired colonel running the farm had been diagnosed with cancer and died, so, at the end of the meeting, I offered Bob the keys to it, but Bob said,

"Keep them. You'll need that place soon. We want it to go back to how it was being run before."

I wasn't sure what that meant and, when I asked, he said,

"Make a game farming concession out of it."

It seemed as though the entertainment industry was high on the priority list of both agencies. I pitched to Bob that we should pull on board one of the instructors called Andries from the Special Forces base in Phalaborwa to run the day to day affairs at the farm. I had made friends with Andries during the brief period I had been there, undergoing my latest training.

Andries was bright and very good at getting the best out of people. Bob agreed and told me he would meet both of us on Saturday afternoon. He poured me a whisky and added,

"You see what you can accomplish if you apply yourself. Stop spending so much time on that hobby of yours, the Hells Angels, because one day you will dig yourself a grave we can't pull you out of."

We made small talk for a while and, as I was leaving, Bob imparted to me one final pearl of wisdom.

"Interpol are making inquiries about you. Fly low my friend."

On the following Saturday afternoon, I met Andries and told him there was someone who wanted to meet him and offer him a job. He laughed and said,

"What are you up to Peter? *Ek ken mos vir julle* (I know who you work for)."

We went to a bar and, shortly afterwards as arranged, Bob arrived and did most of the talking. Andries would recreate the gaming concession on the farm with a view to making a commercial profit out of hunting. He would be paid a salary as farm manager and receive an expense account for minor supplies. All major expenses would go through the accounts department at the Department of Housing. He would sign on for another five years under the command of Bob and his pension would be moved to Military Intelligence. When Andries agreed, I breathed a huge sigh of relief. Things were starting to run a lot better.

I phoned the architect the following morning and we agreed to meet at the house. The house was amazing, located on a slip road only about 100 metres off one of the busiest feeder dual carriageways into Johannesburg. It had no address, so we gave it one. The eighth and first numbers in the alphabet spell HA, so it became Number Eighty One.

The architect was a nice guy and told me he had been given authority to build as soon as he had drawn up the plans. He said,

"Look Peter, everything that you ask for, will be approved."

We decided that the kitchen was too large and it would be better to put up a wall to create another bedroom. The servants' quarters would be modified and linked to the main house by a new structure, giving us four extra rooms. He told me the drawings would be completed within a week.

Chapter 31

A few days later, I had a message from Brett Kebble to call him. When I did, his personal assistant asked if I was available to have dinner with him the following Friday night. I confirmed I would be there at eight. When I drove through the gates of Brett's house, there were bodyguards posted at the front door. In the car, I slipped on a shoulder harness that had been altered to carry a sawn off double-barrel shot gun. At the door, I was told I would have to be searched. I was in no mood for a group of close protection officers to search me, so I brushed past the first one. As he grabbed at me, I hit him and put the shotgun in his mouth. I separated myself from the others with their lead man between us. Brett's butler came out and defused the situation but as I walked past them, one said,

"*Kom by Soutie* (Get over it Englishman)."

In the main lounge, there were faces I remembered from the Sudan mission but a new one as well. He introduced himself as Glenn and said,

"Give me some love."

It was the first time I had met this plastic gangster. It wouldn't be the last. I recoiled and sat down. It was uncomfortable at dinner. Glenn was making his presence known and dropping names of everybody he knew. He seemed very insecure and I disliked everything about him. After we had eaten, I was invited outside by one of the party, where I voiced my concerns about the new loudmouth, Glenn.

"Who is he?"

I was told that Brett had a way of networking new people.

"We have to interact with all different types of people, Peter."

All I could think of saying was,

"I suppose."

We went back inside.

As usual, at the end of the evening we went outside for biscuits and cheese. At some point, Glenn asked me if I would be interested in doing something for him. An uncomfortable silence followed. Eventually Glenn came out with,

"I need you to go to Zimbabwe to make contact with a South African ex-pat. I need you to deliver a contract to him and to bring it back, signed or unsigned."

I told him I was opening a whorehouse at the end of the month and would be busy from then on. Brett went inside and Glenn gave me his business card, asking me to contact him privately as soon as I could. This was not the way things worked, but I kept quiet.

The next day I forwarded his name to both Bob and Marion's respective offices. On both requests I wrote the same attachment, "Who is this prick?" Marion called me personally and told me to meet her at her office in Pretoria the next morning. When we met, she told me Glenn Agliotti was a person of interest. She ended by saying,

"Reel him in, Peter."

The next day, I contacted Glenn and arranged to meet him. The following Thursday afternoon, we met at a coffee shop in an upmarket suburb of North Johannesburg. He wanted me to make contact with a businessman, who had a game farm in Zimbabwe, just north of Harare. I was to give him an envelope and bring the signed contract back to Johannesburg. I told Glenn that the only way I could be sure the signed contract I brought back was the same one I had taken, was to have a copy and ensure no amendments had been made. He laughed and told me to not be so suspicious.

I couldn't help disliking Glenn Agliotti. There was an air of self-confidence about him that made me uneasy. I agreed to go to Zimbabwe, but told him I would expect all correspondence to go through Brett Kebble's office. Glenn objected, telling me it had nothing to do with Brett Kebble. I responded that it had everything do with him, as Brett had introduced the two of us. He could take it or leave it. We agreed that the next time we would meet would be at Brett Kebble's house. Glenn seemed disappointed with my response. I got up and left. Brett

Kebble phoned me that afternoon. He asked me why I was having problems with Glenn Agliotti.

"I don't trust him, that's all."

That was the true answer to the question. Brett told me that, in time, I would understand Glenn's ways. He asked,

"Anyway Peter, will you do what he has asked you to do?"

I told him I would for the usual fee, but that all correspondence would have to go through his office. Brett called me about an hour later and confirmed I could pick up the details from his office the following afternoon. He added,

"I've already paid you."

It was as though he was making sure I was not going to back out. It was nothing like the previous assignments. I picked up the envelope with the contract the next afternoon.

Then I went to see Bob. He was on the telephone for nearly an hour before finally giving me his attention. I told him about Zimbabwe and that Marion wanted me to pursue it. Bob thought for a while and then he nodded.

"Go and do it Peter. I'll give you a contact number in Harare, in case anything starts to go wrong."

I said I was leaving on Sunday night and he confirmed that everything would be in place by the time I flew. I left for the farm that afternoon. When I arrived, I found a new gate had been fitted, manned by armed guards. They were wearing combat fatigues with army boots and webbing belts. They explained patiently they were under orders to let absolutely nobody into the farm. I phoned Andries and he laughed.

"There have been a few changes since you were last here. I'll phone the duty room to let you in."

I had to sign a register in the duty room by the gate and then I was escorted to the hunting camp. I shook my head at the duty room and the register. What had happened to the days when we didn't want attention drawn to what was going on at the farm? When Andries arrived that evening he took me on a tour. He had tweaked the water system and recommissioned the slaughter-house and walk-in fridge. He would be taking over the farm on a full-time basis at the end of June and would begin restocking it by the middle of July. Bob wanted both of us to attend the auctions. I told Andries I was going to Zimbabwe the next evening. He wasn't surprised. It seemed he and Bob were exchanging information freely. I was happy that everything seemed to be working out. The next morning, Andries took me to the shooting range on the farm with a rifle he had modified. The range held many memories for me, especially as I hadn't shot on it since Rob had died. Andries was no substitute for Rob, but it was fun shooting again. It was a start in the right direction.

The following Sunday evening, I walked through Harare International Airport, picked up a rental vehicle and headed north. Bob had given me a telephone number to call when I reached my destination. The number was an office at the Central Intelligence Organisation of Zimbabwe's National Intelligence Agency. All I knew about them was they had formerly been known as the British South Africa Police, Special Branch. I knew for sure there would be very little left of that machine. They were now referred to in South African circles as "C-10s". I arrived at my designated meeting place, the Chinhoyi Caves Motel. It was very nice and the staff very accommodating even though I had arrived late at night. I left my South African passport at the front desk, called the number Bob had given me, announced my arrival and wondered what would happen next. I spent my thirty-sixth birthday in June 2002 by the pool at the lodge, watching two Scandinavian families with small children enjoying the sunshine. I used my credit card to eat some of the finest red meat I had ever tasted and drank myself to sleep that night with the most expensive whisky on offer.

On the third evening, I was approached by an obviously South African male. His waist was bulging from a life of over-indulgence and he sported the red complexion of someone who had hard work getting out of a car. He sat down at my table and asked,

"Are you Glenn's boy?" I said nothing. "You have a contract for me to sign?"

I told him to order a drink and I would take him to my room as soon as I had finished eating. He made small talk about South Africa while I finished my meal. Then, we went to my room. Thankfully, the business was over quickly. I noticed the contracts had signatures already on them. My companion signed all three, gave two back to me and watched as I sealed them in an envelope which he signed across the seal. I was happy to see the back of him and went down to the pool to have a last drink.

I arrived back in Johannesburg the following evening and, after I had delivered the contracts to Brett Kebble's offices, I went home to plan the opening of the whorehouse. At the house that weekend, I met the architect. The alterations had been completed and all I had to do was to sign him off. He told me a maintenance team would contact me to do any minor repairs. What I needed now was the installation of cameras, a theme, a name and a plan.

The next evening, I arranged to meet Kathy, a friend in the sex industry. She looked a little younger than me. It was difficult to tell her age and I never asked. She was tall and blond and looked as though she had taken care of herself. She said she would recruit permanent girls for the house and, on busy nights, would work a roster of part-time girls to cover any shortfall. I explained that what I was doing was an experiment and we would adapt it as we went along. Kathy realised I had no previous experience in the game but was happy to go along with whatever I wanted. The following day we met at the house and Kathy was blown away by it. She appreciated the amount of money that had been invested and became energised before my eyes.

I told her my plan. We would throw a house party every night. There would be an entrance fee and alcohol for sale at the bar. Instead of a customer picking a girl from a line up, there would be a party atmosphere where the customers would socialise with and select the girls. It would be less formal than the usual whorehouse. Customers would feel they were getting a girl into bed because she liked them. Kathy asked for a budget to promote the opening of the house, which I approved. From that evening on there were adverts in nearly every Johannesburg newspaper and social magazine.

On 1 July 2002, we opened the doors. The launch was a huge success. The girls had been carefully selected and the set-up ran smoothly. I was grateful to Kathy and we opened a bottle of champagne later that night, when she signed a long-term contract with the house. The following week, I spent nearly every night at the house, watching the client base grow. It was successful and businessmen from every field were becoming regulars.

I knew I should start the production of the surveillance movie for Marion's office sooner rather than later, so I hired a bouncer I had known for many years and took him into my confidence. I told him he would have to monitor the cameras in the rooms as it was how we were going to keep the business under control. He replied that he would take care of it all and would be available to start the next weekend. We agreed it would not be a good idea to let it become public knowledge that the rooms were being monitored by cameras and microphones.

By the time I met Marion again, I had worked out a demographic and pitched the plan to her. I was going to target personnel in banking. I found them good company. They paid their bills on time and were careless as they tried to make their lives appear more exciting than they thought the general public believed they were. Marion resigned herself to the fact that gathering intelligence in that way was never going to make her feel too good about herself.

Chapter 32

In mid-July 2002, I received a phone call from Brett Kebble asking if I would be available that Friday evening. I replied I would be there at about eight. When I arrived, Brett Kebble was in a great mood. As I walked into the house, I was surprised to see Glenn Agliotti seated in the lounge and a man, whom I had previously met, called John. Glenn was his usual overbearing self, but John was relatively reserved. By the end of the night, I had agreed to fly with John to deliver some suitcases to a copper mine in Southern Zambia.

Andreis, John and I flew out later the same week. When we handed over the suitcases, they were opened to reveal bundles of US$100 bills. I was not surprised as I watched US$1million counted out. When we arrived back at Johannesburg airport, Brett Kebble was waiting for us, looking tired and hungry. He grabbed my arm and said he needed to have an evening with me as soon as possible. I said I would come to his house later the same evening. When I did, Brett Kebble was alone. It was the first time there were no staff milling about. After letting me in, Brett went into the kitchen and poured me a drink. He told me to go outside as he was cooking. He eventually joined me and, as he poured me a glass of wine, he sighed.

"There is someone that I want you to meet Peter and you need to keep an open mind."

It seemed as though he was trying to get this conversation out of the way as soon as he could, so I sat back. I don't think I could have been more surprised by the topic Brett brought up.

"Glenn is my friend, Peter, and he is an important cog in my machine. If he asks a favour, it's in our interest to find a way of giving him what he wants."

I knew immediately that whatever the favour was, I was to be part of it. Brett told me that Glenn Agliotti had made friends with Jacob "Jackie" Selebi, the National Police

Commissioner of South Africa. In 1987, while in exile in Zambia, Jacob Selebi had been elected head of the ANC Youth League. The same year he had been appointed to the National Executive Committee of the ANC. Later, he had been made responsible for the repatriation of ANC exiles back to South Africa. In 1994 he had been elected an ANC Member of Parliament. In 2000, Jacob Selebi had been appointed the National Commissioner of the Police Services (NASCOM). He was to swim in a very bloody shark tank and eventually ended up in jail. I remembered him as the school teacher who, in 1977, had taken the kids from his school onto the streets of Johannesburg to protest about the curriculum being taught in Afrikaans. Now, he was about to be appointed Vice-President of Interpol in the African region. Brett gave me a file titled *Palto* and asked me to read it and get back to him with my thoughts. I didn't take much notice and put the file down next to me. If I had known how important that file was going to be to my future, I might have read it there and then, but I was hungry and it seemed like business was over for the night. Brett's cooking was amazing and we had a great night eating and drinking.

The following morning I opened the file. After reading it, I couldn't help feeling that the more things changed, the more they stayed the same. Palto had been set up by Paul Stemmet. I knew Paul vaguely. He was a well-known bodyguard and martial art expert, who ran his own operations in the South African security industry by day and moonlighted as a reservist policeman by night. On the streets of South Africa, Paul was known to be both a bully and a liar, but it seemed he had all the qualities that the South African Police Intelligence Services were looking to throw a budget at. The Security Company that was registered as Palto was nothing more than a front company for Police Headquarters. I couldn't help wondering exactly what Brett Kebble was getting himself into, but I knew I wanted nothing to do with it.

I took the file to Bob that evening and, as I sat waiting for him to finish reading it, I saw his mood darken with every page. When he eventually looked up, all he said was,

"Shit."

After pouring me a whisky, he asked,

"What do you think?"

"I think that NASCOM is no longer trying to police the gangs. I think that they're trying to become the gang."

He nodded and, again, all he said was,

"Shit."

I couldn't have agreed more.

I thought it was a good time to ask Bob for a budget to be approved for restocking the farm as soon as possible. The hunting season was almost halfway over and I wanted to get as many hunting clients in as possible before it ended. Bob was distracted and said he would leave it all up to me and Andries. I felt I had taken advantage of Bob's distraction by bulldozing a budget decision through. As I was leaving his office, he added,

"Make sure you get that farm working, Peter."

I saluted him and he grinned in a very tired manner.

The next time I went to dinner at Brett Kebble's house, Glenn was there and the mood was tense. Glenn couldn't contain himself and asked me for my opinion on his relationship with the National Police Commissioner. I told him I wanted very little to do with it, as my involvement would be a recipe for disaster. Glenn then came out with what he wanted to say.

"The Commissioner wants to meet you Peter. He can make all your international problems disappear."

I thought about what Glenn had said for a brief moment and then asked,

"Where would we meet?"

Glenn seemed happy at my reply and made a phone call. He had a direct line to Jacob Selebi the South African Commissioner of Police. After what seemed like a very friendly conversation, he put the phone down and, looking at me smugly, he said,

"He will see you tomorrow morning in his office."

I could think of nothing more stupid than being paraded through the offices of NASCOM the following morning and I was worried about the way it was being dealt with. For the first time in that house, I said "No," and went home to bed. The next morning, my house was raided by an Organised Crime Unit, based in Pretoria, and I was arrested and charged with murder. That afternoon, after being given clean clothes and a shower, I was taken from the cells to a restaurant in Pretoria and handed over to an operational police colonel who was sitting at a table with two police generals in full dress uniform. I had seen overkill many times in my life, but that day must have been the cherry on the cake.

I ordered food and sat patiently waiting for the hammer to fall. They handed me a business model that would integrate my security company with Palto and it all seemed as though it was a done deal, which I would accept unreservedly. I wondered what Bob would think about what was going on. I enjoyed the look on their faces as I said,

"No, thank you."

I was released that afternoon and all charges were dropped, but I knew I was swimming against the current. It was best to try to clarify what was going on and the place to start was the source. I phoned Brett Kebble and was put through to him immediately. I asked him to arrange a meeting with Glenn Agliotti as soon as possible. Brett sounded relieved, when he said,

"You are making the right decision here, Peter."

I thought it best to bite my tongue and told him to let me know when and where we could meet. Brett phoned back within the hour and I agreed to meet them at his house.

"I won't be staying for dinner Brett, so make sure that Glenn is on time," was all I said. I felt like a cat on a hot tin roof, where the heat was being applied disproportionately. I was not about to change my mind about integrating my security operation with Palto, so I went to tell Bob.

On a cold winter's morning in the middle of July 2002 on the Highveld, I saw Marion in her office in Pretoria with my report on the success of the first two weeks trading at the whorehouse. After hearing me out, Marion put the report to one side and told me what she wanted. Her plan was that I would find men in the business-world, invite then to the whorehouse, befriend them and discover what made their industry tick. She was very engaging with me that morning and at pains to point out that she was under duress and wasn't comfortable with what she was asking me to do.

I spent the next two weeks at the whorehouse, targeting the banking industry, making friends with some of the regular clients, grading them as gold, platinum or silver customers and setting up a credit system that reflected the status I'd granted them. When I reported to Marion, she dismissed me with the words,

"Keep it as clean as you can, Peter."

When next I dined at Brett Kebble's house, I agreed to escort a man called David, younger and more talkative than John, to the North Kivu Province in the Democratic Republic of Congo (DRC). I took Andreis with me. It was an interesting trip. During it, David, Andreis and I were taken prisoner by a Colonel Laurent Nkunda of the army of the DRC, who will feature again later in this memoir. We were treated well and, after four days, we were escorted to our plane and given back our weapons. As we took off, David announced proudly that Southern Africa had just secured mineral rights for the manufacture of cell phones for the next five years. I knew I wouldn't be at the follow-up negotiations in five years time and didn't care. We were going home.

I delivered a report on what we had seen in the DRC to Bob's offices, in which I wrote that I had never seen such a well organised group of African soldiers led by African officers before. One sentence summed up what I had written, namely that they were a highly motivated, well equipped and well led outfit with what seemed to me to be a chain of command that was not only effective, but well structured.

After that, I continued implementing the plan at the whorehouse. By the beginning of September of 2002, I was ready. Rather than the footage of the sexual activity we had on tape, I used the recorded conversations that took place freely after sex with the girls. The girls always told me that if you want a man's secrets, give him a bottle of brandy and a good looking woman and the rest will fall into place. They were right.

Within a month I had compiled a report on nearly every aspect of those bankers' lives. I knew where their think-tanks were, who was in them and, more importantly, what they were mostly concerned about. It was all too easy. I suppose looking back it was only a matter of time before someone else would want that information and try to take it from me. I submitted the comprehensive report to Marion and left it in her hands as to how to proceed.

Halfway through September 2002, I received an invitation to Brett Kebble's house. That evening I had dinner with a very well educated Englishman and his attentive personal assistant. I was asked to fly back to the DRC the next weekend. I agreed. Then, the Englishman said,

"That DRC colonel wants the exact security detail to be present at the next round of negotiations. Can you make it so?"

I realised immediately he was a military man, and answered,

"Yes, Sir."

As he was leaving, he remarked,

"When you put silk onto a monkey, Peter, you need to watch it closely or the hair will grow through the silk."

I understood and I wondered if he believed it. I decided I didn't care.

Brett Kebble and I were eventually left alone and I could tell there was another agenda. Brett said,

"Peter, the Police Commissioner wants you to take part in the Palto operations. I think it's for the best for all concerned that you do."

I remember looking at him in a different light that evening. There was something wrong and it showed in his voice. I let him waffle on for a while about cooperation and unity and eventually ended a very uncomfortable moment by saying,

"Police hit squads are not what I do, Brett. There's no exit strategy from that world, so no thank you."

That weekend David, Andreis and I flew to the DRC. We landed on an airstrip about fifty kilometres south of the last meeting. We were greeted with a smile and allowed to keep our weapons. We were driven to a temporary camp, surrounded by hard military vehicles. The negotiations must have gone very well, as David came back and told us we were going to have a party with the soldiers. Rwandan soldiers formed a perimeter around us.

First we ate and then alcohol was introduced to the party. The colonel passed out in the first hour and slowly the well organised and well disciplined battalion fell into disarray. Rwandan soldiers started shooting into the air randomly and there was no command structure left awake to stop it.

Andries said,

"Let's hope that they don't turn on us."

As I watched David melt under the threat of drunken African soldiers, I couldn't have agreed more. I eventually took David to our designated vehicle. He looked terrified as he undressed and I felt sorry for him. For him, it was a unique negotiating tactic. Actually, it was just a circus and ended with everyone smiling and shaking hands. However, I'd had enough. I was happy to be going home with another signed contract, but not happy with the new developments that were creeping into the process. I decided on the flight home that it was going to be my last trip for a while. It was only going to get worse and I had to focus on my duties in South Africa. I felt that everything Brett Kebble was doing was getting lax. The attention to detail as to how Africa was changing seemed to be the last thing on his mind and it showed in the way the contracts were being negotiated. For David, it was probably as much adrenalin as his body would ever pump in his life, and it showed in his nervous banter on the flight to Johannesburg. For the three of us and the pilot, our nerves were frayed. There was a much easier way to make a living in Africa, or so I thought.

I prepared a comprehensive report, which I handed into Bob's office that week. I emphasised how well-organised the Rwandan Battalion was and that they seemed to be able to operate with impunity in the DRC. The rest of my report was filled with descriptions of the vehicles and logistics I had witnessed.

The following Friday, I had dinner at Brett Kebble's house. When I arrived there were security personal everywhere, armed with assault rifles of every description. It could not have been more amateur, if someone had invented the word amateur. I walked into the house feeling a little apprehensive and found Glenn Agliotti holding court. Brett Kebble looked a little embarrassed by the show that Glenn was directing. Glenn singled me out and said, in a matter of fact kind of way,

"I am going to need some of your time later."

All I could think of was that some of my time was all he was going to get that night as I nodded and poured myself a very large whisky. When Glenn eventually got around to talking to me, we had finished dinner and I wanted to leave. I had come to this gathering to let them know I wasn't going to be available for any security details into Africa until further notice. I didn't have to bring it up, as it was brought up for me. Glenn told me in front of everyone that if I didn't meet the South African Police Commissioner that week, I would be replaced.

"We are a group that needs to be all on the same page, Peter."

I couldn't think of anything worse than being on the same page as him and all I could think of saying was,

"Then count me out."

As I was leaving the house, I went over to Brett Kebble and said,

"Nice doing business, bud. Let me know if you want to meet me on a purely social level."

I drove to the Hells Angels West Rand clubhouse and, to my surprise, found a huge party going on. As I was welcomed with open arms, I decided there and then to put more energy into the club. I got drunk and used cocaine to keep me as sober as possible. At some stage that weekend, I met a stripper whose stage name was Baby. She hung onto my every word and I forgot about my last supper at Brett Kebble's house.

By the end of the weekend, I had formed a strangely comfortable interaction with Baby and I took her home with me. She was barely eighteen but was a student of the University of Hard Knocks. The most convenient thing about strippers was that they were always unwilling to stay in any one home for an indeterminate period and Baby was no different. On Monday evening, I drove her back to the Hells Angels West Rand clubhouse on my Harley Davidson and attended my first Hells Angels church for many weeks. After church, I invited two Hells Angels to accompany me to the whorehouse. Wade was a West Rand member and Guy was a newly patched-up Nomads member. While Wade was fat with long brown hair, Guy was built like an athlete with a shaved head.

Within in an hour of us being at the house I was sitting at the desk in the office having a meeting with Kathy. Everything seemed to be running smoothly. Most of our clients were bankers and they were bringing more and more of their associates with them from all over the world. I was very satisfied with our progress and started trying to work out exactly how we could best gain intelligence from them. As I was sitting at the desk in the office, watching film footage of some of our most regular customers, we were raided by a police unit. This was not the first time it had happened and, therefore, it did not raise alarm bells, although it was the first time I had been present during a police raid.

I pressed record on all the cameras simultaneously and waited for the police raid to play itself out. I watched as the uniformed policemen rushed into the house. It all seemed very frantic, but as it was new to me I decided to observe. The police unit eventually made it into the office. A Captain Wayne Cookard identified himself to me and arrested me for selling alcohol without a liquor licence. About a half an hour later there was another commotion at the front door. As I was handcuffed to the office desk, I decided to wait it out. Eventually, Paul Stemmit, the head of Palto, walked into the office. He had been very aggressive to the staff and I put a face to the voice that had been handing out commands outside the office. He took the handcuffs off me and told me to wait outside the office, while he completed the investigation. I went over to the bar and ordered a drink. If we were going to be arrested for drinking alcohol illegally, I thought I might as well do it in front of the cameras filming the episode.

It happened very quickly. I remember ordering a drink for a bouncer, whom I hadn't seen in many years. His name was Mickey Schultz. Mickey was a pretty boy and, with blond hair and a muscled physic, he stood out in the crowd. The last time I had seen him, he had been prospecting for The Hells Angels South Africa Nomads. Then all hell broke loose. I remember a loud crack as I was hit over the head with a baseball bat. Everything went blank for a second and, when my senses came back and clarity set in, I realised Mickey was not at all surprised I had been hit from behind. As I grabbed hold of him, I was stabbed repeatedly in the face and body from all sides by a group of men.

As everybody ran towards the exits, I was left for dead. I would later find out I had been stabbed so many times that it was impossible to ascertain the number. As the police were leaving I was surprised at the clarity I had. There was no real pain. Both of my lungs had been punctured and I had a feeling of being drowned. When the ambulance arrived at the house, at first I was pronounced dead by the paramedics. However, all my senses were alert and I felt very little pain beyond a difficulty in breathing. I remember a lot of blood was around me as I was strapped to a stretcher and taken to the ambulance. I concentrated on staying alive by keeping awake. It was only after I had pipes inserted into both of my lungs to drain away the fluids, that I was administered a sedative and fell asleep. When I woke, I was in an intensive care unit, surrounded by Hells Angels and doctors.

For the first time in nearly two months, I saw Charles. He was standing over me. His face was red with anger as he told me there would be payback for what had been done to me. I frankly couldn't have cared less at that time, but felt grateful I was surrounded by members of the club. I could feel my face had been severely damaged by the amount of dressing applied to it. I remember Baby's face crying next to me, as I was given another dose of morphine and fell back into unconsciousness.

I was woken by a plump but very concerned nurse who told me I had a visitor. Although the doctor had not given permission for visitors, the person who wanted to see me had a court order and they had to let the visitor see me. She told me that if I wanted her to intervene, I was to put up my hand and she had the authority to end the visit. Marion entered. She was absolutely distraught and did not hide her emotions. When she broke down and cried, I knew how badly I was injured.

"We have the whole thing on tape Peter and this episode won't pass without repercussions."

I was in so much pain that I smiled through the bandages and managed to say,

"There are things that I have to tell you before you proceed."

As I fell back into a drug-induced sleep, I couldn't help thinking again how much of a fish out of water she seemed. She was in a shark tank and I needed to recover before she started to drown.

Chapter 33

During the seventy-two hours I spent in intensive care, Charles executed three of the men who had assaulted me. The guy who had hit me with the baseball bat was shot outside a nightclub, the evening after I had been attacked. Charles was just being Charles and doing what he thought was for the best for the club and our reputation. I felt helpless and vulnerable. Although I had no idea what he was doing, it created ripples in the security services in South Africa and by the time Marion came back to visit me, she was again distraught. I told her I needed to be fixed up as soon as possible, in order to have a chance of stopping the killings.

Marion arranged for a neurosurgeon, Dr Graham Edwards, to be flown from Cape Town. Her caution turned out to be beneficial for the future appearance of my face as he decided to operate on me that afternoon. He explained that it was necessary to reconnect as many of the peripheral nerves in my face as possible, so as to limit the amount of permanent damage. I wanted to go home and wasn't interested in the cosmetic outcome of the surgery. He told me he would release me the following day after I woke from the anaesthetic and that he would personally conduct the necessary surgery. All I said was,

"Tell Marion that I'm in her debt."

Dr Edwards operated that afternoon and, when I woke, he was sitting next to my bed with a smile on his face. He said,

"You'll live Peter, and women like scars."

I fell asleep knowing I was in good hands. True to his word I was allowed to go home the next afternoon. My fractured left fibula had been plated and there was a cast up to my knee. I was wheeled out by the sergeant at arms of Hells Angels West Rand. It was all done so quickly that it's still a blur. Hells Angels South Africa kept a constant security vigil around me for the rest of the week as I recovered.

Sometime during that week, Charles arrived at my house and proudly presented the bouncer whom I had employed at the whorehouse, tied up and gagged. Charles told me it was up to me whether I killed him or not, but he had been sentenced to death by the Filthy Few. I told Charles to stop for the time being, as there were things that needed to be assessed before anyone else was killed. I was in a lot of pain and only wanted to take painkillers and sleep. I could think of nothing that I would rather do less than kill an old friend for something he had been incapable of stopping that night. I moved Baby into my house and settled down to heal.

Fourteen days later the house was visited by a colonel from the Organised Crime Unit. Baby let him and his partner in through the front gate without asking who they were. As she opened the front door I could hear them giving their credentials to her. I shouted,

"Just let them in."

I was smoking a joint at the time and never bothered to put it out. The colonel walked into my bedroom and said,

"*Rook jy dagga, Peter* (Are you smoking weed Peter)?"

I didn't hide that I was smoking a joint. I believed there were bigger fish to fry other than committing such a petty offence, but they were going to harass me for anything at that point. I was arrested for possession of narcotics, taken to the police station a few kilometres away, put into a cell and informed I would appear before a magistrate the next morning. I was allowed painkillers and settled in for the night, thinking it was harassment that would be sorted out in the morning.

In court the next morning, I was told that if I pleaded guilty to possession of a classified substance I would be sentenced to a small fine. I told the magistrate that I would not plead guilty to possession of such a small quantity of a non-classified drug. It would give me a criminal record and I would have to reapply for my gun licences under the new firearm laws that had been introduced a couple of years before. I asked for a date to be set for trial. I was denied bail and taken back down to the cells.

Marion had all the charges dropped and came to see me that afternoon, just before I was sent to a maximum-security prison. She was very upset about my arrest and made a huge scene in the magistrate's office. He was an old school magistrate and I think he could see how much strain she was under. In fact, what she had done was expose herself to the police unit, which was all the police wanted from the exercise. As she drove me home, I said,

"You just walked into their shit-storm."

She looked at me and replied,

"We still have control of the courts and you've been through enough. There will be no prosecution, but you need to think about the details until we can sort this all out."

I agreed and was happy that she was so committed to me.

A few days before the cast was removed from my leg, I attended church at the Hells Angels West Rand clubhouse. Charles was there with Guy. He told me he was going to a meeting with Mickey Shultz and intended to take him into his confidence and then kill him. I could see no gain in this strategy and told him that Mickey was being looked after by the South African Police Services and, as everyone was on edge, it probably wasn't the best idea. Charles got angry with me and stormed out of the room. It was the last time I would see him alive. Charles was shot later the same evening by a Palto member in an upmarket restaurant in southern Johannesburg. He was unarmed and sitting at a table with Mickey and Nigel, whom he saw as Hells Angels Nomads prospects. Although Mickey claimed to have shot Charles, I later met the person who had shot him, after he had resigned from the police and was about to deploy to a security job in Iraq. What Charles hadn't known was that Mickey and Nigel had changed allegiances from the Hells Angels. They had done a deal with the National Police Commissioner and were protected assets. It was South Africa and Charles had not realised he no longer knew the two guys he was meeting. He was shot once in the chest and died slowly in his own blood. A weapon was found under the table where he had been sitting and so, under South African law, he had been lawfully killed. With Charles's murder, Hells Angels South Africa had been reduced to two

Filthy Few members. Charles had been the epitome of a stone-cold killer, but he was my friend and a huge loss to the club.

My skull had been mended with fourteen staples and the day I had the cast on my leg removed, I insisted on the staples being taken out as well. It was a painful process and I remember feeling very bitter as each staple was extracted. Sitting there, listening to and feeling the staples being removed from my skull, I hatched a plan. I asked Andries to sanitise two assault rifles I would collect that weekend. I decided to kill as many of my attackers as I could. Marion called me that night and implored me to reconsider what I was doing. Everybody seemed to know what was going on. I told her I would meet her the following afternoon and decided to rest the entire operation. In Marion's office, she asked me to leave it all to the registered authorities as Palto was in her sights, but that there was a serious conflict of interest as Jacob Selebi, the Police Commissioner, was pleading ignorance of every incident Palto was involved in.

"He can't plead ignorance for too much longer, or it will start to seem like he has no idea as to what is going on in the country," she observed.

I understood and told her I would leave it all in her hands.

"Leave them alive to give evidence Peter."

All I could think about was how hard it would be to get anything done through the courts. I said,

"I'm going back to the house tonight. I'll let them come to me."

She nodded and said,

"Remember we need to keep it clean."

I went to see Bob the same evening and he told me to give the sanitised weapons back to Andries and he would legally fast-track any weapon I requisitioned. I realised that Andries had been talking to him and I couldn't see any problems with that. As I was leaving Bob's office, he asked,

"Peter, what are you going to do?"

I hesitated, but thought it best to tell him what was on my mind.

"I'm going to set a trap and give Marion a snuff movie."

Bob nodded and said nothing at first. Then he got up, shook my hand and said,

"Good luck, Peter."

Kathy had kept the house going during my absence. In fact, it had become busier, as the attack on me had become the talk of the town. That evening, I rearranged the layout of the whorehouse. I moved the office down into the wine cellar under the bar and, as I kept the cameras rolling in all the rooms, I settled down for round number two.

After the night when I returned to the house, Johannesburg became eerily quiet. Everyone around me seemed to be walking on eggshells. The next day I applied for two new assault rifles and temporary licences were approved almost immediately. I stayed in that house with security provided by Billy and Steve. Billy was the Hells Angels West Rand sergeant at arms. He was the youngest member in the charter but seemed seriously intelligent. Steven Magua was an old bouncer friend of mine. He was not very tall but was built like wrestler and could be described in one word, affable. He had expressed an interest in joining the Hells Angels and, as it only needed two officers of the charter to start the process off, Billy and I voted him in as a Hells Angel South Africa Southbank hangaround. This was the first duty we assigned to him. I issued two-way radios to my two new guards and we sat in for the next move, playing a waiting game.

Years afterwards, I met one of my attackers. He told me he had been informed about my plan and had lost all resolve. He was about to start a fifteen-year sentence for murder and had no reason to lie to me. I knew that the lines in the intelligence world were blurred, but that afternoon years later, I realised how many leaks there had been at the time. He said to me,

"I want to make peace with you, Peter. I have enough enemies where I'm going."

He was released after serving ten years and I remained friends with him.

A few days after I had returned and rearranged the whorehouse, four members from Hells angels West Rand turned up at my house and we formed Hells Angels South Africa, Southbank. We converted my house into a clubhouse and registered our charter with Hells Angels World. I took on the role of president and appointed Rudy, a long time Hells Angel, vice president. Billy became sergeant at arms and the three of us shared the roles of secretary and treasurer. The same day, Guy transferred form South Africa Nomads and Hells Angels South Africa was complete.

Chapter 34

At the end of February 2003, Bob asked me to meet him. I was not really expecting exactly what came up next, but was all ears to anything new. Sometimes it's weird what life throws at you. When I met Bob, he made small talk to begin with, but then he gave me a file titled *Darfur*. He said,

"Take a break from your personal crusade and hurt them where you last helped them."

I took the file home and the next stage of my life began. A major armed conflict in the Darfur region of Sudan had begun a couple of weeks earlier. Rebel groups calling themselves The Sudan Liberation Movement (SLM) and the Justice and Equality Movement (JEM) were fighting the government of Sudan, which they accused of oppressing Darfur's non-Arab population.

Bob was really happy when I told him that I was going to accept whatever he wanted me to do. I wanted to be part of something again and Bob explained that an assignment with the United Nations would wipe my slate clean. He told me to report to the farm, as Andries was beginning a retraining course later the same week.

I arrived at the farm and answered endless questions at the gate. Although the guards knew me, they took great delight in making me go through the entire process. When I told the guard in charge,

"I hold the rank of a lieutenant colonel," he replied with a toothy grin,

"You're not a colonel here, anymore."

Andries came to see me soon after I had unpacked and told me with much glee that I was to expect no preferential treatment while I was in his camp. I reminded him that the camp had been mine before it became his and we laughed over a glass of brandy.

After two months of both physical and mental training, we were issued with new uniforms and told to appear for a passing out parade that afternoon. After lunch I put on my new uniform and added my lapels donating my rank onto the shoulders. The rank was on a blue background and I was now a lieutenant colonel in the employ of the United Nations. I put on my very new blue beret and mustered with the other guys. I noticed that there were three officers that were full colonels and decided to ask Bob for a promotion as soon as I next saw him.

Andries was wearing his rank on his arm which was also on a blue background. After we had been dismissed from the parade ground, Andries came over to me with my orders. I was being deployed to Darfur as a peacekeeper and he told me with a smile that he was coming with me, as he put it,

"Just in case you need someone to dry your tears, Peter."

It made me laugh and we were friends again. We flew out of Waterkloof Air Force Base to a temporary airstrip just north of Nairobi in Kenya. I was taken aback by the number of British soldiers present. The senior officer was a Kenyan brigadier general, but the real power was in the hands of the British colonel. After reporting to the general, I was led to the colonel's office. He told me that because of my previous experience in the south of Sudan, he expected me to direct traffic to every point where I had been before. It seemed simple enough but then he dropped the hammer. We were to escort negotiation teams and under no circumstances was I to order the firing on anyone in the area. We were going in with our hands tied behind our backs and although it wasn't ideal, so long as we didn't let the cat out of the bag about our non-belligerent status, the white UN vehicles and negotiators would be safe. The following week, we and two negotiators would be transported by chopper to a mobile UN unit.

When I told Andries the plan, he was not happy.

"It's like playing poker with a terrible hand."

I couldn't have agreed more but it was the only game we had, so we decided to get on with it. Andries said to me that night as we were preparing to go to sleep,

"If we're bluffing, what happens if we get fired upon?"

I thought for a while and replied,

"If we're in any danger, we'll return fire."

He thought about my answer and, turning over, he left me with,

"What a fucking mess the United Nations have to work in."

The general briefed all the officers the following morning. Governments that had endorsed sovereignty as responsibility for conflict in Africa had shown little inclination to protect civilians suffering at the hands of their own government in the Sudanese Province of Darfur. I switched off after that. I had already been briefed with the truth.

After listening to an overview of Darfur's crisis and to what seemed to be the international society's feeble response, I was unimpressed. To my mind, sovereignty as responsibility meant that NATO and the European Union were going to fail the people of the Darfur region. Was it better to be in Johannesburg waiting for a fight, or to be in Sudan where we were expressly ordered not to fight? I decided that Sudan was the lesser of two evils.

The following weekend, we flew to a temporary refugee camp in central Darfur filled with displaced Sudanese citizens. As we banked in to land, I looked at what could only be seen as chaos down on the ground. Andries lent over me and, looking through the window, gave me a naughty grin.

"This is going to be interesting, bud."

There were volcanic peaks in the distance that seemed to rise up like a range of mountains and foliage on the ground. I said to Andries,

"At least there seems to be water down there."

The heat was a reminder of the last time that I had been in Sudan and the quantity of flies was disturbing. The smell was of a toilet that hadn't been cleaned for a long time. I was offered a tent with the English officers and asked the British colonel if it was possible to billet me in the same tent as Andries. He told me to go to the equipment tent and make whatever arrangements that I needed to make. I was relieved and thanked him. He said,

"Conway, I've been told that you are on police radar in South Africa but there are no South African police here and until there are, I expect you to get on with my officers."

He ordered me to provide logistical help and advice in the ever increasing chaos of the refugee camp and to make myself available to the British doctor, who was running a makeshift hospital for Amnesty International. As I was leaving he said,

"Peter, I'm happy that you're settling in well. Good job! Is there anything you two need?"

I took a chance.

"A bottle of whisky wouldn't go amiss, Sir."

He laughed and the air cleared between us.

"I'll see what I can do." He added, "Those doctors and administrators are not the same as us. Be careful with them and help them but don't let them see your frustrations."

I nodded and saluted him for the first time as if I were one of his team. The following day, Andries and I went into the refugee camp for the first time. There were thousands of Sudanese in temporary cover, with mostly no sides to the tents they huddled beneath to keep dry. There was no privacy and they looked resigned to whatever the future might hold. By then, I had become used to the flies and didn't bother to brush them away.

When we were led to a very temporary hospital, the problems that refugees faced became apparent. The hospital had thirty beds, about one per hundred refugees. The beds were occupied by the very sick and other patients were either sitting around outside or lying in between the beds. Andries looked around and said,

"Well, at least it smells better in here."

He was right, but I wasn't taking too much notice as my eyes were firmly fixed upon the youngest of the white doctors. Her name was Sarah and, as I watched her finish what she was doing, she noticed us. She gave me a dirty look as she walked over to where we were standing. Sarah was probably the most beautiful thing that would ever grace that wet and depressing part of the world. My heart skipped a beat as she got closer to me. The first thing that you usually say in such circumstances is something that later you wish you hadn't. Today was no different.

"We have been ordered to assist you, Ma'am."

She brushed me aside.

"Great! South Africans! I didn't realise things had got that bad."

As she walked past me, she added,

"You can address me as Sarah or Doctor, but I'm not your ma'am."

I looked at Andries, who said,

"Remember our orders, Peter. Don't let them see your frustrations." He burst out laughing. "This is not a place to fall in love, Peter. Any emotion is wasted in this hellhole."

A young English first lieutenant who had witnessed what I had just encountered, smiled and told me that everyone had the same response from her to an awkward opening line.

"Never mind, Colonel. You can only improve from here on."

I laughed.

"Where do we start, Lieutenant?"

He told me that he was having problems recruiting refugee volunteers to clean the temporary toilets, as they were all under the impression that they were awaiting transportation to a more permanent camp.

We implemented more structure in the running of the camp. I appointed a man who had poor working knowledge of the English language as head of translation. He was willing, but progress was slow. By the first evening we had divided the camp into sixteen different areas. Each area was told to appoint a committee by the following morning that we would negotiate with.

As we walked back to the airstrip, I asked the young lieutenant how many troops he had been assigned by the colonel. He told me he was the only officer and had four troops at his disposal.

"The colonel's priority is to secure the airstrip."

By the third morning we had a committee of forty-eight men representing the whole camp and sixteen sub-committees representing the different areas of the camp. We started to exercise a degree of control. We were making friends and, by the weekend, there was a semblance of order in the refugee camp.

On the Friday evening, I was summoned to the colonel's tent. He gave me a case of whisky. It was on his personal expense account and there would be no sick roll the next morning. I saluted him and left before he changed his mind. That night was the first time Andries and I fully integrated with the British officers and the first night in a long time I had felt truly content.

The following Monday morning, a convoy arrived with twenty doctors and medical supplies. We persuaded the committees to work out a schedule to build another fifteen hospitals in each area. I told them that I would requisition the cover and the beds, but that I expected it all to be completed by the following Friday evening. It was rewarding to watch those people come together. All they needed was a structure of sorts. The distribution of food and water was given over to the committee system and there came a point when we started to feel that we were getting on top of the situation. It didn't last.

At the beginning of May, an influx of refugees doubled the population of the camp. There was infighting between the committees and the new arrivals. I was given permission to extend the perimeter of the refugee camp and we extended the committee system as we expanded. But the damage had been done. There were serious rifts within the camp, and we were losing control. Supplies were coming in by road from Khartoum International Airport, but rain had washed away most of the temporary roads and delivery was sporadic.

The colonel was continually busy and, when I went to talk to him, he just barked,

"Make a report, Peter."

I wrote a report and put it in his tent. The following day, I was called to meet him. He told me that everything was getting worse and was not expected to improve. I asked for permission to go to Khartoum the next morning to see if we could fine-tune the supplies from that end. He looked at me.

"You know, Peter, that I was given a report of your behaviour in Johannesburg, before you landed in Kenya?"

I decided not to answer.

"You're doing your best, Peter, but this operation is just a holding pattern. It's not something that we are trying to win. But you can go to Khartoum and I will give you a letter of authority from me. See what you can do. And don't do anything stupid."

He wrote out a letter and gave me the coordinates of the American Marine base on the perimeter of Khartoum International Airport.

"This is where the distribution is coming from. Give this letter to the American colonel, and he will brief you. I'll let him know that you are coming."

When Andries and I drove out of the camp, our Land Rover was white. By the time we reached main roads, it was covered in mud. A few times that day, we heard sporadic small-arms fire, but we just kept driving north. On arrival at the American logistics base, I was ushered to the colonel's office. He explained that the main problem was the Sudanese Government's red tape. Getting the stores from customs to his storeroom had no time frame that could be counted on. I stated what I thought was obvious.

"This is Africa, Colonel. Have you considered offering the relevant officials money?

The colonel shrugged his shoulders, gave me a resigned look and replied,

"Of course. But where do you start? This operation is in its infancy right now and nobody really cares."

He offered me a drink. I sat opposite him.

"Maybe we should leave African bartering up to the Africans?"

He looked at me with interest and I told him what I had in mind.

Andries and I borrowed three different changes of civilian clothing. We swopped our white Land Rover with UN markings for a Toyota Land Cruiser and, with US$1,000 in my pocket, we headed for Central Khartoum. We booked into a suite at the hotel where Brett Kebble had booked for me just over a year earlier. I phoned Bob's office and left the hotel's phone number and suite room number. We ordered room service and two bottles of whisky and waited for a response. When Bob eventually phoned back, he wasn't surprised I was living in a five star hotel. After I briefed him on what was going on, he asked me,

"What can I do, Peter?"

I wanted him to find out who was ultimately in charge of the bottleneck at the airport and arrange a meeting between whoever it was and the American colonel. He chuckled and asked me if I was considering bribing him. I said,

"I'll leave the semantics up to the Americans."

He asked me how long I intended being at that phone number and I told him that I would be there until he got back to me.

"I'll see what I can do."

Andries and I spent the next two days watching American cable TV and eating from a very fine room service menu. Bob phoned back. He had found an official in the Sudanese Customs Department who was willing to inspect the American operation and to speak to the American colonel. I was right. When in Africa, leave the ways and means up to the Africans.

I was not present at the negotiations, but they must have gone well as, from that time onwards, convoys of supplies arrived at the camp far more regularly. There was no easy solution to the condition of the minor roads feeding the refugee camp, but at least supplies were getting through whenever they could. It was a step in the right direction.

For a short time afterwards, there was relative peace between the different groups in the refugee camp, but it didn't last. The young men were questioning the authority of their elders. The elders were questioning the authority of the sub-committees who, in turn, were questioning the authority of the main committee. As the news worsened, the British colonel asked me what I thought would be best way to keep the peace in the refugee camp.

"Martial law?"

He laughed and said,

"Who would be king?"

I replied, tongue in cheek,

"I would be king and I would be a just and fair king."

He told me to hold the line whilst he took instruction from the United Nations. He then changed the subject and I let it go.

Things became worse. There was a murder of a son of a once prominent man. My interpreter told me that it would never be forgiven and a blood feud had been declared. Stupid decisions were not new to me but, given the circumstances, I was taken aback. The murder was something we hadn't seen coming but the reaction was something I never expected. Andries and I sat in on a heated meeting of the main committee.

That night I was woken up by the English lieutenant, who told me that two more boys had been murdered and tensions in the camp were running at an all time high. I asked him to gather his detail in front of my tent and that they should be armed with both side-arms and assault rifles. The situation was insane. We were giving them sanctuary from a conflict area and the very safe space that had been allocated to them was now about to turn into a conflict zone as well.

We first went into the main hospital and I saw the bodies of the two men. They had both been stabbed multiple times. It was an act of brutality and when the families had taken in the ferocity of the murders, all hell would break loose. We called a committee meeting which made things worse. My interpreter was inept and, as he had emotional ties with one of the families that were involved, he was biased to boot. We imposed a curfew and threatened to detain anyone outside their designated area for the rest of the night. That night seemed to go on forever and although I was thankful to see the sunrise, I was even more thankful that we might have bought a little more time.

The following morning, as I was sitting in an administration tent drinking a cup of coffee and wishing I had some whisky, Sarah came and asked if she could join me. Although I never answered, she sat down anyway. Eventually, she broke an uncomfortable silence.

"Why do you care?"

I decided to tell her the truth.

"I'm here on a type of parole, so I'm just trying to do my best in very difficult circumstances."

She nodded.

"That makes sense."

I asked why she cared and, without hesitation, came the reply,

"I've always cared. Do you want to have breakfast with me?"

It seemed a genuine attempt to be nice to me, so I thought it would be a good moment to respond to her comment the day we had first met.

"Breakfast with an English doctor? I didn't realise things had got that bad."

She laughed.

"Maybe South Africans do get judged harshly. I'm sorry."

That morning, as the clouds opened up and, unbelievably, more rain started to fall, Sarah and I became friends.

During the following day, there was an uneasy peace in the refugee camp. The hours flew by and as night approached I knew it wouldn't last. Just before sunset, there was another murder in the refugee camp. The situation was becoming untenable. Sarah came to me from the main hospital.

"I'll introduce you to someone, Peter."

I followed her into the hospital, where she introduced me to an elder of one of the local clans. He spoke better English than I did. It was the first time in a long time that I wasn't being hampered by selective translation. He told me that although my attempt to implement some form of democracy in the refugee camp was commendable, I was fighting a losing battle. I knew he was right. He told me I had to use the old ways to keep control of a situation made up from a demographic spanning over 150 clans. He asked me to take him to a town called Nyala, where he would locate one of the region's elders currently defying the government in Khartoum. If one of those elders gave the word, it would enforce a rule of law in the refugee camp. I told him to give me an hour and went to see the British colonel. We both pored over a map and although given the weather we were experiencing, it wasn't going to be easy, we decided it was worth a chance.

Darfur is approximately the size of Spain. We were right at its centre. Nyala was an urban settlement lying about 120 kilometres to the south-east. Shaking his head, the British colonel informed me there was heavy fighting going on there and he wasn't sure if the banner of the United Nations would be respected by the local militias, let alone by the Sudanese Government forces. Then there was the problem of roads, best described as rivers at that time of the year, and the map would be of no use. However, we decided that it was worth a try and I would leave with the elder at dawn the next day. I noted down the coordinates of the town and went back to the hospital. I told the elder to be ready to leave at dawn and added that the journey might put us both in harm's way. He looked at me with an amused expression.

"You Europeans see danger in what we see as normal here."

Sarah demanded to accompany us. I told her to be ready when we left or we would leave without her. The next morning the three of us left in what could only be described as the pluckiest Land Rover that I had ever driven. It was very wet. We ran into the Sudanese Government forces first, about ten kilometres from Nyala. After nearly an hour of negotiations, they let us through. Then we encountered a group of local militia. They were more supportive, telling my passenger where to find the men he was looking for. It turned out to be much easier than we had hoped and, by that afternoon, a new king of the refugee camp had been anointed.

We arrived back at the refugee camp at about half past nine that evening and shortly afterwards, what could best be described as a loose judiciary had been established under the threat of the men we had seen in Nyala. We were asked to become less involved in the running of the camp's new system and, after consulting the British colonel, we agreed. To say the refugee camp ran smoothly after that would be untrue, but the refugees resigned themselves to the new dispensation.

By my thirty-seventh birthday in June 2003, the fragile peace in the refugee camp had been held by an alliance of force and necessity. The killings mostly came to an end and we had achieved fragile control. In mid October 2003, Andries and I flew to Kenya and caught the first available flight out of Nairobi to Johannesburg. We knew we would not return to Sudan as United Nations peacekeepers. Although we never discussed it, we both realised that the situation in Darfur would get much worse before it got better and we wanted nothing further to do with it.

Chapter 35

After a pleasant month or so looking after our newly established Hells Angels charter, Bob called to ask me to attend a meeting with himself and Marion. It turned out they wanted me to assist another of their agents with an investigation into an alleged plot to murder a specific group of politicians before the approaching elections. The agent was George Darmanovic, whom I knew from my early days in the Johannesburg nightclubs. I can't remember exactly how I had met him many years ago, but I remember liking him and had even attended a few months of boxing training with him.

George had been shot in Angola during the eighties, which had halted a promising boxing career. After his apparent discharge from the SADF, he had become a notorious and vicious street fighter. It dawned on me that the reason he was not occupying a prison cell somewhere in South Africa was not good luck. It was because he had never truly left the military. He was working for Bob. To say the least, this was going to be interesting. I agreed to meet George at the whorehouse that evening.

George had infiltrated a group of businessmen, who were going to fund the assassination of politicians running for mayor in the different councils of northern Johannesburg. He explained he had been hired to do the assassinations himself. He needed proof of payment and intent from one of the businessmen with a view to taking all of them to the National Prosecuting Authority to be charged with sedition. Resigning myself to how happy he seemed to be planning someone's murder, I asked Marion,

"What do you want me to do?"

The plan was simple. We would have the prostitute who one of George's targets was using arrested. She would then be given bail and a job at the whorehouse. She would be told to invite the target to the house, explaining that she couldn't work any other way. We would record the conversations she had with the target and as soon as we had the necessary evidence,

George would drug him. Later the same night, after everyone else had gone home, George would take him to the offices of the Directorate of Special Operations.

Marion was definitely getting her hands down deep in the sewers. It seemed like a long shot, but, by that time, I had become used to long shots working. I again asked Marion,

"What do you want me to do?"

"Bob wants us both on the same page before I sign him off, Peter. It's how it works these days."

The operation ran as smoothly as expected. At first the target was reluctant to visit the whorehouse, but once he had been there, he became a regular. It took about three weeks for him to be drunk and stupid enough to tell the prostitute his plans for fixing the approaching local elections. By December 2003, we had it on tape and it was all over. I received a phone call from Bob the next day. He seemed rattled as he told me he needed to speak to me in person as soon as possible. I knew that whatever news I was going to be given wasn't going to be good. When I arrived at Bob's office, I was ushered in almost immediately. Both Bob and Marion were in the office and the look on their faces told me my prediction of bad news was right on the button.

They informed me that the whorehouse had been raided by the South African Police Services the night after the businessmen had appeared in court. Then came the distressing news. The prostitute had come forward and admitted, under oath, that she had been asked to do it by George. George had been arrested and the police were denying him any visitors, even from the office of the Directorate of Public Prosecution. So, Bob's office, Military Intelligence, Marion's office, the covert arm of the South African National Prosecuting Authority, and the office of the South African Police Services were not seeing eye-to-eye.

When I mentioned this, Bob nodded and said,

"In fact, it's all getting worse than that."

I couldn't wait to hear the rest.

"It's the fact that these businessmen, whom we entrapped, were able to call on the Police Commissioner's office and get an operational response in one afternoon."

It all sounded so petty and the only thing I could think of saying was,

"Where do I fit in?"

Marion took over the briefing.

"We wouldn't ask you to do this, unless it was important, Peter."

I knew that whatever was coming next was not something I wanted to hear.

"After you were attacked in the whorehouse, we informed the Police Commissioner that we had the incident on tape and that we had every intention of prosecuting both the bouncers and the relevant Palto members in the near future."

I thought for a moment and then asked her,

"So, you informed the Commissioner's office that you were running operations out of the whorehouse and, despite that, we still ran that last one there?"

Marion put her head in her hands. Finally she said,

"This whole thing is much more convoluted than you think. There's a real problem with the elections just around the corner."

Again, I asked what she wanted me to do. Marion told me that she had it on good authority that the South African Police Commissioner, Jacob Selebi, was at the top of the list to be appointed the next President of Interpol the following year. Interpol's headquarters then and now are located in Lyon, France.

"There are Interpol members who are against this move and we need to gain an insight into the Police Commissioner's inner circle in France. We want you to travel to Paris and we'll monitor the phones to see what his reaction is, but, more importantly, whom he uses to do what he wants."

It was absolute madness. It could end with me in a French prison for the foreseeable future. They were not only intercepting communications from the offices of NASCOM, but the Police Commissioner's private cell phone as well.

"What makes you think his office will respond to my travelling to France?"

I had to know. Then came the final nail in the coffin.

"We have reason to believe that the whorehouse was infiltrated by Police Intelligence, which is now aware that you were part of the operation to obtain a confession to the intended murders of at least two up-and-coming local councillors. You will not be the only bait we're hanging out there, Peter."

As I processed this, I felt angry. I had no choice but to agree. I was on the Police Commissioner's radar. I supposed that the French penal system would be better than a South African prison before its problems were solved. All I said was,

"Okay, but you buy me a first-class ticket as I want to be drunk and well fed by the time I land in France." And, as I left, I added, "Don't forget about me, when I'm over there."

I flew to Paris the following evening and as soon as I left the plane at Charles de Gaulle International Airport, I was arrested and taken to an interview room.

Over the next ten days, I was interviewed twice. In the first interview, two men, who identified themselves as Interpol agents, asked me very standard questions about my visit to France. They had both my South African and British passports and questioned why I had flown out of Johannesburg on my South African passport but had filled out my landing card on the flight using my British passport. I wasn't rude, but it was one of the perks of legal dual citizenship. I took my time informing them that it shouldn't be up to me to explain international passport law to them. The second interview was more cordial. One of the Interpol agents was a young and very pretty woman, but again there was very little I could tell them.

Around the middle of January 2004, I was visited by Interpol for the last time and, the same evening, I was put on a flight back to Johannesburg.

When I made it back to my house there was an eerie silence. I phoned Steve Magua and he was in a great mood and informed me he was in Cape Town. I told Steve to make up another bed in the house, grabbed my luggage I had taken to France and drove down to Cape Town in just over nine hours.

It didn't take long for the next episode to unfold.

Once I had arrived in Cape Town, Steve and I went to an Italian restaurant in Clifton, within walking distance of his father's holiday home. We ordered food to take away and a drink at the bar. Steve had known the owner of the restaurant for several years and everything seemed to be going well. We were sent complimentary drinks by the owner and I decided to eat my supper at the bar. I'm not sure how it went wrong, but when I came back from the toilets, I saw Steve draw his weapon and start shooting at a group of men next to him at the bar. I remember being more surprised at the speed Steve managed to clear his handgun from its holster, than by the fact he was shooting in a built-up area. He carried on shooting until his magazine ran out of rounds. He then dropped to the floor and changed magazines.

Customers were running in all directions and by the time I got close to Steve, the first incoming shot was fired at us. I shot the man holding the weapon in the chest with a Taurus S & W .40 calibre and he died instantly. The shooting carried on for a while but everybody seemed to be running out of ammunition. The two of us took cover behind an overturned table and although it seemed like forever before the shooting stopped, it was only seconds later. Everything went silent. The smoke cleared to reveal four bodies on the ground. Two of them had been killed instantly but the other two were lying on the floor, moaning within a twenty metre radius of us.

As we were gathering our thoughts, the restaurant was filled with tactical police officers. We were both arrested and taken in separate vehicles to two different police stations. I would find out later that we had been sitting in between two rival gangs at the bar and although we had been oblivious to the situation, we were considered to be collateral damage. As it turned out, Steve had killed three of them and I had killed the other.

We were hauled in front of a magistrate and charged with murder. Steve was granted bail on condition that he would sign a register at a specific police station every day in the area he used as his fixed address. On the other hand, I was refused bail and was transported to Johannesburg in the back of a police vehicle to Diepkloof maximum security prison. I was put into a cell that had been designed for about eighteen inmates. This cell contained fifty men of various ages, all of whom were awaiting trial for serious crimes.

Within days, I had gone from being in a luxury house in Cape Town to an overcrowded prison cell in Johannesburg. I had problem after problem with the other inmates. I was the only white guy in the cell and they all spoke languages I little understood. I was into my third week in the cell, when the doors were opened and a police tactical unit ordered me outside. They put me in chains linking my hands to my feet and I was taken to a transport vehicle. The whole thing was over the top, but I kept my thoughts to myself as I was transported to Police Headquarters. I must have looked like hell as I shuffled into an office. I was pushed into a chair and left alone.

I'm not sure how long it took for the door to be opened, but it was less than an hour and, when I looked up, Jacob Selebi was taking the seat at the other side of the desk. The first thing that came to mind was how badly his uniform fitted him and how the rank insignia he was wearing seemed to fall off his shoulders. I decided not to voice my observations, but let him start the inevitable conversation.

That day, it was the arrogance of Jacob Selebi that struck me. He had been, as I would later find out, appointed the next President of Interpol and was flexing his power. He didn't wait long to give me my options. He told me that Steve and I had been caught in a police intelligence operation to persuade two of the biggest gangs in South Africa to meet and agree a truce to end their war. I had no idea what had gone wrong that night, so I sat in silence and listened. Selebi explained that I had two options.

"My friends need you to courier contracts into Africa, Peter. If you start working for them again, the police and the magistrate will give you bail and drop all charges against you and Steven Magua. The two of you could not have been in more of a wrong place at the wrong time. I can oppose bail and, although under South African law you will probably be found to have been acting in self-defence, I will put you in a prison in Cape Town for the duration of the trial. If you survive there, while being hunted by the associates of the gang members you two killed, I will be very surprised."

I looked at him in a new light. He was the biggest gang leader in the country. The South African Police Services was being run by a gangster. The machine that was NASCOM had kicked up another gear.

I asked,

"What do you want me to do?"

He told me I would be transported back to Cape Town the next day and have a bail hearing as soon as possible. The police and the prosecutor would not oppose bail and, once I was out, I would be expected to get in touch with Brett Kebble. It was the first time that I was truly disgusted by the words coming out of anybody wearing the uniform of a general. I didn't think too much, but said,

"Okay."

I was taken to Cape Town in the front of a police vehicle in clean clothes with no chains. Within an hour of arriving in Cape Town, I was placed in front of the same magistrate who had denied me bail. It was all over in minutes and I drove to Johannesburg very slowly with the pistol that I had used that night on the seat next to me. I didn't go home when I arrived back in Johannesburg. Instead, I went to see Bob.

Bob was totally negative when I walked into his office that evening. He was on the phone and threw a file across his table. The file contained all the newspaper articles on the shooting at the restaurant in Cape Town, with speculation about my reasons for disrupting a police operation. As I read, I discovered that Steve and I had been sitting at the bar between two rival gangs. Police Intelligence had been monitoring them and had made a report that weapons had been drawn, but no shots had been fired until Steve had started the whole thing off.

"They're gonna spin this thing anyway they want Peter," were Bob's first words to me. "Marion exposed that you're working for her office by trying to get you bail."

I looked at him and the only thing I could think of saying was,

"It gets worse."

Once I had disclosed the deal that I had made with the Police Commissioner, Bob was even more negative.

"We're supposed to all be on the same side Peter, not fighting over budget and control."

It seemed the boat had sailed on that plan. I asked him what he thought I should do.

"I'll brief Marion later tonight and arrange for you to have lunch with her tomorrow."

As I was leaving Bob's office that evening, he asked,

"What happened?"

The truth was all that was relevant. I said,

"Shots were fired and I did what I thought was best."

Bob nodded and said,

"This thing needs to be handled correctly. Keep in touch."

The next day I met Marion, who looked like she would rather be somewhere else. She was quick to explain that her attempts to get me bail weren't within her scope of authority, but she had managed to get me moved from the prison in the Cape.

"They were planning to kill you in Pollsmoor Prison, Peter."

I realised she had saved my life and exposed herself and me at the same time. I was truly grateful. Marion had obviously been briefed extensively by Bob and I waited for her to give me the game at hand.

"You are going to have to face your attackers, Peter. If you don't feel comfortable with their terms, then I will help you to get out. They can't jail you for self-defence and your bail will not, under any circumstances, be revoked. Just stay out of trouble."

I asked her what she thought I should do. After a brief pause, she asked if I could work for the group of businessmen that the Jacob Selebi wanted me to work for. She was visibly relieved when I answered,

"Of course."

"We'll get them, Peter. It will take time."

I left her thinking we were going to see where the next stage of the game would be going.

I phoned Brett Kebble's office the following morning and left a message. He phoned me back within the hour. Our conversation was strained as we agreed to meet at an upmarket restaurant in the northern suburbs of Johannesburg. Over lunch, the two of us were uncomfortable in each other's company. I agreed to fly to Mali for him for the same fee and in the same circumstances as the other trips. Before I left him in the restaurant, he tried one last time to bridge the gap between us.

"I had no knowledge of that attack on you, Peter."

It didn't seem relevant any more and I told him to leave the relevant documents with his secretary. I made a point of paying the bill and left. I flew to Mali, where I succeeded in having the contracts signed. The night I returned, I decided that, no matter what the outcome was, I had had enough of running around Africa like a trained poodle for men who had tried to kill me. When I dropped the signed contracts off at Brett Kebble's offices, I told the secretary to tell Brett that I had no intention of working for him again, whatever the repercussions. I drove home wondering what the response from the Police Commissioner's office would be and how fast it would come.

Chapter 36

The hearing of our murder trial was brought forward. I had to appear in court in Cape Town or risk being arrested. One Monday morning, as Steve and I sat outside the courtroom waiting to be called, the last person I expected to see walked in. Brett Kebble sat next to me. He appeared very defeated, looking older and unsure of himself. I had never seen him like that before, so I let him talk. He wanted me to attend a meeting in Stellenbosch, which was less than half an hour's drive from the courts that afternoon. I told him I would let him know after my hearing. He said,

"If you cooperate with us, the police are willing to give a true account of what happened on the night of your shooting incident."

I looked at him and thought, 'What the fuck are you getting yourself into Brett?'

The court hearing went ahead after lunch. Steve and I had our bail extended. As we walked out of the court building, Brett was waiting for us in his car. I looked at Steve and said,

"Nothing ventured, nothing gained."

We were driven to a vineyard in Stellenbosch. It was probably the most opulent farm I had ever seen, but the real surprises were yet to come.

That evening we met and had dinner with Mark Thatcher and a man called Ely Calil. We were served by a butler and the food was cooked by a professional chef. The atmosphere was the same as it was at Brett Kebble's house in Johannesburg. I had seen this dance before and neither Steve nor I were particularly impressed. We both knew that, for certain people, this was the norm.

Everything was very cordial to begin with and, when I went to the toilet with Steve, he said to me that he didn't feel comfortable eating with the son of a member of the English House of Lords. I told him to take Brett Kebble out into the garden before biscuits and cheese were served and they might get to the point a little quicker. Steve chuckled and said,

"Done!"

It was not long after Brett Kebble and Steve followed a waiter out into the garden that the point of my being in that farmhouse was reached. Mark Thatcher first broke the uncomfortable silence.

"My associates tell me you have a working relationship with General Laurent Nkunda of the Armed Forces of the Democratic Republic of Congo?"

My first reaction was, 'So, he's a general now. Another officer selling out to politics.' I knew that both the men with whom I was sitting had the answer to that question, so I said nothing. Thatcher continued,

"We want you to make contact with him again, Peter."

I wasn't taken aback. I had become used to people taking for granted the ease with which contact could be made with someone in an African conflict area. My initial response was,

"I don't work for your associates any longer."

Mark Thatcher smiled and said,

"It's worth ten thousand pounds to you and, if you work for us, we can arrange for the South African police to leak their intelligence reports to the court."

It is amazing how easy it is to manipulate someone in the midst of a crisis.

"What do you want me to do?" was the only thing I could think of saying.

They got straight to the point. I watched men who had never heard the word "No" before, spill out their wishes. Within the space of two weeks, they wanted me to negotiate a weapons purchase with General Nkunda and have the arms ready for collection. At first, as they voiced their thoughts, I concluded they were both crazy. I knew how far removed they actually were from the hot end of what was going on in the DRC.

I replied that if the South African Police Intelligence reports on what had happened that night in the restaurant were leaked to a major Cape Town newspaper, and if that resulted in the charges being dropped against both of us, I would be in. They looked at each other knowingly and we shook hands.

We were driven back to Steve's father's house in Cape Town by a chauffeur. When we finally sat down after what had been a long and stressful day, Steve asked me what it was all about. I told him to prepare for a surprise.

The next morning the *Cape Argus* printed a story about a South African Police intelligence operation that had gone wrong in Cape Town. The following day all charges against Steve and me were dropped and I embarked upon the first stage of my new employers' plan. I flew to Goma airport in the DRC that evening, with a list of the weapons I was to procure written on the inside of a box of cigarettes. The whole process went very smoothly. Looking back, it was too slick to be true. I was collected from Goma airport, which looked to have not much life about it and was driven north. When I arrived at a lodge overlooking Lake Kivu and saw that all the general's soldiers were dressed in American Homeland camouflage, I should have smelt a rat. General Nkunda received me upon my arrival and we reached a deal within the hour.

I was to go back to South Africa and return with US$250,000. The weapons would be waiting for me at Goma airport. I was told the whole list of weapons and ammunition would be available and there would be no hitch in their transfer from a vehicle to the plane. I had completed the first phase of my mission and flew home to Johannesburg via Luanda.

The following morning, I phoned Brett Kebble's office in Johannesburg and was put through to him. He sounded relieved to hear from me so soon and was quick to tell me he had arranged finance for me to buy a new car at a BMW showroom in Northern Johannesburg. I told him I would have to courier the cash back to the DRC as soon as it was available. He told me he would get back to me. I didn't expect to hear from him for a day or so and went downstairs to join the Hells Angels party that was in full swing.

At lunchtime the following day, Brett Kebble phoned and asked me to meet him within the hour at a five-star hotel in northern Johannesburg. I threw on a pair of shorts and a vest and drove to meet him. When I arrived at the hotel, I asked for a table booked under the name of Kebble. When I entered the dining area, there were two new faces at Brett's table.

The first to greet me was called Nick du Toit. The second was the retired Special Air Services major, Simon Mann. Brett Kebble didn't get up and we nodded to each other. Simon Mann is someone it's difficult to like. He spoke to me as though he owned me. Executive Outcomes were all over this deal and I wasn't in the least surprised.

I was handed US$250,000 and went to leave, but Simon Mann had to have the last word.

"Make sure it gets there, Peter."

I looked at him and answered,

"If you had anyone else to do this, you wouldn't be handing me the money in the first place."

As I left the hotel it struck me how stupid it was to meet in such a public place and the fact I was wearing only minimal clothing made it very hard to disguise myself.

I flew back to the DRC with the money. The only thought going through my head was how much these businessmen were paying for weapons I could have supplied at a tenth of the price in South Africa. More importantly the money was in US$100 bills and there was absolutely nowhere in the part of the world where I was heading that General Nkunda could spend it. Once again, it all ran very smoothly and I told the general that a Boeing 727 would be landing at Goma Airport on 7 March. The general chuckled.

"Let's drink. You South Africans can't be trusted when you are sober."

I laughed and agreed with both statements. That evening I got drunk with General Nkunda and, as the sun set over the vast stretch of water that is Lake Kivu, I believe we came close to becoming friends. He was very intelligent and it was easy to get a laugh out of him. He was only a few months younger than I was, but had a very different outlook on the world around him. General Nkunda told me he had studied psychology at university and had been a school teacher after that. He had been ordained as a Christian preacher before becoming part of a military operation many years before. He spoke wistfully about his children and how much he missed them. He said his heroes were Ghandi and George W Bush.

The occasion differed from the first time I had done business with him. He became a little sad about Joseph Kabila, the new president of the DRC, who had succeeded Joseph Kabila's father. He told me stories of helping the then president's father overthrow the first president of what was, at the time, Zaire. Mobutu Sese Seko, he told me had been the hope for that part of Africa during the 1960s but had lost sight of what needed to be done.

"We needed to get rid of him, so we did."

He ended the evening by saying,

"Be careful not to get too involved with what's happening on the other side of this country. All is not what it seems."

I would soon find out he must have known a lot more than he was telling me, but that night, I was left wondering exactly what he meant.

When I arrived back in Johannesburg, I phoned Brett Kebble's office and was told he was in Cape Town. I left a message and he phoned me back within the hour. He asked me to fly down to Cape Town that evening. I told him I expected to be put up in a top hotel as I'd been on the go. It was the first time in a while when we seemed able to put the past behind us.

He said,

"Of course, Peter. Nothing but the best."

That evening, I was collected from my hotel in Cape Town Marina and driven to the same vineyard where I had been taken from the court building on what seemed then to have been a very long time ago. The best way to describe what I witnessed that evening was a reunion of Old Etonians. They had the world at their feet and were living a dream in sunny South Africa. There were also a few South African men present, mostly gathered round a fire burning in the barbeque area near the pool. I made my way across to them and greeted them The first man to respond introduced himself as Crause Smith. I had met him some years before, when Steyl had been the name on his uniform, but I let it go. I wasn't interested why he was using a different surname. I wanted to hand over the details of what I had negotiated in the DRC and return to my hotel.

Eventually, Brett Kebble appeared. As usual, he was taking care of the catering arrangements going on around us. I eventually spoke to him in the kitchen and gave him the report of my procurement of weapons from General Nkunda. Brett Kebble was very distracted and I wasn't willing to be insulted by him being short with me. As I left the kitchen, I remarked,

"Those soldiers in the Democratic Republic of Congo are now wearing U.S Homeland Security uniforms. Whatever you're planning is going through the Central Intelligence Agency."

He looked very weary as he replied,

"If you see this night through, we'll pay you the same amount we paid you for going to the Democratic Republic of Congo."

All I wanted to do was to return to my hotel room, but £10,000 was a lot of money to turn down, just for staying at a party. Sometime after we had eaten, Brett Kebble and I spoke again. I had watched him be his usual, hospitable self all through the proceedings and felt sorry for him as his work-rate keeping the party going had gone largely unrecognised. He said to me,

"We are willing to pay you fifty thousand pounds for you to fly back to Goma with a small team to make sure that the delivery of the weapons goes through smoothly, Peter."

We both knew I wouldn't turn down that amount of money. I agreed to go and I asked him to contact me with the details. I left in the same vehicle that had brought me to the vineyard, with the thought that he hadn't taken to heart my observation about General Nkunda's battalion wearing US military camouflage.

The next day, I returned home to Johannesburg and switched on my phone. Bob had left a message every single morning I had been away. I realised he must be aware that the charges against Steve and me had been dropped in Cape Town. I phoned his office and was put through immediately.

"Come and see me directly, Peter," was all he was willing to say on the phone.

When I entered Bob's office, for once he wasn't on the phone. He pointed to a file on his desk.

"Read this."

The file was titled, *Equatorial Guinea*. I took it to the outer office, poured myself a cup of coffee and started to read. It was very detailed. The first page was headed, *The Wonga Coup*. It was a plan to replace the president of Equatorial Guinea, Teodoro Obiang Nguema Mbasongo, with an exiled opposition politician, Severo Moto. It would be largely executed by South African mercenaries and was being mainly organised by British financers. Large oil and gas reserves had been discovered in Equatorial Guinea. A United States report described that country as the New Kuwait. As I read through the file, I became increasingly disturbed. It was clear that South African Military Intelligence was far better informed than usual. I eventually reached the page on the procurement of weapons. It was spot on. The list of weapons was exactly what I had secured in the DRC.

The South African National Intelligence Agency had supplied an entire intelligence portfolio on me and there was even an analysis of how successful I would be in reaching a deal with General Nkunda. It was not only current, but more amazingly, it was the most concise report on myself I had ever read. The basis of the intelligence on me, was a suspicion that I had been involved in weapon dealing on a regular basis since the early nineties.

There were copies of invoices of aviation equipment bought with money deposited into South African bank accounts from London. The main company being financed was called Air Ambulance and government contracts had already been secured in Equatorial Guinea. The final page was a summary of information and it ended,

"These people want their bread buttered on both sides."

As I put the file down, I knew I was in trouble. It was easy to see why Bob was so upset. I walked back into Bob's office and felt anxious as I sat down. Bob looked up and said,

"Tell me what I don't know."

I looked at him and replied,

"You know much more than I do, but there has been a development."

I explained to him that I had agreed to fly back to the DRC on 7 March to ensure the weapons deal ran smoothly. There was an uncomfortable silence, which Bob broke, saying,

"You've put me in the light, Peter."

I knew then that I was on thin ice and decided that silence was better than excuses. Bob continued,

"One of the few friends that you have left is going to steer you through this mess. He's in charge."

I nodded and asked,

"Who is it?"

"Sean. From tonight he will monitor every decision you make until this stupidity plays itself out."

My relief was overwhelming. All I said was,

"Thank you."

As I was leaving the office, Bob's final words were,

"When are you going to learn that all that glitters isn't gold?"

I turned, stood straight and saluted him.

When I arrived back at my house that night, there was a large Hells Angel party going on. I decided not to act out of the ordinary and joined in. Sean arrived later and let himself in. There were Hells Angels in differing states of drunkenness in every room. Sean smiled at me from the bottom of the stairs. He pointed around the open plan downstairs and asked,

"What's this?"

I smiled back.

"It's a production of sorts."

Sean laughed.

"Who's it for?"

I felt so relieved to see him that I burst out laughing.

"It's for me. Let's try and keep it that way."

We went upstairs. Sean said,

"You really have walked into this one haven't you? These idiots try to kill you one year and you secure an arms deal for them the next?"

I felt a little stupid when it was put like that, but waited for him to continue.

"There's a back door here, bud, we need to find it. Nothing changes with your current involvement. In fact, we're going to increase your level of involvement."

I asked him which side we were playing for and he gave me the same grin I remembered from our first border crossing in Angola.

"The winning side, bud."

Chapter 37

I was to contact Simon Mann, via Brett Kebble, and meet him at the same five star hotel in northern Johannesburg where we had first met as soon as I could. I was to ask for half of my payment up front, before agreeing to fly to the Democratic Republic of Congo. The meeting was arranged for the day after I had spoken to Sean.

As I walked into the hotel foyer, it seemed the entire hotel was filled with intelligence operatives. I had purposely worn a pair of shorts and a vest to be as visible as possible and to look as I had done for our first meeting. It is easy to become paranoid in situations like that, so I focussed on the game in hand. I took a phone given to me by Sean into the meeting to record what was said

Simon Mann was a different person that morning. He congratulated me on what I had accomplished with General Nkunda and seemed a much nicer guy.

"So, are you are coming with us on the first leg of our trip?" he asked.

I shrugged and answered,

"I'm broke. I have no choice."

He gave me a bag containing £5,000, saying he would let me know the travelling details closer to the time. I had lunch with him and we mostly spoke about Angola. That day, Simon Mann came across as very bright and I let him do most of the talking. In fact, I discovered that it was hard not to like him and time passed very quickly. After lunch, I started to get drunk and eventually made an excuse to leave.

"We've heard bad reports about you, Peter, but you certainly know how to get the job done."

As we shook hands, I thought to myself, 'I hope you're on the winning side.' I walked out of the hotel seeing the same people sitting in the same places and wondered exactly who was stinging whom.

On the last day of February 2004, I was contacted by Simon Mann. He wanted to have lunch with me that evening and I agreed. When we met, Mann told me to be on standby from 5 March, handed me £45,000 in cash, a contact phone number and a new British passport. The photo of me in the passport was a copy I recognised from an old British passport photo that had been taken when I had visited Weymouth, England, years earlier. When I got into the car in the hotel parking lot, I passed the phone and passport to Sean. He looked at the passport and, with his usual grin, he said,

"I guess that means the English are on board."

On 1 March 2004, with Sean I visited the BMW dealership Brett Kebble had mentioned to buy a new car. My dad had agreed to sign for the finance and I went all out. I ordered a gun-metal grey BMW 745i with a full Schnitzer conversion. While the sales manager was working out the logistics, timing of delivery and finance, we were interrupted by a man with a heavy German accent. He introduced himself as a friend of Brett Kebble and told the sales manager he would take over the nitty gritty of the deal. He had all the papers ready within the hour and had phoned my dad to confirm a time to sign the papers. As we got up to leave, Sean said to him,

"If you buy me a cup of coffee, I'll give you a plan to streamline your operations in South Africa."

The German looked over at me and I shrugged and threw in my ten cents worth.

"If you buy me a cup of coffee, I'll introduce you to a German Hells Angel."

We all laughed and spent the next couple of hours planning efficiency improvements in the BMW dealership that Sean had been observing, while I was choosing the modifications to my new car.

Later the same afternoon, I collected the £10,000 in cash for attending the party in Cape Town from Brett Kebble's office.

When I arrived home, Sean was sitting in my lounge, reading a newspaper. He looked up.

"We're not going to let you get on that plane, Peter, but it's important you keep up appearances."

I realised then that the operation had been blackballed and I was thankful I was being handled and was not part of the management.

The plan was simple. In a couple of days' time, I was to get high and drunk and phone Simon Mann. I would manufacture an argument with him and promise to give him his money back. We would take it from there. I opened a bottle of whisky and Sean left, saying,

"I'll meet you back here when it's time. Just act normal."

There was nothing more normal than me drinking and doing drugs.

On 3 March, I was well and truly off my head. Sean came around at lunchtime and I was given a written speech to tell whoever answered the phone number Simon Mann had given me. A man with a heavy South African accident answered and I read out what I had been given. Basically, my story was that I had twisted my ankle and needed to know exactly when and where I was to report. I was cut short.

"*Jy is net dronk. Bell my teruig na dat jy a bikie slaap vat* (You are just drunk. Phone me back once you have slept)."

I cut off the phone call and, as I put the cell phone down, Sean looked at me and said,

"Good job. Now switch off your phone. You live in silence until further notice."

I nodded and went to my bedroom, took a sleeping pill and passed out.

The following morning, I went outside to the quarters that housed my staff. I gave the woman that ran my house R1,000 and asked her to buy food and whisky for me over the coming days. I asked the gardener to set up targets at the top of the garden, fifty metres apart from each other. I had sighted in weapons before in that garden and it usually kept everyone away from me. I settled down for the wait.

I didn't have to wait long. On 7 March, the South African news channels began to report about a plane being forced to land at Harare International Airport. At first, it was said that a Boeing 727 had been intercepted by two Zimbabwean Air Force

MiG 29 fighters. I remember thinking that the Zimbabwean Air Force couldn't scramble eggs let alone two MiG 29 fighter jets. I was aware that only the Israeli Air Force maintained that level of readiness. The whole thing was a mess and it was only going to get worse. As the day went on, it unfolded. The Boeing 727 had been impounded by the Zimbabwean Police at the airport and speculation was running at an all-time high. The eight o'clock news reported that Simon Mann had been arrested with two colleagues near the runway, waiting for arms to be loaded onto the Boeing 727. The Boeing had flown out of South Africa, carrying three crew and sixty-four former soldiers.

On 9 March 2004, Nick Du Toit and fourteen other South Africans and Americans were arrested in Equatorial Guinea on suspicion of being the mercenary advance party. At that point, I knew who was on the winning side.

On the morning of 10 March, Sean came round. I was still in bed and, in my bedroom, he told me that Bob wanted me to go to the farm and stay there with Andries until further notice. He had a very stiff whisky. As he was leaving, he added,

"Andries has been briefed so you won't be alone anymore, but be careful how you go, bud. He knows everyone on that plane."

I drove to the farm house and spoke by phone to Andries' wife. She told me that Andries had been ordered to step up the security on the farm and she had no authority to let me in. I would have to wait until Andries got back. This put me into a foul mood and the stress of the previous two weeks boiled over. I reversed my new car around the nearest cover, opened the boot and took out an AK-47 with a drum magazine. I put all seventy rounds into the ground in front of the gate. The reaction was led by Andries. I was allowed in.

"Jesus, Peter. Everyone is strung out. You need to be a little bit more patient," were his first words as I parked my car in front of the farmhouse.

"Fuck you! My patience is at its limits. You knew what was going on yet you thought better than to tell me? While I'm being danced around the Democratic Republic of Congo, I'm actually just a plan B?"

He looked embarrassed. I said,

"I need to be filled in and I can't wait any longer."

Andries nodded and said,

"Go and choose a rifle and we'll go hunting. We can't talk here."

I picked up a Winchester 300 Magnum bolt action rifle on which Andries had modified the front sights. I put a box of ammunition into the pockets on the legs of my trousers and said,

"Let's go hunting, bud. I need some answers."

We drove out to a watering hole nearby. Andries reached into a refrigerated box behind his seat and passed me a beer.

"Let me tell you what I know in one load. Then we can speculate on the fine tuning after you have no more questions."

All I could think of saying was,

"Go!"

He told me that *The Wonga Coup* attempt was all systems go, until about the middle of February 2004. After that everybody knew about it. I asked what that meant and he replied,

"Your high-flying friends that you moonlight for in Africa went one step too far. The fucking South African Police Commissioner is up to his ears in this shit."

I should have known. I asked him to start at the beginning. I took a deep breath and decided not to interrupt until he finished. Andries was someone who I knew would be brief. He was.

"The powers-that-be decided to change their minds. You might have procured the weapons, but when the plan was shut down, Jacob Selebi, the Police Commissioner, decided to change sides. When you went missing last week, the weapons deal was changed. Once the South African Police Commissioner was approached by South African Military Intelligence and told the mission was not allowed, he must have been advised to join the winning side."

I was sick of hearing about the concept of the winning side, but let him continue.

"When you were not available, two operators working for Palto gave Simon Mann an alternative solution for the procurement of the weapons. That solution was Zimbabwe. They took it, but it was a set-up. That way only the guys on the ground get fucked up. The Commissioner is taking full credit for infiltrating the operation and bringing it to its knees."

He ended by saying,

"You got lucky Peter. Let's go and shoot something, as my wife will be suspicious if I don't come home with something."

I had one question;

"How come you know more than I do about it?"

He shook his head and said,

"Think about it, Peter. I recruited the soldiers."

Andries leaned back in his chair as the animals started making their way slowly down to the water in front of us. He ended the conversation by telling me,

"We're gonna have to sit this one out."

That night, just before the eight o'clock news, it was announced that the Zimbabwean Government was considering a request to send their now world-famous prisoners to Equatorial Guinea, where they would be charged and, if found guilty, face the death penalty.

Sean came to meet me on the farm. He lit a joint and lovingly caressed the M14 assault rifle he had brought with him.

"Look Peter, this is what we think. The Police Commissioner is focussing on everybody who has no connection with the businessmen who hired you. He has too much to lose by shining a light on them. His pocket money might dry up. We think his office has run people out to harass, but for the time being, it is probably better to stay out of sight."

I agreed and took a large gulp from the bottle of whisky. I beckoned him to pass me the M14 and fired some shots at plants about seventy-five metres from where we were sitting. Sean rolled another joint, smiled and said,

"Just like old times bud. We look after each other."

Sometime in the middle of May, Sean contacted me with what can only be described as the best news I had received for a while.

"You have slipped the noose, Peter. The Police Commissioner is still being patronised by those businessmen. He can't act on you without them being lit up, so we all agree you're free to resurface."

I got drunk that evening and drove to Johannesburg the next day. I was very happy to see civilisation again.

The first thing I did was to check the Hells Angels correspondence on my e-mail account. There was one from Hells Angels Nomads Brazil asking if I would be attending the upcoming Hells Angels World Meeting that was being held in Rio de Janeiro that year in June. I remember thinking, 'What the hell,' and e-mailed back, "Most certainly."

I phoned my dad and told him that I was home and, although he didn't say much, he sounded relieved. When I put the phone down, I sat in front of the television, put on the news and thought about how much stress my continual disappearances must add to my dad's already stressful life. Now, impending incarceration was on my to-do list, walking through international airports was the best test possible. I phoned Sean next and he told me to come and see him when I was ready.

"I'm at the armoury all day, bud."

Sean lived on a compound situated about twenty kilometres south of my house. I decided to go and see him as soon as I had watched most of the news channels, to see what the headline stories were. The only story I cared about had gone dead. I was happy there was no mention of Equatorial Guinea.

As I neared Sean's compound, I phoned him to let me in. He told me to use the VIP entrance. That was code that he was in the main house and for me to wait for him in the kitchen. When I signed in at the gate, I told the sentry on duty that I was carrying a sidearm on me and had an FN assault rifle on the back seat of the car, which I was returning to the colonel. Sean's security was a lot slicker than at the farm, I was told to park in front of the main house and go straight in. Sean was making two cups of cappuccino coffee when I walked in and was in his usual good mood.

I put the bag with the FN assault rifle in it on the table in the middle of the kitchen and sat down. Sean was a creature of habit and liked to sit at the stove where he could see out of both kitchen windows, with me sitting with my back against the wall in the corner. He gave me a cup of coffee and began,

"So our little black sheep has come back to the flock?"

I had always enjoyed Sean's company and this day was no different. I told him I was planning to attend Hells Angels World meeting being held this year in Rio de Janeiro.

"That Hells Angels shit in Europe was actually a bit more than some localised biker shit. Nobody will talk to me over the phone, so I need to go to Brazil, or it will look like I'm weaselling out of what I have already agreed to do. It might sound stupid to you, but I do need to go."

Sean picked up his two way radio.

"Wayne, can you bring in those papers for PC?"

He brought out a joint and, after some thought, he remarked,

"Well at least we know that the Portuguese is one Government that wasn't involved in the mess that you're in."

Wayne walked into the kitchen with a file of papers. Wayne was Sean's business partner. He was an ex-South African Special Forces operator and he hardly ever smiled.

"Nice to see you again Peter. I will have these papers ready for you before you leave."

The papers were applications to relicense all my weapons. The papers had been prepared so that I only had to sign and initial wherever Wayne pointed his bony fingers. When I finished, Wayne picked up all the paperwork and left, adding,

"I'll see you on the range when you are ready, bud."

I looked at Sean and he shrugged.

"Wayne is a stickler for the rules. Someone has to be."

We talked about the relicensing of my weapons and my proposed trip to Brazil. Then we went through photographs of the mercenaries who had been detained in Zimbabwe. I vaguely recognised a few faces, but hadn't anything to add to the very detailed files Sean already had. Next, Sean brought out two new photos. I recognised the first person immediately. It was Harry Carston. Harry was an operator trained at Five Special Forces in Phalaborwa.

"I know him. He's Andries's friend."

Sean looked at me and said,

"Exactly, but Harry has been working for Palto for the last few months."

He told me that Harry had given Simon Mann the alternative of securing the weapons in Zimbabwe, rather than the DRC.

"The Police Commissioner is smarter than he comes across. As soon as he realised his wallet and reputation were going to take a hit with this whole fiasco, he managed to find a way to come out looking like the saviour of African history, whilst keeping his friends out of it at the same time. Harry gave Simon Mann the new plan and, as they were jittery about you not wanting to fly to the Democratic Republic of Congo to make sure General Nkunda kept his word, they walked into a trap in Harare, bud."

I went cold. After catching my breath, I looked at Sean and said,

"But it was you that gave me the plan to tell the person at the other end of the phone number Simon Mann had given me that morning that I was unable to fly due to an injury."

It was the first time I had seen Sean look embarrassed.

"You know as well as I do that the lines get blurred at times," he replied. "Don't be so naïve. The Americans and the British found common ground with the Government of Equatorial Guinea and decided that the devil that they knew was the better option. The Spanish couldn't pull out without alerting everyone and the South African Police Commissioner needed a way out of embarrassing his friends, so you're in the clear."

Sean dismissed me by telling me I should go to the range as soon as I could and get the competency shoots out of the way. As I was walking out, he added,

"Take the FN with you. We are licensing it in your name as well. It's the first rifle I gave you all those years ago. It's yours."

Sean always insisted that firearms should only be broken in by one person. After that, anyone using them would be at the weapon's mercy. I was still processing what I had been told as I walked onto the range to jump through the hoops stipulated by the South African Firearms Registry to be competent to possess a newly licensed firearm.

Chapter 38

The Hells Angels World Meeting in Brazil was boring. When I returned to South Africa, I moved straight back into my house and attended the whorehouse on a nightly basis for the next week. Then, when I woke one morning in August, it all seemed like a nightmare from my past. There was a sound that can only be associated with military helicopters. My first thoughts were that I was dreaming and, although it is often said, that morning I was totally disorientated. It had been many years since I had heard military helicopters flying that low and at that speed over the suburbs of Johannesburg. They were ready to deploy.

It became even more bizarre as, by the time I had sat up in my bed, there was the sound of three Puma military helicopters hovering over my house. I looked out of the window and saw South African Special Forces soldiers abseiling from two of the Pumas into my back garden. To most people this would seem a strange sight, but to me it was something I had seen many times before. Someone important had pressed the button. As I heard them break open my front and back doors, I opened my rifle safe next to my bed and threw my weapons onto the bed. When they came through the gate that separated my bedroom from the rest of the house with a battering ram, I took off my shorts and lay naked on the floor with my arms outstretched. I was struck with the butt of a rifle on the back of my head and, as I didn't want to be hit again, I acted unconscious. My hands and feet were bound in military tie-downs and a canvas bag was put over my head. At this point a familiar voice shouted out,

"Time check!"

It was Andries and, as I didn't know whether to be shocked or angry, I was both at the same time. I was lifted and put onto the couch, three metres from my bed. I acted as though I was still unconscious. There was a sudden influx of personnel as the Special Forces handed my house over to the police units that had followed them in. Eventually the canvas bag was taken off my head and smelling salts were broken under my nose. It was time to act awake but the smelling salts actually brought out the pain in my head caused by the impact of the rifle butt on the base of my skull. A Maglight torch was shone into my eyes and all I remember thinking was, 'I hope that isn't attached to a weapon.' I had a search warrant shoved in my face, but all I could see with that amount of light in my eyes were black dots. I was then formally charged with the production of illegal arms, dealing in illegal arms, the production of narcotics, dealing in narcotics and under the Mercenary Act.

Two Special Forces policemen lifted me and threw me onto my bed. I lay there watching them ransack my bedroom. A group of detectives came into my bedroom. They told the heavily armed policemen to cut off my restraints and allow me to put some clothes on, as a female prosecutor was about to come in. After I had put on my shorts, Marion came in with a group of armed investigators and ordered everyone that wasn't in her team to leave us alone as she wanted to charge me formally.

"Sorry, Peter, we were only informed about this operation a few hours ago, but I fully intend getting to the bottom of it."

I looked at her concerned face and again realised how much she was outside her comfort zone. I asked for a cigarette and told her,

"Don't compromise any of us, as we both know the longer this goes on, the more mistakes will be made. There was no need for this party to have been thrown. If they had buzzed my gate, I would have let them in."

Marion shook her head and told me that an operation like this was something she had never heard of before.

"They have been waiting for you to come home, Peter. There have been arrests in Cape Town and Durban too. They even arrested Mark Thatcher yesterday evening on the same warrant as you."

She looked close to tears. As I put my cigarette out, all I could say was,

"Make sure I get to the police station alive."

I was taken to the local police station and locked in the largest cell. There were still some belongings of the previous occupants lying around, indicative that the cell had been emptied at a pace not usual in South African police stations. It was obvious our arrests that day were as much of a surprise to the police in the area as they had been for us.

Over the course of the next day, I went through South African Police profiling. This is basically a physical description and a record of any distinguishing marks or scars. I was re-fingerprinted. I was told I would be informed if anything came up at either national or international level. The following morning, I was taken from my cell, put in shackles and taken to the front entrance of the prison. When I arrived at court I was taken immediately in front of the magistrate. A young man heading a legal team told me Brett Kebble had arranged for them to represent me. He was very rude in court as he tore into the case against me. All the firearms that had been found in the house were legally licensed under the South African Firearms Act. The traces of narcotics were consistent with any house that had been the scene of a party for more than three days. He ended by saying,

"The Mercenary Act is still at the committee stage in Parliament and although we expect the accused to be re-charged under the Foreign Military Assistance Act, until we receive any notification of this, our client must be given bail and re-arrested under a different warrant at a later stage."

The prosecution did not object and the magistrate reluctantly granted bail of R10,000. My new legal team then demanded that I be kept in the court holding cells, as they had been given the funds to pay for the bail immediately and had arranged for my transport from the court. I was released that afternoon and received a phone call from Bob telling me to report to his office the next day.

Marion was in Bob's office as I was ushered in. I sat next to her and the meeting began without pleasantries. Marion began with a brief outline.

"Peter, Nick du Toit has made a full confession to the Equatorial Guinea Government, which included his role in the procurement of weapons from an arms dealer in Harare. Although there isn't a lawyer in the world who won't believe his confession was made under duress, it will still count. You are cleared from any involvement in the planning of the *coup* for the time being, but you broke international law by procuring weapons in the Democratic Republic of Congo. The United Nations is baying for blood, but for the time being, we need to steer you through the minefield here at home."

I sat back and closed my eyes. She continued,

"Our biggest problem is the office of the South African Police Commissioner. We have reason to believe that Jacob Selebi was fully aware of the planned *coup* attempt but it's easier to suspect, than to prove. As soon as the plug was pulled on the whole operation, his office went into action. Simon Mann was arrested at Harare International Airport with two members of the National Police Commissioner's Palto hit squad, but we're not focussing on that right now."

Marion stopped and, as she poured herself another cup of coffee, I felt as though I was about to burst with frustration. She continued,

"We have it on good authority that the National Police Commissioner's office not only knew about the plan to send you to the Democratic Republic of Congo, but was behind its planning."

"Why?"

"We believe you ticked all the boxes. You knew someone who could supply a shopping list of weapons in the Democratic Republic of Congo and it completed the mercenary cover story. You weren't co-operating with his friends in South Africa anymore and they needed you to continue flying all over Africa delivering contracts for them. More importantly, the Commissioner needed to make some arrests in South Africa to keep up appearances at home. So, you were the round peg that fitted perfectly into the round hole."

I let it all sink in. Then I asked,

"So I'm being driven by many differing interests?"

Marion shook her head and replied,

"No. It's all about the National Police Commissioner's office looking competent and his friends need to manipulate your co-operation in the future."

I needed a drink. As I walked over to the liquor cabinet, Bob spoke for the first time,

"I'll have one too, Peter."

It was an order. As I drank the whisky, I felt betrayed. There had to be someone more important than me to arrest in South Africa. Marion beat me to it.

"The day we arrested you, I told you that Mark Thatcher had been arrested the previous afternoon under the Mercenary Act. That's the real publicity here and you're not that important for the National Police Commissioner's brownie points. The National Prosecuting Authority has secured a witness who has been given full indemnity from prosecution in return for full and truthful testimony. He has turned himself in and he can prove that he was paid to procure a helicopter with funds from Mark Thatcher. We have proof of bank transfers into this accomplice's account. He sounds like a very reliable witness, so Mark Thatcher is our main target for the time being. For you, it's all about being beholden to the National Police Commissioner's friends. Those weapons were never handed over in the Democratic Republic of Congo, but procuring them is something we will have to deal with at a later stage."

The decision was that I should go back to the farm. I was not to associate with Brett Kebble until further notice. Marion ended the meeting by saying,

"We know that Brett Kebble paid for your lawyers, Peter, but we are in a very grey area and will take it from here."

As I was leaving the office, Bob told me to listen to what Andries had to say before I judged him.

"Be cool up there with him, Peter. I know you brought him in. We want to remain as a team."

When I arrived at the farm later that day, Andries met me at the front door. I said,

"I hope you're going to tell me the reason for leading an assault on my house."

Andries opened a bottle of whisky and, after pouring us both a stiff drink, he sat down and delivered his version of the raid on my house.

"That fucker from the Air Ambulance Company turned himself in to the National Prosecuting Authority and made a deal that led to the arrest of Mark Thatcher. The National Police Commissioner was totally pissed off that his office had not been the first agency to make an arrest in South Africa over this case and he gave his Palto squad the green light to hit you. They were given orders to shoot first and ask questions afterwards."

He finished his whisky and, getting up to pour another one, he said,

"They were going to execute you, Peter, under the pretence that you had resisted arrest."

I reflected on that and asked,

"So how did the army get involved?"

It was the first time he smiled. He shook his head.

"You actually got lucky, Peter. Bob has a better working relationship with the Minister of Safety and Security than the National Police Commissioner. Bob demanded that the South African Defence Force Special Forces should lead the assault on your house that morning, so I was seconded to the unit to lead it into your house and to make sure you lived through the whole thing."

After a while, I smiled and said,

"Your guys have got slow. I could have baked a cake in the time it took you to deploy from those choppers."

Andries laughed.

"The captain in charge was new to an urban assault, so we left him outside. Peter, when we evacuated the area, I made the police units sign for you. You were bagged and tagged so they couldn't kill you."

We finished off the afternoon with a tour of his armoury. Andries proudly displayed a brand new M14 assault rifle. He had added a very large night vision telescopic sight to the railings on its top.

I stayed at the farm for the following week, before returning to Johannesburg for my court appearance. When I arrived there was an agent from Bob's office waiting for me. I was hurried to the Supreme Court, where I was put before a judge in chambers. My bail was extended until further notice and I was told I was not to leave the South Africa until my trial had run its course. I was then driven to the Department of Housing to see Bob and Marion. Marion looked as though she had aged ten years and was very distressed.

"Now that we have your bail extended, we can put this whole thing to bed, Peter. The National Police Commissioner's office are going to take full credit for infiltrating the group of mercenaries on the plane and Mark Thatcher is going to receive a slap on the wrist. The National Prosecuting Authority wants a statement from you, giving details of your involvement, but I'm resisting that as we have a high profile guilty plea and everyone is going to come out smelling like roses."

At this point, Bob joined the conversation.

"You are going to have to go to ground for the next few weeks while this shit pans out, Peter."

On 13 January 2005, Sir Mark Thatcher left South Africa after pleading guilty to involvement in the *coup* plot in Equatorial Guinea. He was fined about US$560,000 and given a four-year suspended sentence. Although he denied all knowledge of the *coup*, he had agreed to a plea bargain and to cooperate with investigators in South Africa. Mark Thatcher had admitted breaking the anti-mercenary legislation in South Africa by providing the finance for the helicopter to be used in the *coup*.

Sean came to my house to celebrate. He lit a joint and then let the hammer fall.

"Okay. The Police Commissioner's office is satisfied that it has made its point in this whole mess. There will be no further prosecutions, as our president is about to have a summit in Equatorial Guinea in the coming weeks with Mugabe

(President of Zimbabwe) and Obiang (President of Equatorial Guinea). The gravy train wins again, bud. You need to stay away from Pretoria for a while, as Marion has got it into her head that she's going after the National Police Commissioner's office. They want you to run a restaurant for them in the northern suburbs of Johannesburg and reel in Brett Kebble and his associates."

I thought about it for a while and asked,

"What do you think?"

Sean was very calm as he handed me the joint and answered,

"You owe her, bud, so you have no choice. Bob is with Marion in this, so it seems the South African Military Intelligence is going to side with the National Prosecuting Authority against the office of the National Police Commissioner."

I knew he was right. I had no choice. I opened a bottle of whisky.

"When do I start?"

Sean smiled.

"As soon as we give you back your weapons."

On 1 March 2005, my weapons were returned to my house, together with every round of ammunition and every holster. I reported for duty as the manager of a very well-known fish restaurant in the shopping centre that used to be the first rave club. Later that week, I phoned Brett Kebble and arranged with his personal assistant for him to eat at the restaurant. Brett Kebble arrived with his new head of security, Clint Nassif. Clint Nassif had been a prospect for Hells Angels South Africa Nomads and I knew him slightly. As they were leaving the restaurant that night, Brett turned to me and said,

"Peter, I need to speak to you. Can you come see me at my house tomorrow night?"

He looked terrible. I felt a little concerned, but now I was back on my master's clock. I told him,

"Only me and you this time. None of your security."

He nodded in agreement and left a huge tip for the staff.

I met Brett Kebble the following evening. So far as I could tell, he was alone in the house. We sat in his kitchen while he prepared two steaks in red wine sauce. Eventually, he opened up.

"Peter, everything is starting to go bad and I'm a little scared. The National Police Commissioner, Jacob Selebi, is about to have a turf war with the National Prosecuting Authority and I'm in it up to my neck. There are some very dangerous people involved in this fight and I don't want my family brought into it."

I asked him what he thought I could do about it and he went silent. After he had plated the steaks, we went to eat them outside. Although it was not a warm night on the South African Highveld, he had no jacket on and seemed very troubled. We ate in silence. When he eventually spoke, he asked,

"Can you protect me Peter?"

After a pause, I answered,

"I don't know Brett. The nest of vipers you have in your camp has already tried to kill me once. What's in it for me?"

Again, we sat in silence as he thought about his next line of conversation. I had never seen him so down. Eventually he spoke.

"I know that you have a connection with South African Military Intelligence, as I did the first time I met you in Luanda." I stayed quiet and he continued, "There's nothing secret in my world anymore and I'm not looking forward to the prospect of spending any time in a South African prison."

When I left him that evening he shook my hand and said,

"Please help me Peter, I'm in deep trouble."

I phoned Bob. As usual, he was at his office and told me to come and see him. When I did and told Bob that Brett Kebble was looking for some kind of deal with the State, Bob shook his head.

"Marion won't go for it. She intends prosecuting him to get him to give evidence against his friend, Glenn Agliotti. She then wants to prosecute Glenn Agliotti so he gives evidence against his friend, Jacob Selebi, the National Police

Commissioner. You know Peter, the only way to get out of your involvement in all this shit, is to help her finish her mission."

The manipulation had begun again. I went home and was woken the following morning by the sound of my landline telephone. It was Marion. She told me she would meet me for lunch at the restaurant I managed. I went in early and the manager, who was actually doing the job I was supposed to do, had everything running smoothly. I signed off a few invoices and waited for Marion to arrive.

She was happy to see me. She ordered a coffee, looked at me and said,

"I need you to give me the same report on Brett Kebble you gave Bob."

I did my best to repeat exactly what I had told Bob the previous night. We ordered a light lunch and she started to speak.

"Your friend Brett Kebble has committed huge commercial fraud over the last few years and he will eventually be charged by my office for it. When we offer him a deal in return for a guilty plea, he will have to give evidence against his gangster friends and they will help me prosecute the office of the National Police Commissioner."

I asked,

"What do you want me to do? He will want an answer, Marion."

She replied, looking as fierce as I had ever seen her.

"Let him stew. He's been a naughty boy and his boards are shortly to start voting for his resignation. He can come to us from a position of weakness and not before."

I couldn't help thinking how she was beginning to fit the profile of her job description. I was glad she was on my side, and asked,

"What do I do next?"

"As usual Peter, you have managed to fast-track your part of the operation. Now ignore him until the rest of it catches up. We didn't expect him to reach for a lifeline quite this soon. Run this restaurant for me and make friends with anyone of interest to us."

I nodded and wondered if it really was a step up from the whorehouse down the road.

Chapter 39

I spent most of my time at the restaurant making friends with anyone who might be of interest to Marion. Mostly there was very little intelligence, but I wrote her reports anyway. I mostly filed, "Nothing to report," and took the absence of communication from Bob's office to mean there was no bad news. I checked my messages and there was a continuous stream from Brett Kebble. One afternoon, I phoned Marion. She told me to come into her offices in Pretoria. Her tone was not happy. When I arrived, Marion told me she was ready to start the prosecution of Brett Kebble and it was time to bring him in to make a deal with the National Prosecuting Authority. I told her that Brett Kebble had been leaving messages on my cell phone almost daily. She answered in a matter of fact tone of voice,

"Kebble has been put in a corner. Go and see him."

I phoned Brett Kebble that evening and was put through to him almost immediately by his personal assistant. He told me he was in Cape Town with his family, but if I could meet him the following evening, he would fly to Johannesburg. The next day, when I walked into his house, he looked terrible. His head of security, Clint Nassif, was hovering around. I let Brett Kebble do most of the talking and said very little. Eventually Brett asked me why I was being so reserved. I told him that if he wanted to talk to me, it would have to be in private. Clint Nassif got upset and there was a brief argument between us. Clint put a handgun in my face but wasn't prepared to squeeze the trigger, so it turned into a stalemate. When Clint turned his back on me, I hit him with a pot that was on the stove and he dropped like a stone. The whole situation was out of control. I shouted at Brett,

"The next time someone threatens me with a gun, I'm going to shoot him."

One of the house staff came running into the kitchen and started to tend to the wound on the back of Clint Nassif's head.

There was blood everywhere and I grabbed the butler and took him to my car parked outside the front door. I called out,

"Brett, when you let me out, you can have him back. If you want my help you can meet me tomorrow at my restaurant for lunch."

I was allowed to leave.

The following day, I was seated in the corner of my restaurant with my AK-47 on my lap, when Brett Kebble walked in on his own and sat at my table. He looked as though he was at death's door and hadn't slept the night before. I told him I was going to take him to Pretoria for a meeting. He nodded and replied,

"Just keep me safe."

I put the AK-47 on the table and answered,

"That's the plan."

That afternoon, I drove Brett Kebble to Marion's office, where he entered into a section 204 agreement with the Directorate of Special Operations, acting for the office of the South African National Prosecuting Authority. The agreement made him exempt from prosecution for every count of fraud pending against him, in return for a full and truthful testimony against his friend Glenn Agliotti and Jacob Selebi, the South African National Police Commissioner and, by then, President of Interpol.

Brett Kebble was offered a safe house, which he declined, telling Marion he would fly down to Cape Town and stay there until further notice. I dropped him off at his car parked outside the restaurant and watched him drive off. Although I felt sorry for him, I steadied myself by remembering the beating I had taken in the whorehouse on the orders of his friends.

Later the same evening, 27 September 2005, Brett Kebble was found shot dead in his car near a bridge over the M1 motorway in Abbotsford, Johannesburg, supposedly on his way to dinner with a business associate. I knew I could have kept him alive if I had paid more attention to what was going on around him, but I'll never know for sure. I should never have left Brett Kebble alone that night, but I did.

Sean phoned me the following morning. He was brief.

"Batten down the hatches, bud. I'll be there as soon as I can."

When he arrived, we went into my kitchen and made a late breakfast. We sat down and ate as Sean gave me the bad news.

"We think that both you and Marion are next. Bob wants you on our upcoming tour into Africa this year. Marion is contemplating taking early retirement as her legal strategy just got murdered at the first post."

I knew Sean was referring to an intelligence-led tour though Africa, masquerading as a tourist adventure. I had been on one before and knew what was expected of me. I asked Sean what was my next move. He told me I was to move in with his team in Cape Town until we were ready to leave in a couple of weeks.

The following morning, I moved to Simonstown in the Western Cape. I was logged into the naval base and surrendered my personal weapons. I was issued with a Heckler and Koch .40 calibre side arm and a M14 assault rifle. I didn't do much for the next couple of weeks and hardly socialised or watched television. The Kebble murder was never very far from the front pages of the newspapers. It was all hard to take in. I read a few books from the civil library near the base and tried not to think about what was happening in Johannesburg. I was resigned to the fact that I was going to be part of a very boring South African Military intelligence operation through Africa, disguised as a tour for wealthy adrenalin junkies from Europe.

The clients had already started to arrive and were booked into a five-star hotel on the waterfront. I was told I was expected to meet them and introduce myself. When I arrived at the hotel, I was surprised by how enthusiastic everyone was to be going on a very long road tour from one end of Africa to the other. They all seemed very pleasant and I began to relax.

When Sean arrived, things accelerated. When every client had arrived, we set off north. Two motorcycles at the point of the convoy would be followed by the Land Cruisers with the trucks bringing up the rear. I was bored before we had even started but applied myself to the task at hand. We meandered to a small railway town called Matjiesfontein. Matjiesfontein is a strange but quaint place situated in the Karoo desert. It wouldn't exist without the railway. My body was happy to be stopping after such a short distance. I kept pretty much to myself until we eventually crossed into Mozambique and spent the night in the capital, Maputo. That evening things changed. Sean came into my room and handed me my sidearm and M14 assault rifle.

"You and I are going into Zimbabwe, bud," was all he said.

We left early the next morning with rally stickers on our vehicles and around lunchtime we made camp just east of the Zimbabwean border. The pace we had ridden and the state of the roads had finally taken its toll on me. I fell asleep almost as soon as I had erected my tent.

As I was preparing to go to bed, Sean told me in a matter of fact way,

"You are coming to Harare with me tomorrow afternoon. Bob is going to be at the South African Embassy there and he wants to talk to you."

I looked at him and replied,

"Some way to break the news, bud, but you're in charge."

The next day Sean and I drove into Harare and we had lunch with Bob at the South African Embassy. Bob confirmed that Marion was contemplating taking early retirement from the South African National Prosecuting Authority and all deals that she had entered into were now off.

While we were having dessert, Bob brought the subject up again.

"Marion is pulling your file Peter, so walk away."

I nodded and was happy to go to sleep that night in a newly washed bed of linen in the South African Embassy staff quarters.

The following day we drove very fast back into Northern Mozambique and then into Malawi. It took another day to cross the border into Tanzania. We slept on the roofs of the Land Cruisers and my body started to loosen up. When we reached Dar es Salaam on the east coast of Tanzania, we stopped, booked into the Movanpick Royal Palm Hotel and waited for the convoy to catch up.

When it did, we slowly meandered north, visiting tourist sites along the route to Cairo. We looked more like tourists than the clients. We eventually reached Cairo in early December 2005 and booked into the Four Seasons Hotel. I took a deep breath, ordered an expensive bottle of whisky and cut myself off from the rest of the convoy personnel.

I was woken just before dawn by Sean. He looked agitated and poured himself a drink from what was left of my unfinished bottle. He said,

"Get dressed, bud. You're on me this morning."

My head was pounding and I must have put on the same clothes I had been wearing when I had gone to bed. At about 06h00, Sean and I drove to the South African Embassy and were ushered into an office on the ground floor. Bob was waiting for us and came straight to the point. He told us that on 6 December, Jacob Zuma, the vice president of South Africa, had been arrested for raping a family friend at his home in Forest Town in Johannesburg. Bob said very little else. He finished with,

"You two are to fly home with me this afternoon as you are the only white people I trust right now. This is an attempt to overthrow our government and everything else is on hold."

We both armed ourselves and, later the same day, we flew out of Cairo on a private jet to Lanseria Airport north west of Johannesburg. Bob said very little to anyone on that flight. A large security detail was waiting for us at the airport. Bob was distracted and I went with the flow. When we left the plane, Sean took over. I don't think I had ever been as proud of Sean as I was that day. He shouted,

"Who's in charge?"

An ANC security guard put up his hand and Sean shouted at him,

"You will be my point until we get some clarity."

Sean directed me to Bob's car. Although I don't know too much about the detail of what happened during the following week, we kept moving and I lived in clothes that were bought from shops in the different cities I visited with Bob. I usually waited outside in the vehicle, while Bob had meetings at what seemed like an endless tour of South Africa. On the way back to Johannesburg from Durban, I moved my rifle to the back of the car and woke Bob. He reached for his flask of coffee and said,

"The prosecutors have been allowed way too much latitude. We have put up with them in the interests of public opinion, but as Marion may soon be leaving office, from now on, we shall only be spectators. They're a bunch of speculators, but we'll win this one."

I didn't care too much at that point and, that evening, I was happy to be allowed to go home.

The next day Sean came to see me.

"Peter, things have changed here. It's all happening much faster than design. You have to make a choice. Bob wants you and me to become members of the African National Congress. Only party members are in any circle of trust these days."

I looked at him and asked,

"What do you think?"

There was a pause before Sean gave me a brief rundown.

"The South African Civil Service is pretty much still run by the same faces as the day when Nelson Mandela took over in 1994."

I'll never forget his laugh when he told me in a matter of fact way,

"Bob and I think some of them are dead but as long as the stamp from their offices keeps touching the relevant paperwork, they are still occupying the same distraction."

I thought about it for a while and asked,

"What are you going to do?"

I had never seen Sean hesitate for so long before answering,

"I'm going to gamble on Bob getting it right, but if you come along there is going to be a bun fight to wrestle the power from the old guard. They won't give it up without a fight."

I think it took me more by surprise that I was having this conversation, than I was with its content.

"I'm in, bud," was all I said.

After a brief silence, Sean finished the conversation by saying,

"You will have to dissociate from the Hells Angels eventually."

We eventually lit a joint and, after some thought, I spoke.

"We'll take as it comes. I hope Bob has the balls for this."

The author's ANC membership card

Chapter 40

Together with Sean, in an obscure office in Cape Town I joined the ANC. The irony wasn't lost on me. I was nearly forty and hadn't even voted in an election, either at local or national level. I was issued with a temporary membership card of a political party that had struggled and had its members murdered for the right to vote. When Sean and I were driving back to our hotel, Sean looked at me and said,

"Welcome to the party, comrade."

I laughed.

"Fuck off, bud. You're as much of a hypocrite as I am, carrying this card."

Bob had moved his office to a building called Compensation House. He was now a brigadier general and on the record as working for the Department of Labour. Security was very tight at the entrance and there were no pleasantries. Everyone in the foyer seemed very suspicious. Bob's office was situated on the fourth floor at the end of the building, as far away as possible from the lift. After I had logged-in my handgun, I was escorted into the lift by two security guards and, when the lift doors opened, I was tag-teamed to two much more aggressive security guards waiting for me.

Almost as soon as I walked into his new office, Bob issued me with a permanent membership card. I looked at it and laughed.

"There is no expiry date on this card."

Bob was in a serious mood.

"That's because you are now a VIP member of the party. There's no off button. You infiltrated us at university, shot us in Angola and sold us weapons before the election in 1994 and have been nothing but a pain in the arse ever since. At least we can trust you to be diverse." Bob smiled and said, "Pour yourself a drink. This will take a while."

I did and spent most of that morning being briefed as to how the South African Civil Service worked. The ANC had inherited a minefield of problems, to say the least.

"There is no way to fire these people without a union problem, an expensive court case and an even more expensive settlement. We have to wait for them to die or become old enough to retire. It seems that nearly all of the political appointments we have put in place over the past twelve years have been contaminated by bad procedure."

I got up and poured myself another drink. This was going to be a long day. I remember thinking, 'What the fuck have I signed up for?' The basic plan Bob's office had in mind was, firstly to observe the problems in motion, and then begin to reverse them in the South African Civil Service.

"We are going to press their buttons at every point and see where it lights up in the civil service machine. Then we are going to do it again and again and see if there's a pattern."

I took it all in and asked,

"Where do I come in?"

"You are at the coal face of what we term the South African Police Services' nightmare."

I looked at him.

"That's huge. Where do I start?"

Because I had such a long and documented criminal history, it had been decided I would make public I was a member of the ANC and see exactly what came my way. It's what academics call "a mutually hurting stalemate". The South African Policing Union (SAPU) had been established in November 1993, only a few months before the first truly democratic elections in South Africa. The Union was high on Bob's agenda to enforce change and I was now to be thrown to these wolves. I had become used to being on the shit end of the stick. I said,

"Yes. Let's do it."

When I left Bob's office, I was given a credit card and resigned myself to go to work.

The whole operation began on 1 April 2006, April Fool's Day. The irony wasn't lost on me and I began by visiting Hells Angel clubhouses around the country. At every clubhouse I visited, I flashed my new political identity and was surprised by the negativity that resulted. Bob had a point and the response didn't take long. I was arrested outside the Hells Angels clubhouse in Cape Town and held without charge. I was released by the weekend, but then I was stopped and re-arrested on my drive back to Johannesburg. I was held and transported to Johannesburg by the South African Police Services for a bail hearing on my outstanding charge of possession of narcotics. Bail was contested by the investigating officer and I was taken to Leeuhoff Maximum Security Prison in Vereeniging, some fifty kilometres south of Johannesburg. The following day I was taken back to the court for another bail hearing and, with no policemen in attendance, the prosecution didn't resist my application and I was released on a bail of R100. I left the courthouse thinking, 'If that doesn't get someone's back up, nothing will.'

I went to see Sean. He laughed when I told him what had happened. He told me that, when he had flashed his ANC ID at the previous meeting of the Legion, a government funded military veterans' association, he had been visited by the South African Police Services the very next day. Sean gave me a cappuccino and shook his head.

"I guess we now know what it feels like to be black."

I remember thinking that it wasn't possible for the plan to have been so successful in such a short space of time. I asked Sean what had happened and he told me,

"The bomb squad sent a senior superintendent with a warrant to search my armoury."

Sean laughed as he recounted how he had led the guy past three deactivated pieces of ordinance he had brought back from Angola, before there was a reaction.

"He told me I needed a permit and I told him to give me the application papers. Looks like we both are on some police shit-list this time, Peter. Take care with this one."

I smoked a joint with Sean in his kitchen and he seemed happy with his situation. He said,

"The fucking office that runs the bomb squad in Pretoria has had the same general in charge for so long, it's gonna take a seismic event to get rid of him. Personally, I think he died years ago and was embalmed in the seat behind his desk, but I'm gonna find out one way or another."

The only thing I could think of saying was,

"Yeah. You already said."

Then, after some thought, I asked,

"Do you believe that Bob is going to be able to pull this off?"

Sean lit another joint and, after a short silence, he replied,

"You'd better hope so, bud. If the South African Police Services get a warrant for an inspection at a military installation, we're all in trouble. One way or another, that office is going to bring me those papers and I'm going to demand clarification at the highest level."

The whole thing was insane. I wondered how many people were flashing ID cards denoting they had joined the ruling political party of the South African Government, who were then immediately harassed by the South African Police Services. It only then occurred to me, how many departments of the South African Civil Service must have been switched on at the beginning of the month. I developed a massive headache and went home. This was going to be a very long war and much dirtier than anything I had participated in before. In a way, it was a *coup d'état* to stop a *coup d'état*.

In June 2006, just before my fortieth birthday, I was called in to see Bob. His first words were,

"We're going to have to let this bullshit court case of yours run its natural course of events. It's just an experiment for both sides."

I looked at him and replied,

"But I'm the piggy in the middle."

Bob smiled.

"There's no real evidence you're being persecuted for being a member of the African National Congress. There are senior members of Military Intelligence who believe the immediate harassment that was put on you after you joined the political party could be explained by old grudges you accumulated in one of your many fights on the nightclub scene. Your trial date for the narcotics charges has been set for the middle of September."

When I arrived home, I called a Hells Angel meeting and, the following evening, I was back in my comfort zone. Hells Angels, prostitutes, drugs and alcohol made my problems seem so far away. At one point during the party, I was approached by an officer of a subordinate motorcycle club and told, tongue in cheek, that his girlfriend would leave him and marry me for my British passport. I asked him to point his girlfriend out and when he did, I saw one of the most attractive girls I had seen for a long time playing pool. She was bent over the table and looked like a child about to become a woman.

"What does she do?"

He looked at me as though I was trying to catch him out and answered,

"She's a hooker."

I looked over at a friend, Billy, who shrugged. I said,

"If she wants to marry me for my passport, scrub her up and send her to my tent because I'm going to have to consummate the marriage."

Early the next morning as I staggered to my bed, this little girl, who was eighteen, was in my shower and eventually crawled into bed with me. Like the girl I met in 2002, her working name was Baby and she moved in with me that night.

Sometime during that period, the next task came along. Sean let himself into my house and into my bedroom. I was still in bed.

"You're up again, Hells Angel."

Baby came out of the bathroom. After one look at her, Sean added,

"I guess we have a keeper here."

I told Baby to go downstairs and make a pot of coffee.

Sean sat down on my bed and said

"You can't keep her, Peter. Your case is too sensitive."

I rolled over in bed and replied,

"I'm off. Ask Bob."

Sean shook his head and replied,

"No. You've been activated and she can't stay."

I got angry with his matter of fact, cavalier attitude towards my life.

"Fuck you all. I have a bullshit court case coming up and now I'm being told who I'm allowed to be with?"

Sean shook his head again and looked me straight in the face.

"I'm not in Africa this year because of the shit that is going on, so suck it up. It's not ideal for any of us."

Having that conversation made me feel caged. I asked,

"There must be a way around this. She makes me happy."

Sean replied,

"Make her one of your agents, or get rid of her."

The following afternoon, I registered Baby as a South African Military Intelligence agent at Compensation House. For the first time since Rob had driven his car off the highway and ended up in a coma, I had a partner. Baby was now on the books. She did a brief course in military training and, after she was vetted, came back to me as an agent with a spanking new Military Intelligence credit card. The first thing she used it for was to book me into a five-star hotel for a belated Christmas. The South African military machine had made her awake during the time she was away and I truly felt content in her company during our time at the hotel.

During our last supper at the hotel, she said,

"All right, Colonel. Where to now?"

I downed my drink and replied,

"We are going on a fishing expedition, girl. Welcome to my world."

Baby didn't last a week on her new game. I was chopping a line of cocaine in my car when I heard the shot that killed her. Baby had walked into a restaurant robbery that was in progression. She was shot in the chest by a Vector assault rifle .223 as she was drawing her weapon. I remember seeing her dead body as I ran past it and fired at the man who had shot her. I hit him once high and right in the shoulder and then again in the chest. As I was standing on his throat to make sure he was dead, a few shots missed me as his associates ran into the darkness.

When the police arrived at the scene, the patrons who had been traumatised by the event were the first people they ran into, so there was no interaction between myself and the South African Police Services. I had managed to lose a partner before we had even begun to work together. She had been stupid enough to get herself involved in something that had nothing to do with us and had died violently as a result. I was so stoned on cocaine that I will never know if the outcome might have been different had we been together that night. I have successfully repressed all memories of Baby since that incident and still feel very sad that I dealt with it that way. I don't even remember her real name.

I wasn't charged with the shooting of her killer, but my weapon was taken from me for ballistic tests. I signed a receipt for the weapon to the first police officer at the scene, went to my car and armed myself with my backup weapon. I returned to the restaurant in a very dark mood and things became worse. When I walked in, I was applauded by the restaurant staff for killing someone. I went straight into the kitchen and forced myself to throw up.

I drove to Pretoria that night and it wasn't a surprise to find Bob in his heavily guarded office. I walked in and, without greeting Bob, poured a stiff whisky from his drinks cabinet.

Bob spoke first,

"Peter, I've heard what happened. I'm sorry."

I was so angry that I nearly choked on my opening sentence.

"She was supposed to be trained, not taught to be confidently stupid."

Bob got up and poured himself a whisky.

"None of our instructors would join the party Peter, so we had to let them go. I guess we're now a product of the hole in the machine."

Thinking about all the no-smoking signs all over the building, I lit a cigarette and said,

"She was only a child."

Bob nodded.

"Like all South Africans, we are living in a very dangerous environment, Peter."

I had to get my anger out.

"You're using cops to train your agents, because for some reason she didn't take cover. She drew her weapon and she was slow."

Bob whispered,

"The lines are blurred, Peter."

I felt it was time to make my point.

"Why didn't Andries train her?"

Bob hung his head.

"Andries has been let go. He refused to join the party."

It all made sense. Anyone new was going to be police-trained. They would invariably try to intervene in any crime that was taking place and their first instinct would be to draw a weapon and shoot.

"Well," I said, "I won't be bringing in any more new recruits."

About a month later, I had my next court appearance on the possession charges. There was a new police officer who appeared and he brought a new arrest warrant in front of the court. I was further charged for the possession of the unlicensed weapon that had been taken from me at the scene of Baby's killing. The fact was, I had been handed back the weapon with an all clear, but it was put to the court that I had been committing crime whilst out on bail. I will never forget the magistrate's words.

"Take the accused to the cells, but I want to see this warrant and the police officer who is leading this new charge, together with the prosecutor, in my chambers right now."

My lawyer came down to the cells and asked me what he should know about the weapon. I couldn't believe it and told him,

"I shot someone and killed him that night and I'm being charged with possession of an unlicensed firearm that was booked into a South African Police register and subsequently returned to me by an order from the Police Headquarters in Pretoria."

When I was taken back in front of the magistrate, he ruled I had not breached my initial bail conditions, as the charges were different. Then he added,

"Everyone involved with these cases must be prepared to come to trial by the end of September of this year or I'm throwing it out of court."

I was released on bail of R500 on the weapons charges and went home. Bob phoned me and told me to come in later that afternoon. When I got into Bob's office, he came straight to the point.

"The general who gave you back those weapons is very unhappy. So am I. A Police Intelligence captain is questioning his orders to give your weapon back to you. Now, we have another police general on our side and another police unit in our sights."

I waited for his next sentence, as I knew something unexpected was coming. He handed Baby's weapon to me.

"Take that girl's weapon to Sean and book it into his armoury. It's technically illegal in your possession."

The next morning, I took Baby's weapon to be logged into Sean's register at his armoury.

Chapter 41

I went home and called a Hells Angel party for the following evening. In fact, the party started early the next morning. We had wine, women and song. At some stage, my road captain came to me and said,

"We're going on a run up the Northern Province this weekend."

He held my attention.

"The road to hell? Count me in, bro. Who do we know to get my Harley working?"

He smiled and said,

"Leave it to me."

There were over thirty Hells Angels, including four prospects, who rode out of Johannesburg that Friday afternoon. I instructed one of the prospects to drive the support vehicle as close to me as possible.

"I'll be riding at the back of the pack and I want you close by me."

I put my new weapons into his vehicle and then started my Harley Davidson for the first time in a very long time. We rode fast out of the city and even faster as we came into more rural areas. When we stopped for lunch, a fight broke out between the Hells Angels members and some of the locals in the town. I was sitting at a table and didn't get involved. It was all drunken stupidity and I wanted no part of it.

We eventually reached the rally site just outside the town of Hoedspruit. I phoned Andries as I was close to the farm. He told me he had moved off the farm and taken early retirement. He said,

"I need to show you something."

I sighed.

"Where do you want to meet?"

Andries asked me where I was and arranged to meet me in an hour. I took the prospects' car and made my way into town. Andries was right on time. When he sat at my table, he explained that his family had been strongly against him joining the ANC and he had decided to do free-lance work for local security companies instead.

"I can't have an angry wife and an angry father and an angry brother all at the same time, Peter. It was best to walk away."

After small talk I asked him,

"What do you have for me?"

Andries reached into his bag and put about a hundred photographs on the table in front of me. They were pictures of men wearing biker colours and I couldn't believe what I was seeing. They were members of Bandidos MC. The Bandidos Motorcycle Club was from Denmark. It had been in a violent gang war with the Hells Angels that had begun in 1994 and had continued until 1997 in many parts of Scandinavia.

"Why were these photos taken?"

Andries shrugged.

"Special Forces were based in the area and they photograph every new uniform that appears here."

As I took this information in, I knew there was going to be bad news.

"Can you get me the behavioural pattern on these uniforms?"

Andries was nonchalant.

"Of course."

I finished my meal and said,

"Fuck!"

That Sunday evening, I slashed the back tyre of my Harley Davidson and put it on one of the support trailers to be taken back to Johannesburg. I commandeered one of the support vehicles and bid my Hells Angel brothers goodbye.

As I was leaving, I said,

"Get an officers meeting organised for this Friday night. Every charter is to send an officer and the minimum requirement is vice president."

I went to Andries' house in Phalabora. Andries gave me a photo-copy of the file that linked the behavioural patterns to the photos he had shown me a couple of days before. It was way worse than I could ever have imagined. Not only were the Bandido's Motorcycle Club in South Africa, but they had bought huge tracks of land and were involved in most of the labour intensive industries in the area.

Andries brought me a cup of coffee and said,

"I know, bud. I've read it. Your guys had better pitch a tent here before it's too late."

I drank the cup of coffee with him and said,

"I've got to leave early in the morning, thank you."

Andries shrugged.

"You know that you can't start shooting them, Peter. They've been here for a while and have been paying off the local authorities since they arrived. They obviously feel confident enough to expose themselves."

I knew he was right.

"Will you help me?"

Andries paused for just long enough to let me know how bad the situation was.

"Get an authorised operation going here and I'll help you make contact with them."

I went to see Bob. After he had read the file and studied the photos, he looked at me.

"So your biker friends have some competition in South Africa, but it has nothing to do with me."

I was angry.

"Yeah. You're right it has nothing to do with you, but this time it has everything to do with me."

Bob poured me a whisky.

"What do you want from me, Peter?"

I finished my whisky.

"I need to go to Copenhagen without any Interpol shit."

Bob was not put off.

"Go downstairs and get something to eat in the cafeteria and come back in an hour'

An hour later, I was back with Bob.

"We have issued you with a temporary passport. You're being sent to the South African Embassy in Copenhagen for a week."

Bob was truly a friend. I couldn't believe he'd come through with this much weight. As I was leaving, he added,

"Keep it clean over there, as you are representing this office."

I smiled.

"I know my duty, Director. Thank you."

Bob smiled back.

"I like you, Peter, but you're willing to risk anything at any time because you don't know enough to be afraid. I don't have that luxury."

That Friday night, we held a meeting of Hells Angels South Africa officers. I showed them photos. The hostility was immediate. The president of Hells Angels Durban South Africa spoke first.

"How do we know that these photos were even taken in South Africa?"

He had a point and I came very close to bringing the behavioural file out. I don't know why I didn't, but I remembered Bob's words when he had dismissed me earlier that week. I dropped it that night. If Hells Angels South Africa were going to put their heads in the sand, I would carry through my plan to go to Denmark.

I phoned Bob the next day and asked him for my passport and a posting to Denmark as soon as possible.

"It's arranged. You leave tomorrow night."

I flew into Copenhagen and was met at the airport by a designated driver from the car pool at the Embassy where I would be staying. A conversation with the ambassador about why I was in Denmark concluded with him saying,

"In every way, keep it clean, son. We don't want any incidents."

I was driven to the Hells Angels Nomads Denmark clubhouse in a vehicle with diplomatic plates. I had brought my Hells Angels colours to Denmark. It was a good decision. When

I was greeted by a very suspicious prospect, I put my colours on and said,

"I need to see Blondie."

Blondie was a Hells Angel I had met on a previous trip to Denmark. Later, he had travelled to South Africa and we had spent a lot of time together. The prospect looked relieved and answered,

"I'll have to make some calls"

I added,

"Tell him that it's Peter."

I met Blondie that afternoon and came straight to the point.

"We have Red and Gold colours all over the northern province of South Africa and they all seem to come from Denmark."

He laughed.

"You arrive at my clubhouse in a big black vehicle with diplomatic number plates and this is your news?"

I shrugged.

"I'm afraid so. My other life."

Blondie shook his head.

"How many?"

I put the photos down on the living room table.

"It seems like six, but it's not the numbers. It's what they are up to."

Blondie briefly studied the photos and looked up.

"Sit down. I recognise them all. It's not ideal but things have changed over the years. We are now obliged to cooperate with the Bandidos up here or face a banning order as we experienced during the last war with them. South Africa is your country and if you don't want them to multiply over there, you're going to have to go to war with them and soon."

I asked,

"How would you begin?"

Blondie picked up one of the photos and handed it to me.

"This is Sean Nielson. His family own the biggest chain of supermarkets in Scandinavia and, although he is the black sheep of his family, that's where their money is coming from. Make contact with one of his prospects and see what their bank does."

I was confused.

"You told me years ago that you didn't want any Bandidos in South Africa. Now you are pretty vague about it."

Blondie handed me a cup of coffee.

"Things change, Peter. You've got to work it out for yourselves over there. We know that you play the role of a Hells Angel only when you want to. Now you want to start a war?"

I realised I had over-reacted by flying to Denmark and changed the subject.

I spent nearly all that week at the Hells Angels Nomads Denmark clubhouse, drinking and partying. On the following Monday morning, I flew to Paris and after spending forty-eight hours with the Hells Angels Nomads, France, I flew back to Johannesburg. The first thing I did, was to go and see Bob. I had no idea how to deal with the Bandido problem in South Africa. I came clean with him.

"I've got to take a look at this, or it could be an even bigger problem in the future."

Bob wasn't listening. I went into one of the offices in the building and took out the behavioural pattern file and read it again. It didn't take long to find something. The Bandidos were selling cycads, a woody plant, dating from pre-historic times, sometimes called sago palms.

When I told Bob, he laughed.

"What have cycads to do with us?"

I stuck to my guns.

"Nothing yet, but I'll make something out of nothing to justify you moving me back there. They're selling an endangered plant. They'll be pissing someone off and when I find out whom, I'll have an ally."

Bob was not impressed.

"What's in it for us?"

"Well these guys own land bordering Zimbabwe and Mozambique. Please work something out for me."

Bob told me,

"You have four weeks and if you don't find anything concerning our borders with Mozambique or Zimbabwe, you're off the clock."

I was relieved to be going into this with some authority from Bob. As I was leaving his office, he looked up.

"You go by yourself and nobody gets killed there until you submit a report." Then he smiled. "After all these years, I know you, so keep it clean as otherwise it might be hard to make anything you do against a rival biker club appear legal."

I drove to the farm the same evening. By now, it was being run by Farnie, a veteran of the old SADF, a decorated non-commissioned officer of the once feared Thirty-two Battalion, known by South African soldiers as the Buffalo Battalion; and by the Portuguese speaking opposition as *Os Terriveis*, the Terrible Ones. He was waiting for me. I asked him,

"What do you know about cycads?"

His face lit up.

"I know something about everything here, Colonel, and what I don't know, I can find out."

I laughed.

"We have four weeks to find something to become operational."

He looked happy. It turned out that there was a cycad reserve within twenty kilometres of the farm. The majestic plants there were some of the oldest and largest on the planet. They were worth a fortune both in the ground and out of it for sale. I had a game but I didn't know what to do next. I phoned Sean.

"Peter, drive up to the front gate of the farm where the cycads are and ring the bell. They're living behind electric fences, terrified of any new influence in the area. If they don't shoot at you, you're in. And just be Peter."

It was what I expected from Sean. I replied,

"How's it going down there with the general?"

Sean hesitated.

"He's one of the good guys, Peter, so go and get us some bad ones. By what I hear, everyone expects you to run into brick walls up there."

I laughed.

"Fuck it, bud. In for a penny."

Sean burst out laughing.

"That's us bud, one hundred percent, so get on with it."

I phoned Bob and he laughed as well.

"You're going to approach a landowner with nothing but a cold canvass? They'll probably let you in and shoot you."

I replied,

"That's the plan."

Bob paused and then, more seriously, he said,

"Peter, be careful up there. That's where I grew up. If you find something I'll send you some help."

All I said was,

"So you're giving me a green light?"

Bob sighed.

"Just do what you do, Peter. We'll take it from there."

Later that afternoon, in my make-shift office, I spoke to Farnie.

"I need you to bring me some of your retired army friends as this might get nasty."

Farnie sprang to attention.

"How many do you want and how much is it worth?"

At that time, it was easy to recruit retired SADF personnel. I replied,

"I only have the authority to feed them for the time being but it might lead to a salary in the future."

Farnie smiled and saluted me.

"I'll have six here by tomorrow afternoon."

I saluted back.

"I want at least one to be a mechanic, but that will do for the time being, Sergeant."

The next day, seven men arrived at the farm.

"The mechanic is a useless soldier, Colonel, but we'll look after him," Farnie told me proudly.

I laughed and asked,

"What do they expect?"

Farnie grinned broadly.

"They want to wear a uniform and be armed, Sir."

I replied,

"Put them on guard duty. I'll get them uniforms and weapons."

I phoned Bob. He was hesitant.

"We can't dress them in military uniforms as that battalion retired before the nineteen ninety-four elections."

We couldn't restore the former glory of a disbanded battalion, but we could get as close as possible.

"I'll dress them as security guards, but I want to arm them as well."

Bob exhaled.

"Phone Sean and make it happen, but don't make it too personal, Peter."

I phoned Sean, who was much entertained by my requests. We decided to put the unit in charcoal uniforms and arm them with Vector R1 assault rifles and .45 calibre hand guns, all of which were delivered the following weekend. Sean phoned me on Monday morning.

"You'd better keep the discipline up, as you're on the radar. I'm sending someone to change the locks and the alarm system on the armoury."

So began my personal operation.

I went to the front gate of the farm with the cycads and buzzed the intercom. A hostile tone answered. I stayed calm and told the voice that I was investigating the harvesting and illegal sales of cycads. He told me I could come in, but on foot and by myself. I remember thinking that these days there was no one in the world as paranoid as white people in Africa. I walked in, unarmed and alone. The owner of the farm was a retired military general. He let me into his house and we drank together. I asked about the cycad trading.

"They're slowly stealing our plants from beneath us."

I took a big swig from the very expensive bottle of whisky on the table.

"Who are?"

He looked old.

"The Scandinavian gangsters who have moved in up here."

"Why haven't you gone to the cops?"

He looked at me as though I were mad.

"Up here, the cops are the biggest gang in town. The Scandinavians are paying them more than they could earn as policemen in a lifetime. This is their pension fund, Peter, and I'm too old to care."

I smiled.

"Do you want to become operational again, General?"

I liked him when he replied,

"What the hell? We're all going to die sometime."

After more whisky, he told me it would be best to look into a cycad dealer in Phalabora. I said I would go there before the week was out.

"Don't go alone. These guys are not going to be an easy victory. Anyway, what's your concern with them?"

"They're the start of an international biker club pitching a tent in my back yard. I don't want them here."

The retired general smiled.

"So you're the Military Intelligence colonel by day, who plays at being a Hells Angel at night?"

I finished off the bottle of whisky.

"Can you allow my transport onto your farm to take me home?"

The general let out his first real laugh.

"We baited two male lions down to the front gate to stop you leaving, but now we're friends, you are going to need a vehicle to get out of here."

I smiled.

"I think we'll be friends for a long time, Sir!"

The whole process went very quickly. In Phalabora, I walked into Sid's Cycads and punched the guy behind the counter. There was a lot of blood and shouting but I had their attention. On the way back to the farm, Farnie was cleaning his teeth with a splinter of wood.

"I see you know how to start a war, Colonel, but only time will tell on how you work it."

I liked Farnie and smiled.

"They're migrants, bud, and you're right. Only time will tell."

Farnie showed concern.

"You white people fight over the most stupid reasons?"

I decided to grant him some insight.

"This is not about plants. It's something bigger than that."

Farnie opened his window and threw out his toothpick.

"It always is."

I looked across at the trained veteran.

"Double our personnel and double up the security on the farm. I'll take care of the budget."

Farnie grinned.

"Yes, Sir."

"And get all our vehicles up and running."

Within forty-eight hours, I had thirteen battle-hardened men at the farm. I phoned Andries to come and see me. He did and said,

"There's a warrant out on you for assault, but that's not your biggest problem. Every Danish national in the area is having an emergency meeting after your interaction at that shop. You need to meet their boss."

"Can you arrange a meeting?"

Andries laughed.

"Why bother with an official meeting. Meet him in your own time and remind him he's in Africa?"

As Andries left the farm, he said,

"Peter, people up here are watching. Make your approach slick and they will carry on watching. If you fuck it up, they'll choose a side."

333

I asked,

"Do you have any suggestions?"

Andries smiled.

"Visit him in his home in the early hours of the morning. That should do it."

Early the next morning, Sean Nielson was woken by the sound of a running tap in his kitchen. As he walked downstairs to turn it off, he realised he was not alone. I was sitting in his lounge with an assault rifle on my lap. He just walked past me. I would be lying if I didn't give him credit for his reaction. He said,

"I think we're going to need a large cup of coffee for this meeting, Hells Angel."

I liked him immediately. He sat down and smiled at me.

"Where do we go from here?"

"Let's create some boundaries."

Sean Nielson was about to become one of my closest friends. He shook his head.

"Let's merge."

These Bandidos were in a foreign land with foreign laws, yet they were very confident. I asked,

"What makes you comfortable bringing me a cup of coffee while I'm armed and you're not?"

Sean Nielson finished his cup of coffee.

"There's no reason for us to kill each other. There's always middle ground."

I stayed quiet for a while. Then,

"Give me some options."

Sean Nielson got up and threw me a set of keys to his house.

"Billet your guys downstairs and spend the night, I have something to show you tomorrow morning."

As he was walking back upstairs, he added,

"If you intend to shoot me, Peter, you will have to do so in my back. I hear that's not your style, but you have me ambushed so I'm going back to bed."

I had to have the last word.

"Next time you come and visit me."

As he was walking into his bedroom he called down,

"I'll come to see you tomorrow, and in the daytime."

The next day, Sean Nielson visited me at the farm. He walked into the house, smiling broadly.

"So you have soldiers looking after you. I had to wait nearly half an hour to be escorted here. I wish I had that luxury."

It was odd how much I liked him.

"If we merge, you can pay for them."

Sean Nielson shook my hand.

"I pay enough taxes and bribes, so let's leave their salary to the state."

I made him a cup of coffee and he spoke business.

"How do we get you to leave our cycads venture alone?"

I answered,

"Just stop it."

He laughed.

"No, Peter. This is a big business and I am willing to cut you in."

Living off a state budget had left me ignorant about profit.

"What do you propose?"

Sean Nielson answered too quickly.

"I will give you fifty thousand rand a month and free access for Hells Angels members to all our game farms."

It seemed too easy.

"Why would you want Hells Angels members on your property?"

Sean Nielson realised he had been a little fast on his offer, but was quick to respond.

"We're not leaving, Peter, so a merger is inevitable. We have nothing to hide."

I saw his point and was taken aback by how sure he was about staying.

"What makes you think I can't force you to leave?"

Sean Nielson sighed.

"You can force me to leave, but you can't get away from the investment we have put into this country."

He was right.

"Let's get drunk today," I said, "and I will take instruction from my club."

Sean Nielson shrugged.

"Let's get drunk, but I need to show you something first."

Sean Nielson made a phone call on his cell phone and arranged a meeting with the person who he was calling.

"Take a drive with me Peter. There is something you should see."

I wondered why he was so persistent.

"I'm gonna bring one of my guys with me."

Sean Nielson smiled.

"Bring them all, if you need to. I'm unarmed and so is the person that we're meeting."

I was uneasy.

"You Bandidos think it's a matter of trust?"

Sean Nielson seemed weary.

"That's why we'll eventually take over. We are not a democracy. We take orders from one man and he says that I have to show you something."

I felt I was being manipulated, but that I had no choice.

"I'll come alone Sean, but I'll be armed and so, if it's a trap, you die first."

Sean Nielson shook his head.

"Whatever makes you happy, Hells Angel. Paranoia is what we bank on and that's why we'll eventually take over."

I let that comment pass. I was intrigued by what he wanted to show me.

"Okay, Sean. We'll use your vehicle and while your hands are on the steering wheel, I'll feel more comfortable."

Sean laughed.

"I'm going to show you how bad your Hells Angels intelligence is, but there is no danger, Mister Filthy Few. We killed each other in Scandinavia in that stupid war and ended up surrounded by populist legislation back home. Let's do it right in Southern Africa."

I took a couple of spare magazines for my sidearm and got into his vehicle.

I was taken to a house in Johannesburg, built for the sole purpose of entertainment. Sean Nielson and I were let in through an intercom and an electric gate. The house was empty, but at the bottom of the garden there was a garage full of people, with a Porsche on a lift.

I was introduced to Graham, the owner of the property. Graham was very English and very proper. I was taken into a very large and expensive house. It had a beautiful bar and a kitchen that could cater for as many people as any embassy I had ever been in. I walked around what seemed like an endless labyrinth of bedrooms with en suite bathrooms.

Sean Nielson asked me what I thought.

I told him,

"It's a whorehouse waiting for whores and customers."

Sean Nielson nodded at me.

"That's the plan, but we need someone to run it."

I sat down on one of the beds.

"Why me?"

Sean Nielson didn't hesitate.

"We need to have common ground so there's no conflict in South Africa. We can all meet here without colours on and co-exist amongst the party that will be going on. What do you think?"

I went into the well-stocked bar and chose a very expensive whisky.

"Sean, for me to spend time here, it will have to be for an intelligence-led operation."

Sean nodded and said,

"That's the plan. You feed South African Military Intelligence what you want and the Hells Angels what they want and the Bandidos what we want."

I handed him the bottle of whisky and, as he drank, I replied,

"I'm going to need to take instruction on this operation."

Sean Neilson was one of the calmest men I had ever met. I suppose it was easy for him to take things slowly, as he had no financial obligations to fulfil and all the time in the world to move forward.

"Of course, Peter, but if you make it happen, I'll make you wealthy and it will be beneficial for all of us."

I laughed.

"Seems like you have it all planned."

Sean Nielson nodded.

"I hate this city, Peter. Too much shit going on, but we need to work together."

That night, when I said goodbye to Sean Nielson, I told him I would consider his offer. I went to see Bob a few days later.

"So you start an operation with cycads and come back to me with a whorehouse?"

I laughed and sat down opposite him.

"They paid me off."

Bob grinned.

"That's how this country works. I'll make you operational in that house but first you have to go with Sean to Mozambique and Zimbabwe. He needs a small team and you're on it."

At that moment, I could not have thought of anything worse than a trip to a couple of countries in Africa.

I asked,

"You think I need a promotion for this one?"

After all the years I had known Bob, we had worked up a very good working relationship and he was in a good mood that night.

"You are already punching above your pay grade. Get this shit up there over with and I'll make your new whorehouse happen."

Chapter 42

The next day, I went to see Sean, not Sean Neilson, the other Sean. He was waiting for me in his kitchen.

"Come and see what I've bought."

We walked out to the garages where he showed me a brand new black BMW M5. I laughed.

"So we're both on the take these days? "

Sean gave a huge smile.

"It gets better."

I shrugged, but was very happy for him. Sean said,

"I just bought the property next door as well. I'm going to breathe life into it and you can live there whenever you want."

I realised what a good friend I had made during the insanity that was my life, but at that moment, I had more pressing things on my mind. I said,

"Let's talk about our trip."

Sean was in a great mood.

"Peter, the reason I asked for you to be on this trip with us is because I don't feel very well."

"What do you mean?"

"In two thousand and four, I got fragged in the chest when I drove onto a landmine in northern Mozambique. My lungs took most of the damage and I can't breathe very well at the moment."

It took me by surprise.

"Why didn't you tell me?"

Sean looked extremely happy for someone who, I would later find out, had only eighteen per cent lung capacity.

"You didn't ask and, more importantly, this country is about to undergo a massive political upheaval and it looks like Bob is on the winning side. This is no time for weakness."

I remember feeling apprehensive. This wasn't my usual profile. I realised how much weight had been placed on my shoulders.

"Peter, I have arranged for a vehicle to be fitted with a maximum capacity secondary fuel tank. Also, I have an agreement with both Mozambique and Zimbabwe that the weapons we are taking with us will be allowed across all three borders. I need you to take control of this game from now on."

I was about to be in charge of something important. I asked,

"What do you want me to do?"

"Peter, I'm going to be on oxygen and sleeping pills for the whole journey. You need to make sure that I get to each meeting on the itinerary, awake and fed. Most important of all, I need on be on time."

"How long before we roll?"

Sean was looking weak.

"We've got to get this shit done in a week."

I knew it must be important for Sean to risk his health like this. He looked even more tired and I made him a cup of coffee.

"What are we going to do?"

"We're going to create a secure platform for our next royal families. Our current president wants to breach the constitution and run for a third term in office, but there's about to be a political *coup d'état* in South Africa."

I said,

"Go to bed, bud. Just give me the itinerary. I'll get you to the church on time."

Sean looked tired.

"One more thing," he said. "We're rolling in South African Defence Force army browns. I took the liberty of having yours sent here. It's been stone washed already."

As we walked to his bedroom, I asked,

"How soon do we leave?"

Sean switched on a humidifier in his bedroom.

"You're in charge, Hells Angel. The other two coming with us are in the house immediately to the left of this one."

I shouted,

"Where's the plan?"

Sean replied,

"On my desk, Lieutenant Colonel Conway. Make it all happen."

We had a week to get Sean to four meetings. Meeting the deadlines didn't seem too difficult. There would be the usual problems, but no matter what, we would be on time. I divided the plan into four stages. The first meeting would be at the South African Embassy in Maputo, the capital of Mozambique, specifically with the Department of International Relations and Cooperation. The South African High Commissioner and names I didn't recognise would be there. It didn't matter who they were. We had thirty-six hours to get there.

I took the keys and went to the office. My uniform was folded neatly on the floor. I had a shower and put it on. I walked to the house to the left of Sean's, where I found two non-commissioned officers in uniform. Both looked hard as nails.

I started it off.

"Evening, guys. We're rolling with LM6s and Heckler and Kock .45 side arms. I have mine in the boot of my car and if you check the register in the armoury, you'll find Sean's weapons. Arm yourselves with the same and don't forget to fill in the registry when you take out the ammunition. Let's start this thing properly. I'm driving and the colonel will be in front with me. There will be no reference to the colonel's health."

They both came to attention and saluted me. I smiled.

"You can desist with the saluting shit as of right now. I'm in charge until we join the dots on this mission and we certainly don't have to make it public knowledge. Make sure the vehicle is ready, because we leave at 02h00. You guys can sleep on the way to the border."

It occurred to me that we were wearing the uniforms of the very same SADF that had escalated trouble in both the countries we were going through. I went back to the office and took out eight shoulder lapels denoting the rank of captain.

I woke Sean just after midnight. It was the first time I had seen him naked. He had marks all over his chest from fragmented bits of an explosion. Sean said,

"Yeah and I've caught a bug. My lungs are barely oxygenating my body. You're my body for the next week."

I helped him to put on his uniform. He laughed.

"So, you demoted me to the rank of captain, Captain?"

We both laughed, as it did seem extreme.

"I'll promote you back to a full colonel by the time I walk you into your first meeting."

Sean seemed very weak.

"I need you to get me through this, Peter."

We had been friends for such a long time and I was worried about him.

"This whole thing is not ideal, bud, but I'm on it," I told him.

So, that morning, four heavily armed Military Intelligence operators left for Mozambique. By the time we reached the South African Embassy in Maputo, Sean was very weak. He had been on a nebulizer throughout the journey and I was feeding him liquid protein drinks and penicillin. As we switched back our ranks, he looked terrible. I almost had to carry Sean into the building. I put him in a bed and took off his uniform. I told the two sergeants to take our uniforms to the laundry and to put on their second uniforms.

"We might not look healthy tomorrow, but we're going to smell pretty, guys."

I changed Sean's oxygen tank and went to sleep on the floor next to his bed. The next morning Sean looked a little better and I helped him dress.

"You're coming in there with me, Peter. There are methamphetamines in the spare wheel of the vehicle. Go and get them and administer them to me."

I took a deep sigh and said,

"This meeting better be important, bud."

Sean briefly looked like his old self as he said,

"Like I said, you're coming in there with me. It won't take you long to see what our mission is."

That morning, the South African High Commissioner to Mozambique moderated a meeting between Sean and the high command of the Mozambique Defence Force. I took notes. The pleasantries were very short before the discussions began.

The Cahora Bassa system is Africa's fourth largest artificial lake, situated in Tete Province in Mozambique. The project was begun by the Portuguese in the late 1960s. The then South African Government agreed that Portugal would build and operate a hydroelectric generating station at Cahora Bassa to bring electricity to the South African border. The South African Government undertook to build and operate the Apollo HVDC converter station which was part of the transmission system bringing electricity from the border to the Apollo station near Johannesburg. All I could think was, 'Fuck! We're securing a national key point situated outside our borders.' The dam was being operated under a joint venture, the Mozambique Government having an eighteen per cent stake and the Portuguese government the other eighty-two per cent, but it was about to change. In the very near future Mozambique would assume control of the whole operation. It made sense that Sean was willing to risk his life for this meeting. We left with signed documents, stating that South Africa would not be affected by the coming changes.

Sean looked at me as we left.

"When do we leave, Hells Angel?"

I felt drained as I replied,

"How do you feel?"

Sean laughed.

"You wacked me up on drugs this morning. Let's get on with it. I fucking hate this part of the world."

We left that afternoon and went on to stage two. South Africa was about to have a political bun fight but the lights would stay on. That evening, when we made it into the urban environment of Beira in Mozambique, Sean was looking the worse for wear. We booked into the Hotel Tivoli and I put Sean to bed, changed his oxygen tank and fell asleep on the floor beside him. Our uniforms were sent to be laundered. I was relieved at how things were running.

During that night, Sean started having violent convulsions and I rushed him to the nearest clinic. We were both in a pair of shorts and must have seemed out of the ordinary. Sitting in the waiting room, I felt conspicuous, but sometimes life throws you curve balls.

The doctor came out.

"Your friend needs rest. He is in an advanced state of pneumonia."

I asked the doctor if I could speak with him. Sean was delirious.

"We roll Peter. What's the schedule?"

"I've got to get you up the river, bud. You're meeting some directors of Shell, tomorrow."

Sean turned up his oxygen.

"Give me an hour and get me out of here, even if you need to use the weapons."

I went back to the hotel to collect the other two guys and our uniforms. I told them,

"Sean wants to be extracted from the hospital."

I felt overwhelmed by the decision that I was about to make. The older of the sergeants came to my rescue.

"I've known Sean since he was a kid, so I'll get him out if you decide to move him."

I made a decision.

"In an hour we make contact with him, but he stays there in that clinic until the last moment. All four of us are leaving in the morning. We are on the clock."

The following morning, Sean looked much better as I argued with the duty doctor for his discharge, which eventually he granted. Sean put on his uniform, gave me a resigned look and said,

"Let's go, bud."

Later that day, Sean and I met directors of Shell. Sean was high on methamphetamines during the meeting, but, by the end, he had secured that fuel would be delivered to the Special Forces and South African Infantry bases in Phalaborwa for the next five years.

"We just secured energy for our borders, bud."

"What's happening back home Sean? Why is this important?"

"Just let me rest, Peter. We carry on with your timetable. I'll tell you what you want to know when I have more strength."

The third leg of the journey was into the northern part of Mozambique. We drove fast and I was exhausted when we reached Nampula. We were booked into a game lodge about thirty kilometres south of the airport. After I put Sean to bed, I went to the bar for a drink. I was surprised to find Bob there. I felt too tired for a debriefing.

"How's he doing Peter?"

"He's doing great, but he's killing himself doing it."

Bob bought me a drink and said,

"I'll take care of the meeting up here. It's one of my friends from the days of exile. Let Sean sleep and if his condition doesn't improve by tomorrow afternoon, we'll evacuate him home."

I sat next to Bob, feeling very tired.

"What about the final meeting in Zimbabwe?" I asked.

Bob ordered another two whiskies.

"I have brought the information with me and, if you have to send him home, then you're taking the lead of this operation."

I felt a degree of dread.

"You know I'm not a negotiator?"

Bob looked tired as well.

"We're spread thin at the moment and you're going to have to do your best. Meet me in the morning for a situational report. We'll take it from there."

I remember saying,

"Buy me another drink. I have to get back to his room."

Bob watched me finish another shot of whisky. Then he said,

"There is change coming at home, Peter, and you'll be rewarded for your effort."

I got up to leave.

"I want my friend to survive this trip and I want an operation approved for that whorehouse."

"I'll take care of tomorrow's meeting, but if Sean's health doesn't improve during the night, there's a plane leaving from this airport tomorrow afternoon. I want him on it. I'll brief you and you'll have to hold the line in Zimbabwe."

It all seemed more clinical than I was used to.

"I'll see you in the morning," I told Bob.

The next morning Sean's health had improved, but he was still weak. I gave him breakfast.

"It's time to inject me again, Hells Angel."

"Bob's here. He is substituting for you today."

Sean looked fired up.

"And you agreed?"

"He holds the rank of major general, Sean. What option did I have? Would you have liked me to mutiny?"

Sean smiled.

"How much oxygen do we have left?"

It was time to break the news to him.

"We have enough, but I'm under orders to fly you out this afternoon on Bob's plane if I think your health isn't improving."

Sean sat up in his bed.

"You will not fly me out of my own operation. I'll finish this game even if I die doing it."

I was between a rock and a hard place.

"All right, what's the plan?" I asked.

Sean looked at his oxygen tank.

"Turn this thing up and let Bob deal with today. When you see him later this morning, tell him I'm okay."

I sarcastically saluted him.

"Roger that, Colonel."

In all the years I had known Sean, I had never felt so alienated from him.

I met Bob just before noon. He told me,

"I've just secured compliance with the guys that run the north of this country. Our energy is secured during the coming political turmoil in South Africa. Read this file. It's been updated and shows our current position right now. How's our man?"

I made a split-second decision.

"He's much better today."

Bob closed his eyes.

"You're two peas in a pod. I need him out in the field, but if he dies, I expect you to finish the game."

When I woke Sean up that night, he was stronger. I was relieved.

"I have an update file from Bob's meeting this morning for you. That's the good news. We have got to leave early for Harare tomorrow morning. That's the bad news."

Sean was surprisingly upbeat.

"Just put me back in uniform and get me there. Get yourself a bed tonight."

I put an array of food next to his bed. Sean started to eat the fruit salad I had brought him.

"I'll sleep here on the floor, tonight."

"Good job, Peter."

I switched on CNN and answered,

"You're a fucking prick, Sean."

We made it to Harare with a day to spare. Sean was off oxygen by then and full of his old bullshit. I was both relieved and, as he played the blues on the CD changer and laughed at my demeanour, irritated. The ice was broken when Sean said,

"You'll make a good nurse one day, Hells Angel."

For the first time that trip, I laughed with him.

"Fuck you! I should have sent you home."

Sean met the Zimbabwean Department of Energy on time and in surprisingly good health. It went well. There was a consensus that the electricity for Zimbabwe from the hydroelectric scheme at Cohora Bassa would not be under threat during the approaching political upheaval in South Africa. Everybody was satisfied and I felt a burden had been lifted from my shoulders.

The next morning, Sean was at full strength and called a meeting over breakfast. He announced,

"Fuck going back to South Africa until this political shit is over. I have a very good friend who has a hunting concession just east of here. We're on a state budget and he needs the income, so let's lie in the sun and get drunk." He turned to the two sergeants and said,"You two can kill whatever you can find."

As I walked away from the table, I asked Sean,

"What's going on?"

Sean was back to his former self.

"The Zulus are about to take over the African National Congress. As we're party members, let's take a holiday from it all."

We were good friends again.

"I'm just glad I kept you alive."

Sean grabbed me by the elbow and shoulder.

"Thank you, Hells Angel."

I came to attention.

"Any time, bud."

Chapter 43

On 2 January, we left to go home to South Africa. As soon as we crossed the border, I switched on my cell phone for the first time in what seemed like ages. There were mostly messages from friends, but one from a major who worked in Bob's office in Pretoria. I phoned him first.

"Bob wants to see you as soon as possible. Your operation in Johannesburg has been approved."

My life was back on the clock.

"Tell him I'll come and see him tonight."

Sean looked over at me and said,

"When are you going to learn not to switch on your comms before you even unpack?"

I smiled and accelerated.

"I think this is good news."

I saw Bob that evening. He looked stressed.

"Well done on that last job, Peter."

"It was Sean that really got it done."

Bob replied,

"Get a drink Peter. We're approving your whorehouse, but there's to be a new spin on it."

I poured myself a large whisky, sat down and waited.

"Peter, Military Intelligence, Police Intelligence, the National Intelligence Agency and the South African Secret Service are going to work with African National Congress Intelligence to make this political transition as smooth as possible."

I laughed.

"Well, we already know it isn't possible. What's the plan?"

"You are now an operator for African National Congress Intelligence. You report to me and I report to the new African National Congress Executive Committee. We're going to give you a budget and expect you to interact with white businessmen, discovering their feelings about the current political situation. I expect a daily report as soon as you get that house up and running."

"All right. You want me to report on the emotions of the white people who still hold the purse strings of the South African economy?"

Bob nodded.

"Yes. We need to know what the whites are thinking, as we go through this mess."

I shook my head.

"Who the fuck thought it was a good idea to effect the transition of the ruling party just fifteen months before a general election?"

Bob looked tired.

"Those are the cards we've been dealt and we're going to have to bluff until the election. Everything you do from now on will be for cash. There's a suitcase filled with money outside. Pour us both a drink, Peter."

When I left Bob, I phoned Farnie.

"Get me the same unit back together that was on the farm and find someone else to look after it. You're all coming to Johannesburg in the next seventy-two hours to be security at my whorehouse."

I also phoned Billy, who was still a Hells Angels, and asked him if he would run the whorehouse whenever I was not there. He agreed.

We opened the new whorehouse at the end of January 2008. I recruited the women by going through classified adverts in the national newspapers. I hired those I thought had the right looks and, more importantly, the right mind-set. I offered them more money than they could ever make on the streets. I hired mostly white girls as, at that time, I believed white businessmen wouldn't fraternise with black or coloured prostitutes. I would quickly find out I was wrong, but that was my thought process at the time.

So it began. The Scandinavian Bandidos would give me notice of when they would arrive and I called Hells Angel meetings at the house to coincide with their visits. No one was allowed to wear colours and, to my amazement, both sides discovered common ground.

More importantly, I fraternised with businessmen from every spectre of the South African business world and spoke politics with them. I wrote a report every day for Bob and sometimes even profiled the specific people I was talking to. Their feeling about South Africa's political future was very negative and I didn't try to sex it up. I mostly wrote verbatim what was said in my conversations with them.

I struck up a relationship with a girl named Terry, who was a natural at feeding relevant information about men. Everything was running smoothly.

On 20 September 2008, Thabo Mbeki announced his resignation as president of South Africa. He explained that the ruling political party, the ANC, had recalled him by a decision of its new Executive Committee. The recall came after a South African High Court Judge, Christopher Nicholson, had ruled that the president had improperly interfered with the operations of the country's National Prosecuting Authority, including the prosecution for corruption of the then incumbent president of the ruling political party. Kgalema Motlanthe was appointed interim president of South Africa until the approaching general election.

I woke up to the news on television. Bob phoned me.

"Get in here as soon as you can."

Although I had a huge hangover, my life was not governed by my physiological state.

"I'll take a shower and be there within an hour."

I sat on the end of my bed and thought, 'Now the stupidity begins. Fuck!' Compensation House was eerily quiet when I walked in. The phones were ringing, but not being answered. There were faces outside Bob's office I had not seen for many years. I presented myself to Bob's personal assistant and joined them. The telephones continued to ring unanswered. When I eventually walked into Bob's office, he was sitting in front of a television set. I sat next to him. There was a large pot of coffee in front of me. I poured a cup and waited.

"Peter, your operations at the whorehouse have been up-graded to restricted operations by our new president. Do what you have to, but get me information on this shit."

I stayed quiet until I finished my coffee.

"It's a major fuck-up isn't it, General?"

He looked terrible.

"We don't know for sure why that judge made the ruling he did this close to the election. We don't know what his motivation was, nor about the timing, nor, for that matter, which side he's on."

I sat in silence for a while, watching CNN. Then I said,

"He's on the side of the white tribe of South Africa."

Bob was looking worse and worse as the news broadcast what could only be interpreted as a political *coup d'état* in South Africa. Bob looked at me.

"The whites are fragmented. I want you to up your operation with the lawyers. We need to know what's going on in the legal sector and I need answers now."

I stood up.

"I'll get onto it, Sir."

I had never seen Bob look so fatigued.

"Peter there's a phone outside. It has my number on speed dial. Phone me every time you have any news."

I was driving back from Pretoria when, as I made a right turn into the street of the whorehouse in Johannesburg, an armed man ran out of the shadows and stood in the middle of the road, pointing a very old Star 9mm parabellum at my car. I realised that what I had been taught many years before was true. You're at your most vulnerable close to home, because you start to unwind and switch off. I was nearly home and now I see a guy with a gun in his hand, pointing it at me.

My first thought was, 'That fucking relic probably won't even fire and even if it's been maintained and is operational, he probably doesn't have access to ammunition to waste a round on me. He can wait for the next car to hijack.' So I accelerated and was wrong on both counts. A round came through my windscreen as the guy that shot it was struck by the front of my vehicle and then by the windscreen. The strange thing is that he bounced off the windscreen. The windscreen shattered but remained intact and all I was thinking was, 'That's why I pay the little extra for a BMW.'

I had two LM6 assault rifles next to me on the seat. One was in factory condition, the other had modifications. I picked up the rifle with the laser 'scope fixed to the dust cover. Another man broke from the tree cover of the fence line the first guy had come from. I killed him with one shot. He didn't have a chance. I waited for about ten minutes, knowing that the response time for the police would speed things up. I switched the rifle selector onto automatic and sprayed the area the two had come from. There was nothing.

I got out and approached the guy I had driven into. I was surprised to see he was still holding his pistol. After three major impacts, he had managed to keep the weapon in his hand. I remember thinking, 'You probably would have made a better soldier than a criminal.' I put my left foot on his weapon hand and spoke to him in anger.

"You picked the wrong fucking car to try to hijack tonight, bud."

Then I killed him.

Although it's legal under South African law to fire at anyone presenting an imminent threat to life, you are only lawfully allowed to kill with a weapon legally registered with the Central Firearms Registry. I had all the boxes ticked, but knew it might be a stumbling block. I went into the house. At the sound of police sirens, I phoned Bob on his speed dial. He answered immediately. I told him what had happened. He took a deep breath.

"You had to kill them both?"

"I'm afraid so. They were shooting at me."

Bob exhaled.

"I'll take care of it. I can hear the sirens. Let them in."

The only white policeman in the detail walked into my room.

"Funny thing, Peter," he said. "I do a check on the number plate of your car and find you're a Hells Angel. Then I get a call on my radio as I'm let in and I'm told you hold the rank of a superintendent in the South African Police Services."

I had to laugh.

"Do I? I'm not sure if that's promotion or not."

I looked at his equipment he was wearing and added,

"Well you're wearing expensive rigging for a lowly police constable?"

He laughed.

"Yip. My unit has eyes on this place all the time."

He turned around and, as he walked out into the garden, he said,

"Come with me. I'm not arresting you, but I think you should see this."

We went back to where I had shot the two guys. Their bodies hadn't been moved. We drove past and turned into the house at the end of the road. There was an ambulance there and paramedics were administering trauma control on an elderly white couple. I said nothing, but the policeman I was with started talking with venom in his voice.

"They burnt him with an iron and they both raped his wife. Seems like robbery isn't enough these days. We've been hunting these pricks for ten days. Well done."

I felt very sorry for the couple and the policeman took me to where they were being put into the ambulance. He called the elderly man over and told him,

"This is the guy who killed those two."

The man looked at me. He looked like he was in total shock.

"Thank you, son," he said.

I didn't know what to say, but felt I had to say something.

"My pleasure, Sir."

They had tied him up and put a hot iron on his leg and then made him watch as they had raped his wife. Fucking cavemen! Sometimes I hated Africa. I was taken back to the whorehouse, where I opened a bottle of whisky and drank it very quickly.

A couple of days later, I went to visit the elderly couple who had been so badly traumatised that night. I rang their buzzer and was let in. The man made me a cup of coffee. His wife didn't come out of the bedroom. He said,

"We obviously heard the shooting outside and knew it was the police."

I closed my eyes. I told him,

"I'm not really a policeman. I'm an old soldier who's lucky enough to have access to specific weapons."

He got up, pulled out his wallet and gave me his business card.

"I'm one of the partners in a legal firm called Group Twenty-one. We represent the African National Congress on a retainer. If you ever need legal help, that would be all I can offer as thanks."

I couldn't believe my luck.

"I need your help right now, Sir."

He walked over to me and said,

"Anything, son. As long as you stop calling me Sir and start calling me Brian."

I laughed.

"Okay, Brian. I need to take instructions from my master, but I might call that favour in."

As soon as I left, I phoned Bob.

"I think I might have hit the mother lode."

Bob replied,

"Come and see me immediately."

Chapter 44

The next day, I walked into Bob's office. As usual, he was on the phone. When he finished, he asked,

"What's your big news?"

I sat down.

"You remember those two guys I shot a couple of nights back?"

"Go on."

I started to tell him what they had done to the couple. Bob stopped me.

"Peter, I have a full report on what happened from Police Intelligence. Get to the point."

I took out Brian's business card and put it on the desk in front of him.

"Run his name. I think you might see my angle without my saying any more."

Bob made a few calls. Then he said,

"Yeah, Peter. He's a heavy hitter and his firm works for us already."

I smiled.

"Should I bring him to you? We don't want to lose anything he has to say?"

Bob thought for a while.

"No. It's too soon after the incident he's been through. His mind will be elsewhere for the immediate future. Make some fresh coffee. I need to make some calls."

I put on the TV. When Bob put down the phone, he came and sat next to me.

"Our new president wants to know what this guy and his circle of friends are saying about the political transition, not as lawyers talking to clients, but between themselves. Give it a couple of weeks and then start networking them in a social way. This operation has been elevated to CLASSIFIED."

Two weeks later, I called on Brian. He let me in. I sat down in his lounge.

"How are things going, Brian?"

Brian didn't look well.

"My injuries are healing, but my wife won't speak. She just stares out of our bedroom window and shakes."

I felt for him.

"That's shock, Sir."

He looked as if he were about to cry.

"You have no idea how our lives have been turned upside down."

"I don't, but I can imagine."

A woman's voice called out,

"Can I speak to you, dear?"

Brian stood up.

"I'll be right back."

I nodded. A shortly after Brian left, he came back into the room.

"She wants to talk to you in private?" I nodded and, as he left the room, he added, "Please be kind."

"Of course."

His wife came into the lounge and put a cup of coffee on the table between us.

"What is your name?"

"Peter John Conway, Ma'am."

There was a moment of silence.

"So you killed those two men who did this thing to us?"

"That's correct, Ma'am."

She poured me a cup of coffee.

"Are you a good man, Mr Peter John Conway?"

I thought before replying,

"I do my best, but it isn't always easy. I live a very convoluted lifestyle."

She burst into tears.

"They hurt me in every way. Physically, emotionally and psychologically. Can you tell me how you killed them?"

I thought, 'Oh fuck!'

"You want me to tell you specifically how they died?"

She was calming down.

"I need to know that they aren't coming back for me. I'm terrified and I somehow need to know for sure."

It made sense. I decided to keep it short.

"The short one shot at me while trying to hijack my car. I drove into him and when the taller one broke cover, I killed him with one shot. After about ten minutes, I raked your fence line with automatic fire and there was no more movement. I then went to the back of my car. The short one was still armed, so I shot him in the chest."

There was an uncomfortable silence.

"So, are you sure they're dead?"

I answered immediately,

"There is no doubt, Ma'am."

She nodded.

"In your opinion, where do we go from here, Peter John Conway?"

I gave her the best advice I could think of.

"Get out of this house for a while, as it has too many memories for you to heal in."

She kept quiet for a while.

"I don't feel safe out there."

I wasn't too proud of myself as I went in for operational advancement. I phoned Billy at the whorehouse.

"Do you remember the house where I shot those two guys, just up the road from the whorehouse?"

Billy laughed.

"Yes, Peter."

"I'm here right now. Send an armed member of the security detail up here immediately, please."

I took Brian outside and explained that I had arranged an armed guard for them for the foreseeable future. Brian sat down.

"Peter, it's time to discuss why you're doing this for us."

I sat next to him.

"Brian, I need your help."

Brian answered,

"Anything that is within my financial power will be yours."

I shook my head.

"This isn't about money. It never has been." I launched into my pitch. "I work for an intelligence agency under the command of the Department of Defence…"

Brian interrupted.

"Before the incident at this house that fateful night, I was consulting with the South African Presidency at least three times a week. I've always known what you do. I had a copy of your file sent to me as soon as I was released from hospital."

"So you have a security clearance?"

Brian was resigned to where I was going.

"Obviously Peter."

I smiled. He asked,

"What do you want me to do?"

"I need you to introduce me to your immediate friends on a social level, so I can compile reports on their opinions."

After some thought, Brian asked,

"Why? Your office answers to the Presidency and all my associates work for them. The Presidency is the main client for our registered partnership. Why doesn't it ask us outright and we bill them for our opinion?"

I took a breath. My whole game hinged on my answer.

"Yeah, for sure they can, but they want an opinion at a social level. Not one that's on the clock."

Brian said,

"I don't think I can do that, Peter. I've been working with the same people the whole of my adult life. Why would I have reason to betray their trust?"

I persisted.

"You won't be betraying them, Brian. I'll only report on the physical profile of your friends, so name, average age and job description. The rest will be my analysis of their opinion at a social level." I continued, "I want to interact with them and their friends and form an opinion at an emotional level."

Brian asked,

"And how do I know you'll give a truthful analysis of their opinions?"

I had only one answer to that.

"Brian, you know this change of government is going to be based on tribal reversal, so help me keep these politicians less paranoid. If they know the opinion of the demographics in your social circle, there might be more confidence in a smooth transition."

Brian picked up his phone and walked off into the garden. I could hear him talking on the phone. When he came back, he said,

"I am not able to get a straight answer from anyone as to the rank you currently hold, Peter."

I knew he was baiting me.

"I only ever served in a forward base as a captain. Then I was given an administrative rank as a major. The South African Defence Force retired me in 1999 and bumped me up to the rank of lieutenant colonel to make it more attractive for me to take a lump sum, instead of a pension. When I was re-activated, they were stuck with me at that rank. I'm only upper middle management and so my analyses of your friends are only going to be an opinion on an opinion."

"Okay. I've decided to help, but I'll be watching you interact with my friends and if you abuse my introduction by asking leading questions, I'm going to pull the plug on the whole thing. I'll have a dinner party here at seven o'clock on Friday night. You can arrive at any time."

I breathed a huge sigh of relief.

"Thank you. Now I'm going to instruct your armed guard and then go and get myself high at the whorehouse down the road."

I attended Brian's dinner party on Friday night. It got off to a slow start. Everyone was tip-toeing around Cathy. It was the first time they had all been together since she had been raped and they were uncomfortable. Brian eventually addressed the topic.

"Peter is the guy I told you all about. He is the one who killed those two outside our walls."

A man started a conversation with me.

"Peter, Brian tells me that the armed guard we had to get through at the gate outside was put here by you?"

I looked at the man who had given me my first specific profiling question of the night.

"I have a registered security company and Brian and Cathy are my friends."

He continued,

"I would like to employ your security company to give me the same service."

I paused before answering and looked at Brian. He nodded.

"You don't have a private security company in your area?" I asked.

"Yes we do and we all pay handsomely for their signs to be on display around the area, but I still don't feel safe."

I asked him his name.

"John."

"Well, John, the reason you don't feel safe is because it's not in the interest of the private security industry to make anywhere safe. It would make them redundant overnight. Fear and consumption go hand in hand. I would need a time to access your property."

John asked,

"Can I talk to you outside?"

I followed him to a bench in the garden. It was a warm evening and where we were was very pleasant and sedate to have in your back garden. He started.

"Okay, Peter. Let's put our cards on the table. Brian mentioned you were coming. I consult the South African Presidency every morning. I have access to all the information I need, to give both current and good advice." I stayed quiet, waiting. "I know you're a lieutenant colonel working for Defence Intelligence and answer to a general with an office in Compensation House in Pretoria."

I paused briefly before I remarked,

"You're very well informed, Sir."

"What is your mandate?"

I answered immediately.

"I'm to compile an assessment of your friends' social opinions and provide information on the upcoming elections."

John enquired,

"What do you know about the impending decision to be made by Deputy Judge President Louis Harms in a few hours time?"

I felt slightly intimidated.

"In response to a representation on behalf of Jacob Zuma, the current president of the African National Congress, Judge Harms is about to rule on two aspects of an appeal. The first is whether or not Jacob Zuma had the right to be invited to make a representation to the National Prosecuting Authority before it decided to reinstate charges of bribery and corruption against him. The second is whether Judge Nicholson was correct in implying political meddling by the previous South African president, Thabo Mbeki, as regards the charging of Jacob Zuma."

John was happy.

"All right. It seems Defence Intelligence is doing okay. I will start the conversation off at the dinner table and you will ask no leading questions. Don't forget I will be reading your report only minutes after our president does."

I stood up.

"Thank you, Sir."

"Wait. There's another issue we need to discuss."

I sat down again.

"Are those guards rotating around Brian's house all ex-Thirty-Two Battalion soldiers?"

I was somewhat taken aback.

"Yes, Sir. I think it's better to use them for what they are trained to do, rather than leaving them to die of boredom or lung disease up in that asbestos mine in Pomfret."

John smiled at me.

"I want three of them to live with me over the next few months. You can bill me whatever you want."

"Consider it done by the end of the week."

The following morning, as I was performing my ablutions and listening to the news, I heard read the judgement that Judge Harms had handed out on the president of the ANC. The charges against Jacob Zuma had been re-instated and the findings of Judge Nicholson's interpretation of the South African constitution over-ruled.

I stepped out of the shower and made a mental note to acquire a new uniform. South Africa was about to have a brand new civil war.

I phoned Sean.

"Get me a uniform. I think it's about to begin again."

Sean sounded very serious as he asked,

"When can you come and see me? How close are you to Johannesburg?"

I hadn't heard that tone in his voice for a very long time.

"I'm at my house. I'll see you in less than twenty minutes."

Sean led me into an operational room that had obviously been dedicated to the new political problem. There were photos on an operational wall of Zulu men in rural areas, wearing red headbands and Zulu men in urban environments, wearing black T-shirts with, '100% ZULU BOY' printed on them. I looked at Sean.

"So the transfer of political power from one royal family to the next has just been helped by the South African judiciary. There'll be a war. It's how it works in Africa and we both know that. It was always designed to fail."

Sean sat down and said,

"The problem is that this isn't between two different political parties. It's a fracture within the African National Congress. That fracture needs to be addressed by the party internally, not by the judiciary. They left their destiny in the hands of old white judges and did not anticipate a divisive outcome."

"I don't give fuck, bud. I'll pick them off at the fence line when they come for me."

"That's the thing Peter. It actually might come to that."

John phoned me about an hour after the news of Judge Harms' verdict had hit the country. He told me,

"I'm at home all day. Come and see me, please."

I went to John's house immediately and walked in. John started the conversation.

"You've heard the news?"

I sat down and replied,

"We have some trouble coming again."

John asked,

"What is the Defence Intelligence's plan?"

I remember thinking, 'How can you be so well informed yesterday and not be able to access the information in my office this morning?' Then it dawned on me. These lawyers had lost the case for the president of the ANC and possibly they were on the wrong side and therefore in danger. I recognised my lever.

"Look, I will provide you with a defence of your house and your family, but we're all running out of time. I need your cooperation."

John realised he was at the short end of this conversation.

"What do you want me to do?"

"We can't wait for your associates to open up to me at dinner parties. I'm going to need you to write reports for me on the emotional response of your friends to what's going on."

John responded,

"Okay, you got it. When do I get my guards?"

I answered,

"I'll stay here until I can get someone here."

John relaxed.

"Just keep my family safe. I'll feed you any information that your office wants."

"Are we friends, John?"

He answered,

"I hope so. We will defeat the decision handed down today. Just keep my family alive through it."

I made a few calls and then explained my plan.

"It's best if I move you and your family in with Brian and Cathy for the time being. That way my resources are less stretched. I'll arrange for the detail to get your kids to school and back and even leave an armed guard at the school. You will have to run all operations from the house."

John was open to the suggestion.

"What do I tell my family?"

"Tell your kids we are playing a game and your wife the truth."

John nodded. I kept the conversation moving.

"Start to make ready. We move at dawn. I'll run your family's life from day to day from now on. The whole country is dependant upon your skills right now."

By the following afternoon, I had moved the four lawyers representing the ANC and their families into the thankfully large property owned by Brian and Cathy. I surrounded them with a ring of steel. They all knew each other and the transition was smooth. They gave me a list of their needs and I drew up a duty-roster. By 15 January 2009, I had isolated and secured the think-tank that was the legal thought process for the ruling political party of South Africa. The ANC had it all secured by the very people who had been trained many years before to kill them. I fell asleep that night absolutely exhausted.

Chapter 45

I spent the following days and weeks observing the security detail move around and listening to John's instructions to the gate through an auxiliary radio. Every morning, I took an envelope from John to Bob in Pretoria. I watched the news as South Africa began to tear itself apart again. I ate every night with the people who were living on the property and I began to integrate with them.

On 6 April 2009, the South African National Prosecuting Authority dropped all charges against Jacob Zuma, president of the ANC and the next president of South Africa. New revelations had emerged of serious flaws in the prosecution case, namely intercepted telephone calls, showing that the head of the Directorate of Special Operations and the former South African National Director of Public Prosecutions had conspired over the timing of the charges, presumably for political advantage. I remember thinking, 'Marion got out just in time.'

At Brian and Cathy's house, I walked into a temporary conference room where John was sitting at a desk, poring over paperwork. I said,

"Evening, bud. Well done."

John looked up.

"This thing is not over yet, not by a long shot."

I sat down, opposite him.

"Well at least we have our next president taking office without charges over his head."

John was in a good mood.

"We've decided to stay together at this house until after the election."

"Well, we'll keep to the same plan. You must be paying for the most expensive private security operation in this country's history so, as long as you're feeding information to my boss, I'll stay with you all. It's going to start getting cold at night very soon, so ask everyone to make a list and I'll send someone shopping for clothes."

John gave me a cup of coffee and asked,

"How long do you think that it's going to be dangerous out there?"

"The transfer of power from the Xhosas to the Zulus won't happen overnight. Only the vote will. There were always going to be casualties and, as the police lose control, it will keep getting worse for years to come."

John said,

"Transition is never an easy process."

"I hope you've learnt your lesson about putting important matters before *verkrampte* (conservative) white judges. Everyone is going to have to wait for them to retire. I've watched an operation going to hell by trying to prise them out of office."

John asked,

"Do you want to get drunk with me, Peter?"

"I'm going to get drunk for the rest of my life. The only thing I have a choice over is who I get drunk with. So the answer is: Yes, of course I'll get drunk with you. You're a very interesting man, John."

John brought out a bottle of whisky from his desk, looking like a naughty child.

"My wife is going to go mad. She hates it when I'm drunk."

"Fucking women and their sensibilities! Just tell her I held you down and poured it down your throat. She's far too bright to believe you, but it's your job to concoct an argument, so I'm sure you'll do okay."

By midday, we were both drunk.

"What's it like to go to war Peter?"

I asked why he thought I'd been to war.

"I had a detailed file pulled on you. You know, I even know what you did in Angola." He asked again, "What's it like to go to war?"

"It's just like what you do in a courtroom, but with much less blood."

John opened a second bottle of whisky.

"Please tell me, Peter."

I looked John straight in the eye.

"The real problem is voluntarily motivating yourself to get into a ready position. Once the killing starts, it's over before you know it. Your training takes over. I know that sounds corny but it's true. The next problem comes after you have murdered people in the field. You feel anxious for the rest of your life, because, when you understand the mortality of a human being, you realise it could all be over for you before you even hear the sound of the shot."

"So you just stay drunk?"

"That's what works for us."

After some thought, John said,

"Well at least you're a functioning drunk."

"So we're still friends, John?"

"I think we'll be friends for a very long time, Peter."

I stood up to leave.

"I really hope so, bud."

John remarked,

"You know if the African National Congress doesn't get two thirds of the popular vote, it won't own the constitution and then it all starts again."

I didn't care. It had been a very long time since I had thought that far ahead. I said,

"Just relax for the next month and I will help you cross that bridge when you come to it."

Later that evening, Sean phoned me and asked me to meet him at his house. When I walked into Sean's kitchen, he was pecking away at his laptop. I hadn't seen him in a while. He was happy to see me. He poured two whiskies.

"Come outside to the pond. I'm going to brief you on a mission in Cairo. We need you to leave the country, because the police are about to arrest you for murder. This is not a punishment. We need a military attaché in the Embassy in Egypt during the elections and while you're there, we're going to work things out for you. Get out of Dodge, before they find a reason to pull you in."

I wasn't happy.

"They want to arrest me on a bullshit charge this close to an election? What about my operation down here?"

"You've gotta leave, bud."

I felt completely manipulated.

"Why do you think there are cops stupid enough to arrest me living around that many lawyers? Especially the one who just came up with the strategy for clearing the name of our next president? I fucking hate Cairo."

I watched Sean roll a joint and I waited for an answer.

"Because there's trouble coming up."

"So what is the job?"

The fun died in Sean's eyes.

"You will fly up there with a South African National Defence Force detail and secure our embassy. Then make ready for the shit that's going on up there."

I said,

"Fuck! Is the South African Police Services making decisions for the Department of Defence these days?"

Sean shook his head.

"Until our next president appoints one of his friends as the next police commissioner, you've gotta be somewhere they can't touch you. There is a large file on Egypt in my office. Put Billy in charge of that house security and spend the weekend reading that file. You leave on Monday morning."

Chapter 46

On 9 May 2009, Jacob Zuma, President of the ANC, took over the office of the Presidency of South Africa. Even after a much smaller turnout of voters than expected, the ANC won a two-thirds majority of the popular vote, although not quite enough to change the constitution.

I spent until the second week in August in the embassy in Cairo, collecting local opinions about the political situation in South Africa.

One afternoon, Sean phoned. He sounded very business-like. I asked,

"What's up bud?"

There was a pause and a sigh.

"I'm bringing you home tomorrow. Egypt is about to blow and we're replacing you with a full colonel. He's going to need time to acclimatise." There was a pause. "You're going to be arrested and charged with murder as soon as you land at the Air Force Base."

I thought for a while.

"What if I decide not to be arrested tomorrow night?"

Sean laughed.

"Are you gonna fight them off?"

I didn't see the funny side of the conversation.

"Maybe."

Sean laughed again.

"We've taken care of it. Grant will arrest you and hold you in Sunnyside Police Station. We have a surprise for that unit in the courts the next morning."

Grant was an old friend. We had worked together as bouncers when we were young and he had gone on to be promoted through the ranks of the South African Police Services. I knew he presently held the rank of captain and commanded a tactical response team.

I realised I was operational again and said,

"Don't leave me in there too long, bud. I'm not in the mood to be interrogated by some idiots from Cape Town."

When we landed, Grant was waiting for me in the administration block. He had a wary smile on his face.

"Welcome home, bud."

I smiled too.

"I'm thinking of resisting arrest."

Grant shrugged.

"Look around you, you're surrounded." Grant reached out for my rifle. "I've got to disarm you, Peter."

I looked at him.

"Would you open fire on me?"

Grant looked very unhappy.

"Those are my orders, bud. You have been classified as armed and dangerous and to be treated as such."

I handed Grant my rifle and side arm. I spent that night in an interview room on the second floor of Sunnyside Police station in Pretoria, drinking whisky and playing cards with Grant before falling asleep.

At about six o'clock the next morning, Grant received a communication, instructing him to produce me in front of a magistrate in Johannesburg at nine o'clock. He woke me.

I was walked up from the court cells into the Johannesburg Magistrate Courts at exactly nine o'clock that morning. I was feeling rather foolish in my military fatigues. When I arrived at the top of the stairs from the cells, I looked around and wanted to burst out laughing.

The four senior State advocates I had secured in the think-tank were all to my left, with another face I didn't recognise next to them. They made no attempt to interact with me and I sat down. The magistrate came in and we all stood up. I was addressed as Lieutenant Colonel Conway and informed that I could be seated if I wished.

The prosecutor made a hell of a case on behalf of the State to deny me bail. Then, one by one, the four senior advocates assaulted the prosecution's case. As they went along, the prosecutor was attacked on every level. I think John even attacked him on a personal level, citing how few convictions he had secured during his career. The magistrate eventually put an end to the bloodbath,

"Because of the severity of the charge, I'm going to set bail at one hundred thousand rand and I require the defence to give me a fixed address for the accused while he's on bail."

John stood up.

"I'm paying the bail on my credit card and the accused will be living with me until the next hearing. I'm asking the court to order that the evidence the police unit has on the accused be handed over to the defence team within twenty-four hours. This is a serious charge and we feel the Crime Intelligence Unit must have seriously investigated the accusation, so we're not asking for too much."

The magistrate agreed that the law of full disclosure had not been adhered to and that all the evidence the State had would have to be disclosed within twenty-four hours.

As I was walking out of the court with John, I said,

"Thank you, bud."

John gave me a huge grin.

"I've been doing submissions for so long, I was worried about being able to litigate."

I burst out laughing. He continued,

"So that's what a magistrate's court looks like now, I'd forgotten."

I carried on laughing.

"I've arranged for Billy to pick you up. Go and do your thing, but we all eat together tonight. You taught me that."

I got into the car and Billy handed me my assault rifle.

"Welcome home, my brother."

That evening, I sat down to eat with John and his family at his house. One of my security guards at the gate waved me through with a huge smile. The four families had returned to live in their own houses and Billy had arranged for the unit of security guards to be split between them, with one on duty during the day and two rotating the perimeter at night.

John sat next to me.

"Well, we're going to smash this case and that's even if you are guilty. Then we're going to break up the police unit that made the case, but your unit is about to be handed over to the South African Police Services. These guys can be dispersed but not fired. One day you might get a bullet in the back from one of their friends."

I didn't think the day could get any worse under the circumstances, but it did. John passed me a copy of a message from the new National Police Commissioner to the South African Presidency. It was a request to have all budget and personnel from Defence Intelligence transferred to his office.

I gulped down my whisky and John poured me another one.

"Do you have any idea where these charges come from?" John asked.

I shook my head and John continued,

"Well, we'll know in the morning."

"What if they don't disclose in the morning?" I asked.

"If they don't comply with the court's ruling, then I will see to it that the entire unit is charged with perverting the course of justice. They will comply."

I drank my whisky.

"What's the plan after that?"

"This case will be heard in the Supreme Court in front of at least one judge and probably two assessors, so I intend bringing an urgent application. That way I can cherry-pick the judge."

I knew what he meant, but he verbalised it.

"I'm going to call in markers from old friends for a favourable judgement for you and, at the same time, I'm going to compromise my ethics for the first time in my career."

I knew this decision was a hard one for John to have made.

"Thank you."

"I never thought I would ever do something like this, but it is a pleasure, Peter. That's enough for tonight. I'll see you in the morning as soon as I get back from the office with the police docket." As I turned to leave, John added, "You can take the bottle, Peter."

Just before midday, John arrived back at the house and I went to see him in his office.

"Sit down Peter." He handed me a bottle of whisky. "They have got you. That guy you killed outside that restaurant. That's murder."

I opened the bottle of whisky.

"But the police unit at the scene never even charged me?"

John was in lawyer mode.

"You have signed State documents displaying knowledge of the South African Firearms Act and you have even certified students on a shooting range. You know you can't shoot someone more than once when they're no longer an imminent threat to anyone's life. Once your first shot hit him in the shoulder, there was no way he could have used his rifle again and he was therefore no longer an imminent threat to anyone. When you then shot him in the chest, under South African law, you murdered him. The State has a case."

I drank a quarter of the bottle of whisky, before enquiring,

"Does the police docket show he had just murdered my partner who was officially an operative for Defence Intelligence and that she was only eighteen years old?"

John shook his head.

"No. I'll only bring that up in mitigation, because I want you to plead guilty. It's too risky to litigate this fucking thing."

I lay down on the floor.

"How long am I going to get?"

John sat on the floor next to me.

"I have already taken this matter from the Magistrates Court and it has been accepted for trial in front of a judge with two assessors in Johannesburg Supreme Court. I went to university with the judge and I trust him. He is going to accept your guilty plea and then listen to mitigating circumstances."

I repeated,

"How long am I going to get?"

"After I mitigate the circumstances of the shooting, you will receive a suspended sentence and some restrictions we haven't worked out yet."

"What kind of restrictions? Are they going to find me unfit to possess a legal firearms licence?"

John didn't hesitate.

"No. They want you to resign your commission in the South African National Defence Force."

I looked at John.

"The prosecution will object to such a light sentence."

John smiled.

"That's the real kicker here. I've known the prosecutor since high school. He's going to object in the most bumbling fashion possible and his objection will be overruled."

"That's a lot of movement in one morning, John."

John seemed tired.

"I never thought I would do this, but it's done. Do you trust me, Peter?"

I took another deep swig from the whisky bottle.

"I trust you. How long is this whole thing going to take?"

"You will plead before Christmas."

It was arranged that I was to plead guilty on 8 November 2009 in the Johannesburg Supreme Court.

I went to see Sean.

"So you have finally found yourself in a corner you can't get out of. It was always going to happen eventually. If you had shot him and stepped on his throat until he died, it wouldn't have been murder. Legislation, Peter. We get taught it and we are expected to adhere to it."

I sat down and took a joint from Sean.

"I'm pleading, bud. Throwing myself on the mercy of the court."

Sean took the joint from me.

"You know the outcome is rigged, don't you?"

I took the joint back from him.

"That's the general consensus. If only I was a better shot with a handgun, he would have been dead with the first shot, but the light was bad and I was angry."

Sean rolled another joint and burst out laughing.

"Thank God you can kill from a rifle position, otherwise neither of us would be alive."

"Yeah, with a rifle I'd have been able to squeeze the trigger, but up close I've always taken it more personally and I tugged the trigger. I fucked up."

On 8 November, I pleaded guilty to murder and my bail was extended until sentencing.

As I walked out of the Johannesburg Supreme Court building, John spoke to me for the first time that day.

"We start on your mitigation on the third of January. When I get home from the office, please come and see me. I will have all the answers by then."

On the afternoon of 3 January 2010, with my future hanging in balance, I was told by John that if I gave a truthful testimony on the witness stand in the Johannesburg Supreme Court in front of a judge and two assessors, I was assured of being sentenced to fifteen years, suspended for five years.

On 27 January 2010, at exactly nine o'clock in the morning, I took the oath and John started leading me in my testimony. The proceedings were held in camera. I answered John's questions with more passion than I had ever felt in any courtroom I had ever been in before. The truth was, had I been a little less drugged-up, Baby would not have been by herself outside that restaurant and I could have killed the shooter with just one round. I hadn't been sober and she'd been killed because of that and that's tragic. That morning, as I answered specific questions, I realised I was more to blame for the death of the freshly trained Defence Intelligence operator than I had initially considered. It wasn't her training that had let her down. It had been me. I answered John's questions truthfully all morning and felt totally drained when the court adjourned at lunchtime.

I was sitting outside the courtroom eating a sandwich, when John came over and sat next to me.

"You're doing fine, Peter. All they want is the truth."

I looked down at the floor of the corridor.

"I really fucked up that night, didn't I?"

John handed me a cup of coffee.

"The thing is, Peter, we need to learn from our mistakes."

On 31 January 2010, I was sentenced to fifteen years, suspended for five years. A date was set for a military tribunal to decide on the future of my commission. The judge passed the sentence for the intentional but unpremeditated murder of a man who had just murdered a young female operative in the employ of the Defence Intelligence Department of the SANDF.

I walked out of court relieved, but knew that a military judge would find me unfit to carry the rank of lieutenant colonel. I looked at John as we walked to the car park.

"Thank you, bud. Let's hope the military court doesn't take my life away from me."

John nodded.

"My pleasure, Peter. We have a partner who deals with military courts who will represent you, but don't hold your breath. They intend to retire you."

I nodded.

"I know, but tonight, I'm going to get wasted at the whorehouse down the road."

The military court found me unfit to represent the SANDF in any way and, with one swipe of the pen, I was de-commissioned. The lawyer who was representing me didn't stand a chance. He was repeatedly told to sit down and I was addressed as Mr Conway with no rank against my name. The military judge, who handed down my sentence, observed,

"Mr Conway's actions were not only specific, but deliberate."

I remember thinking, 'I wonder how much time you've spent in a forward area, Colonel?' I was stripped of all rank and benefits and classified as unfit to be an officer.

The next day, I went to see Bob. I was held at the door by the security detail and Bob came downstairs to fetch me. He said,

"We're being integrated into the South African Police Services next month and I will need a word with the minister so that you can still be retained as a consultant by this office."

I was feeling as though I had been thrown to the wolves.

"Give him two words. 'Fuck' and 'off'. I'm going to carry on what I've been doing all my life. I'm going to sell intelligence, women, weapons and drugs to the highest bidder."

Bob laughed.

"Well if you give me an hour, I will have a suitcase of cash here for you. I'm buying intelligence."

Chapter 47

Sean Nielson came to my house the following morning. It was very hot, I remember.

"I'm prepared to invest in whorehouses and strip clubs all over South Africa, if you will run them for me."

I replied,

"I'll have a cold shower and come upstairs and have breakfast with you."

We decided to start our new venture in Bloemfontein. We found a suitable property for sale on the internet and made a bid. It was perfect and I acquired it the same day. I phoned Sean Nielson from the property and he made a bank transfer that afternoon. We had title to the premises by evening.

I phoned Billy.

"We have just expanded brother. I need you to come to Bloemfontein."

I loved Billy's reaction.

"I'll be there in less than three hours."

Billy and I spent the next week phoning prostitutes from ads in the local newspapers. Out of some forty girls who responded to our calls, we hired twelve. Over the following month, Billy and I opened whorehouses in Pretoria and Cape Town.

One day I got a call from Bob.

"Come and see me Peter."

That day, as I was escorted into his office, Bob looked healthy. As always, he was on the phone.

"Sit down Peter. Other than us, who do you sell information from the whorehouse to?"

"Only you get reports from me. I mostly sell the clients' secrets back to them."

Bob sat down in front of the television and I sat next to him. Bob poured me a huge glass of whisky.

"You're selling your customers' secrets back to them?"

"The real trick is to not let the girls know when they have valuable information so, after a payment, that's the end of it."

Bob was silent for a time.

"They want me to commission you again Peter. I don't have a choice but to try and get what they want. We're answering to a new minister these days and that means another committee in Parliament."

"What brought this on?" I drank my whisky. "They want to fuck me over one month and expect me to comply the next? Fuck them! I'm doing okay out there and even enjoying life right now."

Bob shook his head.

"I know Peter, but sometimes success is not always a good thing. Being too successful has put you back on the map and you have information coming in, so they want you back on the payroll," Bob poured me another whisky. "You have to meet my mirror in the police and listen to what he has to say."

I wasn't ready to be managed again.

"No. I'm not coming back and anyway, working with cops won't be successful, as they're too obvious."

I left Bob's office and went to the farm for a week. It was three o'clock on a Thursday morning when I arrived back at the whorehouse in Johannesburg with Terry. The front gate was open and the electricity was off. That wasn't unusual as Johannesburg was undergoing what the State called load-shedding. It was an excuse for switching an area's electricity off, as they tried to catch up with the demand for electricity which heavily outweighed the supply. But, I should have known that something was wrong, as we had invested heavily in generators. There should have been some lights on, but I was tired and distracted. After I locked the car, I walked into a man pointing a revolver at me. Terry had walked off in the opposite direction towards the kitchen to get me some food and I thought, 'Fuck!'

I was told to throw my side arm towards him and sit down. I sat down and was told by a very calm voice to call the girl back. I remembered my staff sergeant's advice from my training when I was seventeen.

"There is no ideal outcome to being taken hostage, but they will take their eyes off you at some stage. When they do, try to kill as many of them as you can and then take cover, but always fight."

I had never seen myself as a victim before and I wasn't going to start that morning. I shouted,

"Terry, come here."

As Terry came around the corner, she froze. I saw my chance and drew my secondary handgun from the small of my back and shot the guy. He fell to the ground. I launched myself over my car as I realised there were two other guys in the shadows.

The first shot hit my left elbow. It was a glancing blow and I remember it felt like a burn. The first round caused me to change my trajectory which meant the second round missed my torso and grazed my right leg. The two guys who had taken shots at me panicked and ran towards the garages at the end of the property. I didn't take a shot at them, as it was very dark and I had seen how ineffective my pistol was at close range, let alone at a distance.

I screamed at Terry,

"Come here, now!"

I picked up my primary side arm from the ground.

Terry shouted,

"Peter, are you there?"

I shouted,

"Find the keys on the ground and open the house. I'll cover you."

It seemed like forever, before Terry shouted,

"I'm inside."

I made my way to the door leading to the main bedroom.

"Open the gun safe and get me an assault rifle."

Terry asked,

"Where are the assault rifles from the car?"

I was not in the mood for questions.

"It's question time later, girl. Just focus and get me another rifle."

I sat on the bed and covered the door, as I could hear voices outside. Terry handed me a Vector LM6 .223 assault rifle and a full magazine of rounds. I couldn't see her as it was too dark, but could hear from her breathing that she was in a state of panic. I put the magazine into the assault rifle and made it ready.

"We're in charge now. Just control your breathing." I steadied myself and asked, "Do we have a torch next to the bed?"

Terry answered,

"We have all the things you wrote on the list next to the bed."

I was proud of her. She was thinking again.

"Get me the small torch and the roll of duct tape."

It was very dark outside and I attached the small hydro torch onto the end of the barrel of the assault rifle, switched it on and looked at Terry.

"Now we're *really* in charge."

I walked outside the bedroom door and illuminated a group of men at the top of the garden with the torch. I opened fire, hit some of them and they ran off.

I walked to where the original gunman was on the ground. He was dead. I shouted,

"Terry, come here. It's all over."

Terry walked over to me from the main bedroom. I saw she was in total shock, but she took the assault rifle from me and said,

"I can't believe you shot at them like that."

I felt sorry for her.

"We live amongst animals. People try to kill me and you have to fight back at some stage. When the police arrive, I'll do the talking. Do you understand?"

Terry was in a bad place mentally.

My leg was bleeding. The round had torn my jeans and my blood was all over the carpet. We used the torch to find my medical backpack. I phoned Bob.

"Just had an armed robbery attempt on the house in Johannesburg. Send me a blessing. I may have killed some of them."

Bob was immediately on his game.

"Which is the nearest police station?"

I told him and he said,

"I presume this favour means you're back on board?"

"Make it go away and I'm back."

I heard Bob talking on another phone. Then he came back to me.

"We are sending a Crime Intelligence officer to you right now, but you need to stay quiet until then."

"No shit. Just get him here fast and I will work for your mirror."

I was making a field dressing of sorts on my knee when the police sirens sounded loudly. I shouted at the first police torch to come close to the main bedroom window,

"I'm armed and I'm wounded, so don't come near me as I don't trust you."

The policeman shouted,

"Calm down! Police headquarters are sending someone to speak to you. We have multiple hostages in the garage. We need to question them. I'm in charge of the crime scene and I'll deal with them first."

Terry went into serious shock.

"I feel terrible Peter."

"Just stay quiet and I'll do the talking."

About an hour later, a large reaction police unit arrived. I watched as four Special Forces policemen got out of a car. They secured the area around my bedroom and the team leader spoke to me through the bedroom window.

"Peter, we're here to help. I'm coming in. Don't shoot me."

He walked in with his hands in the air.

"My name is Wayne and I'm here to help. We have a directive from Pretoria to clean up this mess. If you're wounded, I have a paramedic on the premises and he'll take care of any injuries."

Then, he said,

"Fuck, Peter. You shot them as they were dispersing. One is hit in the back and died just outside the wall."

I answered,

"Yeah. This road and I have a history."

Wayne looked at Terry.

"She needs medical attention."

Terry was shaking uncontrollably on the bed.

"Yeah, bud. Her name is Terry and she needs an IV with some diazepam. Don't interrogate her."

As the morning unfolded, I discovered that the staff of the whorehouse had been tied up in the garage and beaten, one by one.

I remember thinking, 'We need to get some security back here.'

Wayne came into the room, by which time Terry was sedated.

"We have one dead outside this room, one dead right outside the property and two were found wounded in the area."

I asked,

"What are you going to do with the wounded?"

Wayne answered,

"I'm going to torture them until I know what the motive of this attack was and then I'm going to kill them. This place has been deemed sanitised by Pretoria."

My knee was seriously painful.

"Can you get someone to administer me some painkillers? And Wayne, have fun. I think we're going to be working together from tonight."

Wayne smiled.

"By what I've seen here, it will be a pleasure, Peter."

Sometime later, as I was feeding Terry water, Wayne came back to speak to me.

"It's all cleaned up Peter, but you need to speak to my general."

"How do you communicate with him?"

Wayne smiled.

"The motherfucker never sleeps. He wants to talk to you on my cell phone within the next hour."

I got up off the bed.

"Let's go outside. This girl has seen and heard enough for one night."

I took the phone.

"Morning, General."

He spoke to me in Afrikaans.

"I hear you are now part of my team. I'm in charge at all times and I want you to present yourself at police headquarters within seventy-two hours."

I answered,

"Yes, Sir, and thank you, Sir."

He said,

"You have seventy-two hours. After that, if you don't come in, you're on my shit list."

"Yes, Sir. Of course, Sir."

The general added,

"And Peter, get that girl's head right. I don't want any loose ends."

I wasn't sure if he was ordering me to kill Terry, but the order had some latitude. I handed the phone back to Wayne.

"Another fucking general who sleeps in his office?"

Wayne laughed.

"He can be your best friend or your worst enemy. This country is burning and he holds the threads to life and death. By sending us to clean up this mess, he must want you, Peter. Stay on his good side and we will get on just fine. My shift ended just after I was called onto this scene, so there's an intelligence agent outside waiting to speak to you as soon as you're ready." Wayne finished by saying, "This seems to be just a random robbery, but everybody is dead. There'll be no comebacks. I'll see you in the office."

I approached the intelligence officer who was waiting for me by the garages where the staff had been held hostage.

"Morning. I'm Peter."

He was very tired.

"Here's your calling card. You have until noon on Monday to present yourself or you will be in prison by Monday night."

"You always get your way, don't you?"

He smiled.

"People like you are the easiest to manage. We keep you out of prison and you do our bidding."

Chapter 48

I thought, 'So now I'm a cop. I wonder what the Hells Angels will think about that.'

I went to see Sean. When I walked into his kitchen, he was on his laptop again.

"Afternoon, Hells Angel."

I sat down and took a joint out of the ashtray. Sean was blunt.

"You're now part of a Delta Team. The South African Presidency has decided to fight crime in South Africa with lethal force. You're the administrator of a team."

I was issued a Vector LM3 assault rifle with a twenty-one inch barrel and a huge telescopic sight fixed to it and later the same evening, Sean introduced me to my new team,

"This is Lieutenant Colonel Conway. You will address him as Superintendent Conway and, as of now, he's in charge."

I stood up. It felt strange addressing a unit of policemen. I was struck by how young they were.

"You have all been briefed. Are there any questions?"

They answered in unison,

"No, Sir."

Over the following five nights, we enforced the will of Bhekokwakhe "Bheki" Hamilton Cele, the new South African Police Commissioner, who, it was rumoured, filled the vacancies we created with his friends.

On the fifth night, I was glad it was over. The next morning, I was very tired and I gave my last order to the team.

"I have arranged transport for you all to go home. We muster back on the first of July so go and take some time off."

I threw my report on Sean's kitchen table.

"I'm going to the farm. I'll see you at the end of the month. Let's hope those kids get through this shit in their heads."

Sean nodded.

"We were doing this shit in Angola when we were as young as them."

I picked up my car keys.

"But then, the reasons for us doing it were much clearer."

As I was driving back to the farm, my dad phoned me.

"I'm coming to see you. Where are you?" he asked.

I hoped it wasn't bad news.

"I'm heading to the farm."

He was determined to see me in person.

"I'll meet you at the restaurant there in three and a half hours."

I was tired of running to a schedule, but responded,

"Okay, Dad. I'll be there."

When my dad arrived, he came straight to the point.

"We have sold the house and are moving back to England."

Although I knew it was selfish of me to be against their decision, I was taken aback. I said,

"Yeah. This country is becoming a war zone. When do you leave?"

My dad was direct.

"Your mom leaves very soon and I am going to stay to finalise our affairs."

I looked at my dad.

"You're leaving because of me and I'm sorry, Dad."

My dad shook his head.

"We were always going back. You just made it happen quicker."

I could see my dad was agitated.

"Let's go and get drunk, Dad."

My dad knew me very well.

"You have just done something bad, haven't you?"

All I could do was smile.

"I have long since forgotten the difference between what's good and bad. I just do what I'm told to do."

My dad smiled at me.

"All right, Peter. Let's go and drink it off."

The following month seemed to go very quickly. Some time in July 2011, my mom left South Africa to live the rest of her life in England. I drove my mom to the airport and she seemed very happy to be leaving. I slept that night at my dad's new home. In August 2011, Dad flew out of South Africa and, as I was driving him to the airport, I looked at him in the passenger seat of the vehicle.

"I'm very tired, Dad."

My dad must be one of the least sympathetic men I have ever known.

"You chose this life, Peter. You have got to keep going or you walk away."

I remember rubbing my eyes.

"I'm sorry I was the reason that made you leave South Africa."

My dad shook his head.

"So am I."

I watched my dad leave and felt very alone.

Chapter 49

Bob called me.

"Get here as soon as you can. This is urgent, so don't fuck around."

I drove to Bob's office. As usual, he was on the phone. When he'd finished, he handed me a file.

"Sit down Peter and read this."

I flipped through a file on a Crime Intelligence officer and was bored.

"What does this have to do with me?"

"He wants you either on his team, or in prison."

I re-opened the file and read his operational reports. I flipped to the last page and saw how large his budget was.

"Why the fuck would anyone get a budget this big?"

Bob shrugged.

"He's the National Police Commissioner's blue-eyed boy at the moment. When we got his file, he was alerted within twelve hours."

"Why me?"

Bob shook his head.

"You're known in the world he's operating in. He sees you as an asset or a potential threat. I need an answer, Peter, as we have to negotiate with this Crime Intelligence officer. We need a starting point in negotiations."

"No. I'm not doing it. All he does is get people arrested and turn them into informers. I draw the line in the sand right here. Just let me go to the farm. Let's see if he is brave enough to come and get me himself."

Bob shook his head at me again.

"I think you're making a mistake, Peter."

I smiled.

"That's what I do best. I make mistakes."

That evening Sean and I ate together.

"What are the most important things you need to worry about in this world, Peter?"

I looked Sean in the eyes.

"Ego, booze, women and money, Colonel."

Sean nodded.

"Well you have managed to fuck up on all of them this year, but thankfully you have a good military record, so we're going to run an experiment. This guy has the ear of the National Police Commissioner, so we need to take care over our approach. You will have to meet him very soon and I'll come with you."

I was pissed off.

"So we have no exit strategy for me?"

Sean shook his head.

"No, Peter. Look at the size of his budget. That amount of power comes with huge fallout if you don't comply."

"Give me a couple of days and I'll meet him."

As I was walking to the kitchen, I turned round to Sean.

"By the look of his file, he's a prick, so I might stick a bullet in him."

Sean laughed.

"I might put a second one in him."

"Then let's kill him."

Sean smiled.

"One step at a time, bud."

I asked,

"Why would the second black South African Police Commissioner fund a white Afrikaans boy so heavily?"

Sean was tired.

"They're observing him, before they steal his game."

"This is going to be a short leash for me, isn't it?"

Sean answered

"I'm afraid so, bud. Go and get some sleep. I'll arrange the whole thing."

I was watching the news, when Sean came into my room the next morning.

"We have a confirmed time to meet this Crime Intelligence operator on Sunday. He'll meet us when he gets back from church."

I laughed.

"With a Bible in one hand and a gun in the other."

Sean laughed as well.

The next Sunday, we found the Crime Intelligence operator's house using GPS co-ordinates and, when we arrived, I was shocked.

"Look at this place. Only the South African Government would be stupid enough to fund it."

The grounds were large and the house had high ground behind for an evacuation situation. Sean looked over at me as we parked.

"Don't be stupid and say anything you might regret. Let him do most of the talking."

I laughed.

"Trust me. I have very little to say to this guy."

Thankfully, the conversation with the agent was very short. I was asked to entrap a well-known tough guy in Johannesburg. I said very little. Sean said nothing.

When we left, Sean asked,

"What do you think?"

I answered,

"I think he's the lowest form of man. He's never spilt blood in the same mud as us, fuck him. The guy he wants me to tee-up has enough information on me to pull me tighter into his bullshit."

Sean nodded.

"I agree."

He handed me a joint he'd rolled that morning. I took it.

One morning the following week, Sean came round to my house. Something was wrong. Sean sat next to me.

"Bob is dead."

I reached over to my bottle of whisky.

"Is that a fact?"

Sean was not himself.

"Yeah. I'm afraid it is a fact."

"How did he die?"

Sean was very distracted.

"He was in a car accident."

I couldn't believe it.

"They are starting to cull us, bud, so we have got to get out of this country."

Sean shook his head.

"Don't jump to conclusions, but you need to eat to get strong."

I jumped up.

"It's okay for you, as your uncle is probably running this shit."

Sean wasn't himself.

"You're probably right Peter, but I don't know."

I was suddenly feeling better.

"Get me out of here, and I mean by tonight."

"I already have. I've got you a job in Lubumbashi in the DRC, handling a security team that's holding a copper mine."

I felt myself again.

"When do I leave?"

"Tonight."

"Who am I working for?"

"It's a subsidiary of Executive Outcomes. It isn't easy to sell you any more these days. It's all we have."

I got up.

"I'll take it and I'll watch this shit happen from the Congo."

I boarded a small aircraft that evening. The pilot was in a very good mood as he asked,

"Evening, Colonel. Would you like food on this flight?"

I laughed.

"You know I can kill you with immediate incapacitation?"

The pilot laughed.

"You guys don't scare me. I'm one of the few people who's actually prepared to move you guys around."

I asked,

"How do we get from the landing strip to the mine?"

"The landing strip is located in the mine and I'm the only plane in and out."

I smiled at him.

"In which case, you and I are about to become friends."

He nodded and said,

"Yes, Sir."

As we circled to land, I glimpsed the size of the mine. It was huge, with one perimeter along a riverbank. On the ground, I was greeted by a white South African,

"Evening, Colonel."

I looked at him.

"What rank did you hold?"

He came to attention.

"I retired as a first lieutenant, Sir."

I walked past him.

"How many personnel do we have?"

The lieutenant stayed at attention.

"We have sixty-five, including the kitchen staff."

"Gone are the days of large spheres of influence," I said. "Muster them, Lieutenant."

He was taken aback.

"All of them?"

"Yes, all of them. I want to see how fast you can do it."

Because everybody was too dispersed, the muster took some twenty-five minutes. When I addressed them, they were all older than me.

"Okay. We are too stretched out, so as of now. We must all stick together. We don't need to hold the perimeter. We just need to hold this command position. Ten of you will do weapons training every day on a rotational basis."

I looked at the lieutenant, and said,

"Make it happen."

The lieutenant asked,

"What are the operational procedures?"

I liked him as he was enthusiastic.

"Stick them together. If our perimeter is breached, draw the intruders in and kill them."

The lieutenant came to attention.

"Yes, Sir. I understand, Sir."

I added,

"And nobody salutes me under any circumstance."

Sean phoned me the next morning.

"What do you think Hells Angel?"

I laughed.

"These guys were too spread out and it's a massive perimeter. My plan is to hold the centre ground. One of the fence lines to the south is along a river, so if we get assaulted from that direction, I'll kill them myself, if they get that stupid. Who am I up against?"

"Only criminals, bud. There's no real threat."

I laughed and Sean became direct.

"They found strychnine in Bob's blood."

I drew a breath.

"You know, that's bullshit. Bob was a drinker. He never took LSD."

Sean sighed and said,

"That's the official story."

I went outside my tent.

"Lieutenant, muster everyone."

The muster took just under half an hour. I stood in front of them.

"It's not good enough gentlemen. You've got lazy and I'm the only person here allowed to be lazy." I knew I was taking the bad news out on them but I kept going. "We are going to have a horn installed and, whenever it sounds, I want you here in less than five minutes. Everybody sticks together, as of now." I looked at the lieutenant and said, "Let's try and be a fucking team."

In June 2011, I spent my forty-fifth birthday in a tent in the DRC. I didn't even have any alcohol.

I spent the rest of the year looking after the security at that mine and, later on, at another mine nearby.

On Christmas Night 2011, I phoned my dad in England.

"Merry Christmas, Dad. How are you?"

My dad has never been good with words.

"I'm with your mother. Do you want to talk to her?"

"Of course."

My mother came on the line.

"Are you safe Peter?"

"I'm safe as I can be, Ma."

She said,

"Remember, there will always be an England. Remember that and stay out of trouble."

All I could think of saying in reply was,

"Merry Christmas, Ma."

My mother answered,

"Merry Christmas, Peter, and remember that you will always be my little boy."

On 3 January 2012, I phoned my parents' home phone number again. My mother answered the phone, which meant my dad was not at home.

"Happy birthday, Ma."

My mother hates the phone and I knew the conversation would be brief.

"Are you safe Peter?"

I answered,

"Yeah, but I feel lonely."

Like my dad, my mother was not one for sympathy.

"You chose your life. I'm sure you'll survive."

I ended the conversation.

"Hope you have a good evening, Ma."

My mother laughed.

"I'm going to have a hot bath and go to bed. I don't like January up here."

Chapter 50

The mines started working well. It was not pleasant being around so many different personalities. Everyone was trying to attract attention to gain promotion. I spent most nights in my tent and most days in the air in the helicopter.

In June 2012, a few days before my birthday, Sean phoned me.

"I'll be in Harare next week. Come and see me."

By that time I had grown sick of the rut I was in. I answered,

"I'll be there for my birthday. What hotel are you going to be in and am I paying for a room?"

Sean was in a good mood.

"I have a suite in the Rainbow Towers. Just present yourself and they will take care of you."

I thought to myself, 'The Sheraton Group. Somebody has a budget again.'

"I'll see you in Harare before nightfall on the twelfth."

I arrived at the hotel on 12 June, the day before my forty-sixth birthday, and was taken to an empty suite. Sean walked in and said,

"Let's have lunch together. We need to talk, as things have changed."

I knew it.

"Well then, we eat here?"

Sean was very serious.

"Yeah. We need to talk. You have to come home very soon."

I looked up.

"Why?"

Sean opened a bottle of whisky and took a huge gulp. He handed me the bottle.

"How many of those engineers working on the mine, do you think, are spooking for their respective countries?"

The question left me puzzled.

"All of them are?"

Sean nodded.

"We don't need someone with your experience there any more. We can put a much junior officer in your place because all you do is feed us logistics. We are trading information with the other countries that have people there, so you will be more effective at home."

I handed the bottle back to him.

"What will be the game we're going to play?"

Sean was quite for a while before he said,

"We are going after criminals again, but this time it's going through the courts and we are going to make it public through the newspapers."

I took the bottle of whisky from him.

"So we become cops again?"

Sean nodded.

"The South African Police Services have been running our lives for a while, Peter. You know that. Just accept it and come home."

There was a brief pause, before I said,

"How long do I have, before you replace me?"

Sean answered,

"End of the month, so come home, bud."

"I don't have too much choice do I?"

Sean drank from the whisky bottle.

"No you don't, but let's go downstairs and eat in the restaurant tonight."

I arrived back at the mine landing strip on a Friday afternoon. I don't know why the day of the week mattered to me, as the mine was working every day, all day.

I landed in Johannesburg on 1 July 2012 and went straight to Sean's compound. He greeted me with,

"Morning, Hells Angel. It's good to have you back."

I sat down.

"Okay. What are we doing today?"

Sean gave me a stack of files.

"We're doing them."

The only name I recognised on the files was a member of Hells Angels Johannesburg. I tossed the file aside.

"I'm not doing that one and he will know he's under investigation by the time I leave this office."

I sat in the kitchen and read through the other files. Sean walked back in and I asked him,

"What do you want me to do?"

Sean was in a bad mood.

"Do what you do, Peter. Go out there and gather some intelligence. You can't leak any information to any of your biker friends."

I stood up.

"Yes, Colonel. Of course, Colonel. Where are my clothes?"

Sean answered,

"Everything is in your bedroom packed neatly in your cupboard. Keep it like that."

I had a shower and shaved my beard and head. I put on a pair of jeans for the first time in a long time but couldn't part from my military boots. I put on a Hells Angels T-shirt and then put on my Hells Angel colours. I walked into the Hells Angel clubhouse in Johannesburg. It was empty, apart from a prospect and two prostitutes asleep, left over from the last party. One of the prostitutes was very pretty and I woke her.

"Change the linen in one of the rooms. Then get undressed and wait for me."

I then woke the prospect and asked him,

"What drugs do we have?"

He looked at my colours and saw the Filthy Few flash.

"I can have cocaine here in less than twenty minutes."

I nodded.

"Then get on with it."

The first line of cocaine I had snorted in a long time hit me like a ton of bricks so I drank a bottle of whisky to level my head out. I then had sex with the girl, who had waited for me in one of the bedrooms. I went to the bar and got another bottle of whisky.

"How old are you, girl?"

"I'm twenty."

I nodded.

"This world you're in is fucked up. Get out of it, if you can."

I remember her answer.

"This is my life."

I nodded again.

"Then, if this is your life, at least you're good at it."

That night I got very drunk with two Hells Angels members and the three of us drove to a nightclub where one of the names on one of the files worked as a bouncer. I waited for a fight to break out and then got involved in it. When the bouncers came running over, I pulled out a Glock 23 with an extended magazine and put my back up against the nearest wall. Everything stopped.

The bouncer said,

"I know who you are, Peter. Let me get these guys out of here and I will buy you a drink."

I spent the rest of the night drinking with him. The following morning I went to see Sean in the armoury.

He asked,

"Make contact, bud?" I smiled. "Of course you did. Which one of them did you choose?"

I sat down and picked up an AK-47 that was being upgraded.

"The bouncer."

Sean nodded.

"Of course."

I put the AK-47 down.

"I'm feeding you what they're doing and then some police detective can turn them. I presume that's what you want?"

Sean smiled and said,

"That's all we want. To increase our sphere of influence, but after that, you stay in their company, Hells Angel."

I felt trapped.

"I fucking hate being in nightclubs these days."

Sean laughed.

"Do you feel old, out there?"

I nodded.

Over the next few months the names on my designated files were arrested and all took a State deal. It was both disappointing and rewarding at the same time.

Eventually the bouncer, who I had befriended first, was arrested for inflicting grievous bodily harm. He held out in a maximum security prison and his lawyer eventually got him bail.

I laughed with Sean.

"There's always one who's actually as tough as he acts. I'm proud of him."

Sean laughed.

"No operation is a hundred percent, but we have made enough hay in the newspapers. I'm going to run his trial in *The Sunday Times*."

I was tired of being in the city.

"What do you have for me, next?"

Sean knew that question was coming.

"The guy we replaced you with at the copper mine is not happy there and he has a very influential father. Do you want to go back?"

I took a half smoked joint from the ashtray and lit it.

"I could think of nothing better. How long before I leave?"

Sean replied,

"Tomorrow?"

I laughed.

"That will do me just fine."

I went back to the mines, but I did not stay long there. Around the end of August 2012, Sean phoned me.

"Morning, Hells Angel. You're going to have to come back to South Africa sometime in October."

I felt dread.

"Why?"

Sean paused.

"You are going to have to give a character assessment in that bouncer's trial."

I opened a bottle of whisky and drank.

"I just tee them up for you. If the cops and the prosecution don't know which club to use to hit them with, then I'm not helping with that game any more."

Sean sighed.

"They are fucking useless."

I answered,

"It's not my problem. I did what you asked me to do. Why not let one of them slip the net? He's displaying more bravery than the others?"

Sean took a huge breath.

"We need the whole group at the same time. You have been subpoenaed to give evidence in this fucking court case, so you have to come back for a hearing."

I asked,

"Who subpoenaed me?"

After a pause, Sean replied,

"The National Prosecuting Authority, bud. You're their witness."

I drew in a deep breath.

"They will fuck this whole thing up as soon as I give evidence for the prosecution. My reputation will be ruined."

There was another pause. Then Sean said,

"It's an international subpoena, bud. You have no choice."

I was angry.

"There's always a choice."

Under a week later at the mine, the South African National Prosecuting Authority served a subpoena on me. I flew back to Johannesburg the next day and went straight to Sean's compound.

Sean said,

"Morning, Hells Angel. You got here early."

I sat down.

"I'm not doing it, bud. Find me a way out."

Sean shook his head.

"These cases have been the highlight of the newspapers. There is no way out."

I picked up a joint from the table and lit it.

"That's the point. This guy is only looking at getting a suspended sentence and a fine. He hasn't broken yet. I have to expose myself in open court for this bullshit?"

Sean nodded.

"That's where you come in and link him to the others."

"I'm being forced to become an informer on the national stage," I stood up. "I'm not doing it and if you put me on the stand as a prosecution witness, I'll fuck the whole thing up."

Sean asked,

"What are you going to do?"

"I'm going to pack some of my civilian clothes in a small bag and move to England."

Sean nodded.

"There will always be place for you here, so I hope you come back."

"You come and visit me, bud."

Back home, I booted up the computer on my desk. My sister was the first person I thought of. To this day, I have no idea why, but she was someone I could trust.

I sent her an e-mail.

"I'm leaving Africa and moving to England."

Her reply came almost immediately.

"That's a brave decision."

I laughed to myself and thought, 'If only you knew.'

THE END

The author is on the left

AFTERWORD

Marion Monica Sparg

Marion Sparg was born into a middle class white family in East London. At first a journalist, she engaged in left-wing anti-apartheid politics and, in 1981, went into exile in Botswana. Via Zambia, she entered Angola, where she received military training with the ANC. On return to South Africa, in November 1986, aged 28, she was sentenced to 26 years imprisonment for planting limpet mines in three police stations. In 1991, as apartheid was drawing to an end, Marion, together with others, was released from prison. Following the first inclusive general election in 1994, Marion served in various public offices, culminating in her appointment in 2000 as the Chief Executive Officer of the National Prosecuting Authority. In 2007, following the events of 2003, 2004 and 2005, described in *Thy Will be Done*, Marion resigned that office, since when she has worked in the private sector in Johannesburg.

Simon Francis Mann

On 27 August 2004, following his arrest in Harare on 7 March 2004, Simon Mann, together with 69 others, was convicted in Zimbabwe of attempting to buy arms for an alleged *coup* plot and sentenced to 7 years imprisonment. After serving 4 years of his sentence, Mann was extradited to Equatorial Guinea, where he was tried, convicted of arms charges and sentenced to 34 years imprisonment. On 2 November 2009, Mann was pardoned by President Teodoro Obiang Nguema on humanitarian grounds and released from prison. On 6 November 2009, Mann returned to England, where it is believed he continues to live.

Servaas Nicolaas 'Nick' or 'Niek' du Toit

Like Simon Mann, Nick du Toit was tried in Equatorial Guinea and convicted of arms charges. He received a sentence of 34 years imprisonment. On 2 November 2009, together with Simon Mann and three others, he was pardoned by President Obiang. It is reported that he now lives and works in Yemen. Of the eighteen men convicted and imprisoned in Equatorial Guinea on the same charges, only five survived to be released.

Jacob 'Jackie' Selebi

In January 2008, Jacob Selebi was charged with corruption in his native South Africa. He was put on extended leave as South African National Police Commissioner and resigned as President of Interpol. In July 2009, Selebi was replaced as National Police Commissioner by Bhekokwakhe 'Bheki' Hamilton Cele. On 2 July 2010 Selebi was found guilty of corruption and, on 3 August 2010, he was sentenced to 15 years' imprisonment. On 2 December 2011, Selebi's appeal against sentence was rejected by the South African Supreme Court of Appeal. In July 2012, Selebi was released from prison on medical parole and, on 23 January 2015, Selebi died, reportedly of a stroke.

Glenn Agliotti

In November 2010, Glenn Agliotti was tried in Johannesburg and acquitted of the murder of Brett Kebble. To date, no one else has been put on trial for it.